LOST COUNTRY HOUSES
OF SUFFOLK

During the twentieth century some forty of Suffolk's country houses vanished, a few by fire, but more through demolition. This book relates their tragic stories, with lavish use of engravings, images and pictures to bring to life what has now gone forever. It offers an account of each house, its history, its families and its architects, with a description of the buildings, and particular information on how it came to be destroyed. The houses are put into their wider context by an introductory chapter, covering the economic and social circumstances that caused difficulties for the owners of country houses at the time, and comparing the loss in Suffolk with losses in England as a whole.

LOST COUNTRY HOUSES OF SUFFOLK

W. M. Roberts

THE BOYDELL PRESS

First published 2010
The Boydell Press, Woodbridge
Paperback edition 2023

ISBN 978 1 84383 523 3 hardback
ISBN 978 1 83765 071 2 paperback

The Boydell Press is an imprint of Boydell & Brewer Ltd
PO Box 9, Woodbridge, Suffolk IP12 3DF, UK
and of Boydell & Brewer Inc.
668 Mt Hope Avenue, Rochester, NY 14620–2731, USA
website: www.boydellandbrewer.com

The publisher has no responsibility for the continued existence or accuracy
of URLs for external or third-party internet websites referred to in this book,
and does not guarantee that any content on such websites is,
or will remain, accurate or appropriate

A CIP catalogue record for this book is available
from the British Library

This publication is printed on acid-free paper

Designed by Tina Ranft

CONTENTS

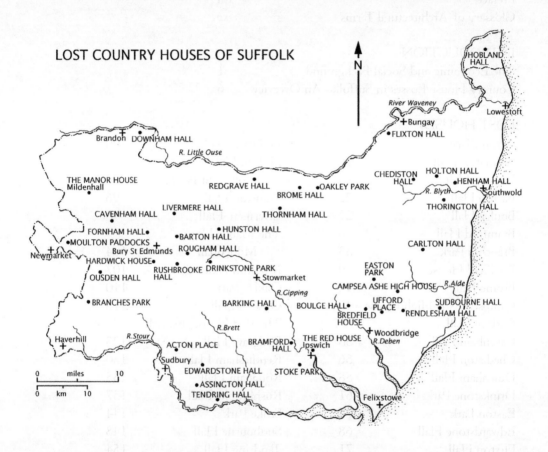

LOST COUNTRY HOUSES OF SUFFOLK

N

JHOBLAND HALL

River Waveney

Lowestoft

+ Bungay
• FLIXTON HALL

Brandon DOWNHAM HALL

R. Little Ouse

CHEDISTON HALL•   HOLTON HALL
              •HENHAM HALL
R. Blyth   ‡Southwold

THE MANOR HOUSE
Mildenhall

REDGRAVE HALL•   •OAKLEY PARK
         BROME HALL•

THORINGTON HALL

CAVENHAM HALL   LIVERMERE HALL•
THORNHAM HALL•

FORNHAM HALL•   •HUNSTON HALL
•MOULTON PADDOCKS   •BARTON HALL
Newmarket   Bury St Edmunds   ROUGHAM HALL•
HARDWICK HOUSE•

CARLTON HALL•

•OUSDEN HALL   RUSHBROOKE   DRINKSTONE PARK
HALL   +Stowmarket

EASTON PARK

CAMPSEA ASHE HIGH HOUSE   R.Alde

R.Gipping

•BRANCHES PARK   BARKING HALL•   BOULGE HALL•   UFFORD PLACE
                         BREDFIELD   •RENDLESHAM HALL
                         HOUSE   SUDBOURNE HALL•

R.Brett

Haverhill   R.Stour

ACTON PLACE   BRAMFORD HALL•   THE RED HOUSE
Ipswich   R.Deben

+Woodbridge

Sudbury

EDWARDSTONE HALL   STOKE PARK•
•ASSINGTON HALL
TENDRING HALL

Felixstowe

0   miles   10
0   km   10

LIST OF ILLUSTRATIONS

18 Cavenham Hall: the garden front. *Reproduced by permission of Suffolk Record Office, Bury (HD1325/63).*

19 Chediston Hall: the entrance front. *Reproduced by permission of Suffolk Record Office, Ipswich (HD78:2671).*

20 Downham Hall: the entrance front.

21 Downham Hall: the garden front.

22 Drinkstone Park: the entrance front. *Reproduced by permission of Bury St Edmunds Past & Present Society (Spanton Jarman Collection K505/2323(2)).*

23 Easton Park: the courtyard. *Reproduced from the Easton Park (Fforde) Collection at the Suffolk Record Office, Ipswich.*

24 Easton Park: the Georgian garden front. *Reproduced from the Easton Park (Fforde) Collection at the Suffolk Record Office, Ipswich.*

25 Edwardstone Hall: the entrance front about 1850. *Reproduced by permission of Suffolk Record Office, Bury HD526/42/2).*

26 Edwardstone Hall: the north front. *Reproduced by permission of James Darwin.*

27 Flixton Hall: the entrance front in 1752. *Reproduced by permission of Suffolk Record Office, Ipswich (PT163/4).*

28 Flixton Hall: the entrance front. *Reproduced by permission of Bury St Edmunds Past & Present Society (Spanton Jarman Collection K505/1936).*

29 Flixton Hall: the garden front. *Reproduced by permission of Bury St Edmunds Past & Present Society (Spanton Jarman Collection K505/1937).*

30 Fornham Hall: the garden front about 1825. *Reproduced by permission of Suffolk Record Office, Bury (1511/105).*

31 Fornham Hall: the entrance front. *Reproduced by permission of Bury St Edmunds Past & Present Society (Spanton Jarman Collection K505/2437(2)).*

32 Hardwick House: the entrance front. *Reproduced by permission of Bury St Edmunds Past & Present Society(Spanton Jarman Collection K505/1005).*

33 Hardwick House: the garden front. *Reproduced by permission of Bury St Edmunds Past & Present Society(Spanton Jarman Collection K505/1003).*

34 Henham Hall: the house in 1824. *Reproduced from H. Davy,* Views of the Seats of the Noblemen and Gentlemen of Suffolk, *by permission of Suffolk Record Office, Ipswich.*

35 Henham Hall: the house viewed along the terrace. *Reproduced by permission of Bury St Edmunds Past & Present Society (Spanton Jarman Collection K505/2311).*

36 Henham Hall: the dining room. *Reproduced by permission of Bury St Edmunds Past & Present Society (Spanton Jarman Collection K505/2314).*

The author and publisher are extremely grateful to the Scarfe Charitable Trust for their generous financial support for this volume – as with so many good Suffolk causes.

PREFACE

MY INTEREST IN 'LOST HOUSES' stems back to the 'Destruction of the Country House' exhibition in London's Victoria and Albert Museum in 1974 and the accompanying book of the same name. Looking back over more than thirty years, I think that there were two things that fascinated me when I saw the photographs in that exhibition and in the book.

The first was that so much of the country's heritage had been lost. Of course, I recognised that some of the houses were not architectural gems and many were so large as to be economically unsustainable in the twentieth century. Nevertheless I wondered how anyone could have destroyed some of the houses depicted, houses designed by the great builders and architects of past centuries often with magnificent interiors by master craftsmen. The second was the knowledge that the houses portrayed had, in their hey-day, played an integral part in the life of the communities in which they were situated, employing large numbers of people both in the houses and on the surrounding estates. I wondered what the impact of the destruction of the 'big house' had been on the people who owned them and worked in them.

My interest in the subject remained but was rekindled by the publication in 2002 of the late Giles Worsley's book *England's Lost Houses* and the related exhibition at Sir John Soane's Museum. My wife and I were, at that time, contemplating moving from north-west Essex to Suffolk, and the idea of engaging in some research into Suffolk's lost houses appealed to me. I wrote to Giles Worsley, who responded encouragingly and made the point that it would be particularly worthwhile to seek out information on the reasons why specific houses were demolished. These have proved difficult to ascertain: whether I have in any way succeeded is for others to judge.

Most of the research has been undertaken using local sources particularly archive material in the branches of the Suffolk Record Office at Bury St Edmunds, Ipswich and Lowestoft. I am indebted to the staff of those offices, too many to name individually, for their assistance. Their help in guiding me through the catalogues and suggesting sources of information has been invaluable, and their services (which have included the provision of many of the illustrations) have been offered with unfailing courtesy and forbearance. Without their assistance this book could never have been written.

I am grateful to Dr Colin Pendleton of the Suffolk County Council

Archaeological Service for providing me with information from the Service's Sites and Monuments Records, and to staff at the National Monuments Record, the Royal Institute of British Architects, the Victoria and Albert Museum (Drawings Collection) and Sir John Soane's Museum. I also thank staff and volunteers at local museums, local historians and parish recorders.

A number of individuals have helped me by providing illustrations, and I offer my thanks to Michael Bidnell and James Darwin (of the Georgian Group), Matthew Beckett, the late Mrs J. Burn, John Harris and D. E. Johnson.

People who have connections (past and present) with properties whose history is recounted briefly in this book have provided me with information, and I also thank them for their help: Caroline Cowper (Bredfield House), the Hon. Jill Ganzoni (Stoke Park), Julia, Lady Henniker (Thornham Hall), Tim Holt-Wilson (Redgrave), the Reverend Christopher Kevill-Davies and Dr Robin Darwall-Smith of Magdalen College, Oxford (Hobland Hall), Alastair and Lavinia Robinson (Ousden Hall), and Lisa Russell and Tim Kaye (Downham Hall).

I am grateful to Joe Mordaunt Crook for agreeing to let me quote from his work on Sydney Smirke and to Phillip Judge for preparing the map. I also thank William Sanders for reading an early draft of this book and for his comments and corrections. I would also like to express my thanks to Dr John Blatchly for suggesting additional sources of information, for his corrections to my text and other useful comments.

To Caroline Palmer of Boydell & Brewer Limited, who accepted this book for publication and who guided me through the latter stages of its writing, I express my gratitude for her encouragement and advice. My thanks also go to her colleagues who have been involved in its production.

I HAVE BEEN ENCOURAGED to write this book by members of my family and by many friends, and I thank them for their interest and for spurring me on to complete this project.

To my wife, Patricia, who has put up with my many absences from home and my seclusion in my study and with detours on journeys peering out of the car window looking for the cedar trees, which were one of the hallmarks of nineteenth-century gardens and survive to show from a distance the sites of lost houses, this book is dedicated.

Bill Roberts

Great Chesterford, Essex, 2002 – Long Melford, Suffolk, 2009

GLOSSARY OF ARCHITECTURAL TERMS

Adam	in the style created by Robert and James Adam (eighteenth-century architects)
Alto relievo	high relief (as in highly decorative plasterwork)
Apse	semi-circular or polygonal recess with domed ceiling
Baluster	short pillar (used in a set, balusters support the handrail of a staircase)
Balustrade	row of **balusters** supporting a rail to form a **parapet** on a terrace or balcony
Band	line of projecting stone or brickwork running round a building horizontally, normally between floors (also termed a **string course**)
Barley-twist	design of brickwork, usually for chimneys, resembling the twisted sugar confectionery of that name
Bas relief	ornamentation that is raised from the surrounding material only to a small degree
Battlement	indented **parapet**
Bay	(i) vertical section of a building, usually the width of a window and its surrounding structure (ii) projecting part of a building, normally (but not exclusively) of one storey at ground floor level
Blind (arches)	arches that are bricked up, either wholly or with a window or door set in the infill
Bow	curved section of a building projecting forward from the main structure
Campanile	bell tower, often designed in imitation of the type of tower common in Italy
Canted bay	bay with sides that slope back from the front to the wall from which they spring
Caryatid	figure used as a pillar to support an **entablature**
Casement window	window the opening section of which hangs from one of its sides
Colonnade	covered passageway between two buildings open to the elements on one side the roof of which is supported by columns
Corinthian	one of the architectural orders devised in ancient Greece in which the capitals of columns were decorated with acanthus leaves and scrolls (volutes)

Cornice	(i) projecting ledge with moulded underside at the top of a wall or other structure
	(ii) band of stone, brick or plaster, often decorative, which covers the join between wall and ceiling
Cross-wing	the section of an 'E' or rectangular 'U'-shaped house joining the two or three projecting wings and normally accommodating the hall
Crow-stepped	the profile of a gable end where the masonry or brickwork is stepped down rather than having a clean line
Cupola	small dome
Curvilinear	structure with curved lines
Dormer	window projecting from the roof of a building to provide light and ventilation to an attic room
Dressings	stone or brickwork worked to a finished face and used at the angle of a building window or other feature of a building
Drip mouldings	projection over the top of a window or door to keep rain from area below
Dutch gables	gables that have a convex top section and a concave lower section
Encasement	the cladding of the walls of a building with masonry or bricks when the old walls are retained
Entablature	the structure between the top of a wall or capital and the structure above it; traditionally in three parts: architrave (at the bottom), **frieze** and **cornice**
Frieze	see **Entablature**, but also used to describe a band of decoration normally at the top of a wall
Gable	the vertical inverted 'V' end of a roof
Grecian	in the manner of the architecture of ancient Greece, a style that was much favoured in the second half of the eighteenth century
Hipped (roof)	the term used to describe a roof where the junction of two faces is protected by leadwork, tiles of semi-circular section or slates of 'V'-shaped section
Ionic	one of the architectural orders developed in ancient Greece in which the capitals of columns were decorated with scrolls (volutes)
Keystone	the central stone (wedge-shaped) of an arch
Lantern	glazed structure superimposed on a roof to provide light to the space below

Mansard (roof)	roof with two slopes, the lower one steeper than the upper
Mathematical (tiles)	tiles used as a cladding for walls, simulating brickwork but also ornamental
Minaret	slender turret in a style associated with the architecture of mosques
Modillion	projecting bracket under a **cornice**, particularly in the **Corinthian** order
Mullion	the vertical bar in a window
Ogee arch	arch composed of sides with concave sections at the top and convex sections at the bottom
Oriel	glazed structure projecting from an upper floor of a building in the form of a bay, which provided additional light to the room
Palladian	Antonio Palladio (1508–80), an Italian architect who designed in the styles of ancient Greece and Rome. His four books on architecture formed the basis of the revival of classical building design in succeeding centuries
Pantile	clay tile used for roofing, curved in two sections, one curve being larger than the other
Parapet	low wall at the edge of a balcony or at the top of a wall at the junction with the roof
Pavilion	building (often used for entertaining) adjacent to the principal structure and attached to it by a passageway or **colonnade** (also described as a 'wing')
Pediment	(i) triangular structure supported on columns or **pilasters** forming the centrepiece of a section of a building (ii) triangular hood over a window or door
Peg tile	rectangular clay tile used for roofing and fixed with pegs
Piano nobile	the principal floor of a large house, containing the state or entertaining rooms
Pilaster	column (rectangular or a segment of a circle) affixed to a wall either for decoration or to support a structure (e.g. **pediment**) over it
Pinnacle	small ornamental turret, usually ending in a pyramid, cone or small steeple
Plinth	(i) the square projecting base of a column (ii) the projecting part of a wall immediately above ground

Polygonal turret	small tower attached to a building, normally at its angles and rising from the ground to above the roof line of a building; usually of eight sides and capped with a domed or **ogee**-shaped roof
Porte-cochère	an open-sided porch of sufficient size for a carriage or car to be driven through it
Portico	a porch supported by columns normally **pedimented** (with four columns it is described as tetrastyle, with six columns it is described as hexastyle)
Quadrant (arcades)	a **colonnade** that is curved
Rococo	an ornate form of decoration in plaster, wood or other material that was favoured in the eighteenth century
Salt-glazed	bricks with a glazed surface produced by applying salt during the firing process
Scagliola	imitation marble made from a mixture of plaster, pigment and glue used in Britain for decorative purposes from the late seventeenth century
Screens (passage)	the passage that was placed at the end of a great hall to provide access to the kitchens
Segmental	the term used to describe a **pediment** over a window or door that is a section of a circle
Spandrel	the triangular space between an arch and the rectangle in which it is placed, the longest side of the triangle often curved
String course	a line of projecting stone or brickwork running round a building horizontally, normally between floors and sometimes ornamented (also termed a **band**)
Stucco	plaster (which may be embossed with decoration) used for surfacing a wall
Transom	the horizontal bar in a window; sometimes the light above the bar
Venetian (window)	a design of window that has rectangular sections at each side and a central round-headed window in the centre
Wainscot	wooden panelling or boards lining the wall of a room
Wrot	old spelling of 'wrought' (as in wrought iron)

INTRODUCTION
The Social and Economic Background

'A NOTHER BIG HOUSE DOOMED' — thus, in March 1957, the *Suffolk Chronicle & Mercury* announced the prospective demolition of one of Suffolk's large country houses, Branches Park, in the west of the county. This was not the first such report that the newspapers had carried, nor was it to be the last. From the end of the Great War through until the last quarter of the twentieth century large houses continued to be demolished, and it was not until changes in planning law and the development of new uses for large properties stemmed the flow of destruction that the considerable damage which had been done to the county's historical, architectural and artistic heritage came to an end.

That damage, which occurred right across the country, was graphically portrayed in 1974 in an exhibition at the Victoria and Albert Museum and in the accompanying book *The Destruction of the Country House.*[1] The book listed some 700 houses in England which had been pulled down or destroyed by fire and contained illustrations of nearly two hundred of them. Through the exhibition and the book the extent of the catastrophe that had occurred was brought to public attention. Not all the houses were of great architectural merit nor were their contents of particular distinction. However, many of the houses were the work of great architects and were set in gardens and parks designed and improved by the best-known landscape gardeners of past centuries. The principal rooms contained plasterwork and fittings which were the work of the leading craftsmen of their day. Their furnishings had often been made for the houses, and the pictures that adorned the walls told the history and demonstrated the artistic taste of those who had owned the properties over the generations.

The loss of houses in Suffolk mirrored losses throughout the country. Medieval, Tudor, Jacobean, Georgian and Victorian houses disappeared, their contents dispersed and their fabric put 'under the hammer'. The reasons for individual losses were many but the sociological and economic background in which they occurred was similar.[2] The place of the country house and its owners in English society had changed. The abolition of the 'rotten boroughs' by the

Reform Act of 1832 and the moves towards a universal male franchise as the nineteenth century progressed reduced the power of landowners in national government. In the second half of the century the creation of elected local government bodies removed from them and the clergy (who were often the sons of landowners) their dominant place in local politics and in rural society, so that the 'big house' ceased to be the centre of authority. Some landowners continued to play a prominent part in local government through membership of County Councils after these were created in 1888, but they were exercising influence rather than power.

Wealth based on industrial and financial enterprise burgeoned, and in national politics the dominant consideration became the protection of property rights generally rather than those based on landed interests alone. The magistracy, which had been almost exclusively recruited from landowners and the clergy, was increasingly opened up to men who had made their money in trade. A higher proportion of people lived in towns, where nonconformity flourished and the influence of the Established Church was less than in the countryside. The concerns of urban people were different from those of village dwellers living close to and dependent upon the landowning class. Great Britain became an industrial nation rather than an agricultural one.

The last quarter of the nineteenth century was a period of declining agricultural incomes from which there was no recovery except during the Great War, and that recovery was only temporary. The availability of grain and meat supplies from overseas resulted in the nation being less dependent on its own agriculture except in time of war. The result was not simply a decline in landowners' incomes but also in the capital values of their estates. The introduction of death duties in 1894 and the fiscal proposals of the Liberal Government when Lloyd George was Chancellor of the Exchequer after 1909 were seen particularly as an assault on the landowning classes. Many estates became increasingly encumbered with debt, and the practice of providing jointures for widows and daughters drained funds away from the land.

Paradoxically, at the time when these trends, particularly the decline in agricultural incomes, were affecting the resources of the landowning classes the age of 'country house living' reached its apogee. In the second half of the nineteenth century huge gardens were maintained, large numbers of servants were employed, and extravagant entertaining was undertaken. Houses were extended to provide additional guest accommodation, and extensive service wings were built, only to be superfluous within a few decades. The Great War saw the end of the sumptuous lifestyle for which the owners of country houses had been noted in the previous half-century. Manpower drained from the land to serve in the Armed Forces with huge loss of life (to which village war memorials testify), and many of the survivors never returned to their former employment. Women left to work in factories and many did not take up domestic service again.

Secondary houses, which could be let in late Victorian and Edwardian times, found no market, and sales of outlying parts of landed estates (a trend which had started even before the war) to pay off inherited debt and fund jointures reduced the income required to maintain them. Families died out in the direct line and houses were inherited by people with other properties and no inclination to take up the burden of unremunerative ones. Social and political trends coupled with financial stringency created a situation in which houses which might, without the additional accommodation built in Victorian times, have remained manageable became simply an encumbrance to their owners. The result was a spate of country house demolitions in the years between the wars when a substantial trade in architectural salvage developed, mainly with the United States.[3]

It has been suggested that the deaths of sons of the landed families in the Great War also contributed to the decline of the country house, although this does not seem to have been a major factor in Suffolk and was probably less significant than some commentators have suggested.

The problems of country house maintenance were highlighted in the 1930s when the Marquess of Lothian, the owner of Blickling Hall in Norfolk, pleaded for the National Trust to extend its work to save threatened houses. This led to the development of the Trust's country house scheme, which allowed continued occupation by the owners of houses while the Trust maintained the property, thus ensuring continuity with the past as well as public access for the future.

World War II brought relief from the demolitions of the inter-war years. Many large houses were requisitioned by the government to provide quarters for servicemen and women or for prisoners of war. Others were used for institutional purposes, such as nursing homes and schools. These uses, however, came at a price. Routine maintenance was not undertaken and the fabric of houses deteriorated both from neglect and from misuse sometimes verging on vandalism. After the war government compensation to make good neglect and damage was meagre, and high levels of taxation precluded the provision of funds from owners' other resources. Deterioration continued and the owners had little incentive or the means to return to restore their properties to their former use. It is not possible to establish how many houses might have survived if wartime damage had been fully compensated because the uses to which their owners would have been able to put them are not known. Whether they would have been able to live in them and maintain them must in many cases be a matter of doubt. As John Martin Robinson, the architectural historian, has written: 'Many houses lost in the 1940s and early 1950s were delayed war victims.'

The fate of country houses as part of the country's historic and architectural heritage, if not the fate of their owners, was recognised by the post-war Labour Government when the National Land Fund was established in 1946, followed two years later by the appointment of the Gower Committee charged with considering arrangements to preserve and maintain 'houses of outstanding historical or architectural interest which might otherwise not be preserved'. The National Land Fund was subsequently enabled to fund death duties discharged by the transfer of houses to the government. At least the problems facing country houses had been recognized, and grants from public funds became available for repairs with public access as the *quid pro quo*. At the same time the National Trust assumed the ownership of a substantial number of houses. Yet despite this recognition of the need to preserve historic houses losses continued until the end of the 1960s.

Not all the losses of country houses in the first seventy years of the twentieth century were the work of demolition contractors. In these as well as in earlier years there had been losses through fire, and Suffolk was not exempt from that scourge. The negligent use of candles and oil lamps and faulty electrical installations had taken their toll. Where only a shell survived reinstatement was normally not undertaken and the remains were cleared away. In any event historic interiors had been irreparably damaged and rebuilding would only have created a new house. The skills of eighteenth- and nineteenth-century craftsmen needed to reconstruct historic interiors had been lost, and their rediscovery had to await the reconstruction of parts of Windsor Castle and of Uppark in Sussex after they were severely damaged by fire late in the twentieth century.

Not only during the years of World War II but throughout the twentieth century country houses were taken over by schools and colleges and by public bodies and commercial enterprises as training establishments and head offices. This often did little to preserve historic interiors and the properties were denuded of their contents but, at least, the fabric was preserved. The conversion of substantial houses into apartments started in the 1950s when the Country Houses Association acquired a number of properties to provide serviced accommodation principally for retired people. In the last quarter of the twentieth century a considerable number of houses were restored as apartments and their stables and other outbuildings converted into houses.

The authors of *The Destruction of the Country House* wrote in 1974 with dire foreboding of the future for country houses: looking back over the last thirty-five years it can now be said that, despite the institutionalisation of so many properties, the final years of the twentieth century have not turned out, in a period of economic prosperity, to be as bleak as they feared it would be. The reduction in taxation levels during the Conservative administration after 1979 and the high levels of income enjoyed after 1990 created a new market for large houses. Owners of historic houses have developed imaginative ways of using their properties to create the financial resources for their preservation. Houses that had been let for institutional purposes have been taken in hand by their owners and restored. New country houses are being built from resources earned in financial and commercial ventures in the same way as the building of many of the houses pulled down in the twentieth century had been financed in earlier centuries.[4]

Some country houses, however, remain at risk as buildings bought by local authorities and other public bodies for offices, hospitals and other institutional purposes are replaced by modern purpose-built properties. Proper maintenance of these houses has often been neglected, and their restoration to private use or conversion to apartments and other uses will impose substantial financial burdens. While these may be met by 'enabling developments' in the gardens and grounds such new building may save a house but damage its historic setting. There are likely to be less funds available from other sources in the years ahead, and how these houses will be protected remains an open question.

Country House Losses in Suffolk –
An Overview

AS WE HAVE SEEN, THE SOCIAL AND ECONOMIC CHANGES of the late nineteenth and the first half of the twentieth century imposed on the owners of large houses pressures that a considerable number were only able to address by selling their properties for demolition and not restoring those that were burnt down.

It should not be thought, however, that the twentieth century was the first one in which country houses were pulled down, although in the past the motivation for doing so had usually been different. Over the centuries the history of such houses has been the story of new houses replacing older ones. Many were built on or near the sites of and some incorporated parts of their predecessors. Medieval houses were replaced in Tudor and Stuart times, and these replacements themselves gave way to Georgian and Victorian mansions. It can be said that this sequence of building, often reflecting the aggrandisement of the owning families, their desire to display their wealth and architectural taste or, more mundanely, to live in a more commodious residence than their forbears, was undertaken with little or no concept of preserving old buildings if they had outlived their purpose. Life in the great hall with a small number of private chambers was superseded by a more genteel style of living, with servants well segregated from their masters and mistresses. Such social changes were reflected in the design and decoration of houses, and if that meant demolishing the buildings inherited from earlier generations they were swept away. In cases where parts of these houses were retained and incorporated in later buildings they often became the service quarters. In others the 'old' house totally disappeared with the site being re-used or the 'new' house being built at a completely different location on the owner's estate.

There is, therefore, a long history of houses being 'lost': houses demolished in Georgian and Victorian times are just as much lost as those demolished more recently. It was, however, the scale of the demolitions and the seemingly wanton destruction of part of the country's heritage in the twentieth century to which 'The Destruction of the Country House' exhibition in 1974 drew attention.

It is not known precisely how many country houses were demolished in England in the twentieth century. In the book *The Destruction of the Country House* the authors listed over 700 (including losses by fire and partial demolitions) in England, but they did not claim that their list was exhaustive. Subsequent research has taken the number up to 1,200 recorded in Giles Worsley's *England's Lost Houses* published in 2002.[5] He, too, did not claim that his list was definitive and surmised that the total number might have reached as many as 1,700. In any event arriving at a precise number must be an impossibility because much depends on what criteria are adopted for a lost house to qualify for inclusion.

An analysis of Worsley's 2002 list shows that a small number of demolitions and fire losses occurred in the first two decades of the twentieth century, with numbers building up considerably in the inter-war years. During World War II the number of losses dropped as many houses were requisitioned by the government for military use or taken over by institutions seeking accommodation away from parts of the country at risk of enemy action. The end of the war saw a rise in the number of demolitions, with the peak period for losses being the 1950s and 1960s, reaching in most of those years between twenty and forty and possibly as many as fifty in 1955.

This book recounts the history of forty country houses in Suffolk which were lost by demolition or by fire in the twentieth century. The problem of deciding what criteria to adopt in considering whether or not a house should be included has necessitated the definition of the terms 'country house' and 'lost'. The houses described in this book were houses of historic or architectural interest or were the 'big houses' in the villages in which they were situated and the centre of the estates that supported them. Defining 'lost' is more difficult. Some houses were totally demolished or were destroyed by fire, but frequently service wings, stable blocks and outbuildings survived and were converted into dwellings or other uses. The houses of which an account is given in this book are all ones where the principal residential accommodation was lost by demolition or fire in the twentieth century.[6]

Of the forty houses described in this book six were totally lost or severely damaged by fire. Of these the service wings of Carlton Hall and Assington Hall were converted into houses, Hobland Hall's ground floor was initially converted to offices and stores but subsequently pulled down and at Thornham Hall (which had previously been substantially reduced in size) a tower survived. Barton Hall and Hunston Hall were almost totally lost. One house, Rougham Hall, was bombed during World War II.

Of the thirty-three houses demolished nine were pulled down in the inter-war years and twenty-four after 1945. The ratio of pre-World War II losses to post-war losses appears to have been broadly in line with the figures nationally.

The precise circumstances in which individual owners decided to sell up cannot now be known as surviving documentary evidence in the public records is sparse and the people concerned are no longer alive. There were some houses that had long been secondary residences often let to tenants, their estates being the asset that provided income for their owners. Others passed through inheritance to people who had their own properties and had no interest in another, particularly when the one they inherited was likely to prove a financial incubus at a time of high taxation. It has already been noted that wartime occupation by the Armed Forces had caused considerable damage to and deterioration of houses for which compensation was inadequate. The prospect of taking in hand an historic property in poor repair at a time of high rates of taxation must have been daunting for many families, and disengagement was the only practical solution. The possibilities of selling to a new owner better placed financially to take over such properties and renovate them did not exist. These latter considerations must have weighed heavily on the minds of country house owners, particularly after World War II, during which nearly all the houses had been requisitioned.

Of the country houses demolished in the inter-war years four were inherited by people with other landed interests, three had been secondary residences for a long period of time, one was a house that fell into an intestate estate after the last member of the family to live in it died and one was vacated by the younger brother of the owner and had become redundant.

The demolitions after World War II are less easy to categorise and the analysis that follows is inevitably tentative in nature. Nine were put on the market following the death of their owners either without direct heirs or with heirs who were unwilling to take them over. Five houses were secondary properties, their owners having other houses in which they lived, and one house had been in institutional use since the 1920s.

One was sold after release from wartime use, the owning family having decided not to return to live in it. The remainder appear to have succumbed through a combination of problems, with a major factor being the damage occasioned by wartime occupation by the Armed Forces.

In very few cases were the owners themselves directly involved in the demolition of their houses. Normally the house and in many cases the whole of its estate was offered for sale. The agents' sales particulars tended to stress the suitability of the house for institutional purposes as well as for continued occupation as a private residence. The extent to which this was 'wishful thinking' or an opinion held *bona fide* is hard to determine, but it is difficult to avoid the conclusion that in most cases demolition was not far from the minds of the owners and their advisers.

The outcome of these sales was often purchase by a syndicate which purchased on a speculative basis and then arranged sub-sales of parts of their purchase and demolition of the main house by specialist contractors. Alternatively sales of the fixtures and fittings were arranged, followed shortly afterwards by sale of the remaining fabric on the basis that specific elements such as roofing materials, floor boards and leadwork were offered in lots and the remaining structure then sold to a demolition contractor. The apparent reticence of most (but not all) sellers to acknowledge that their sale was likely to lead to demolition was often mirrored by the reticence of buyers to acknowledge publicly that their purchase was a speculative one. It may be that sellers felt some pangs at the prospect of the dismantling of part of their inheritance. Buyers probably had few scruples about the part they were playing in the destruction of part of the county's heritage: their interest was to make a quick profit.

One point that needs to be borne in mind in considering the fate of Suffolk's lost country houses is that not many were of such architectural distinction or historic interest that there was any real prospect of them being saved for the nation. It is unlikely that, even in more favourable times, more than a very few would have been candidates for transfer to the National Trust or to English Heritage.

Of the houses whose destruction is, in architectural terms, particularly to be regretted there are three that deserve special mention. Rushbrooke was one of the finest Tudor houses in Suffolk, altered and embellished by Sir Jermyn Davers when he inherited it in 1729; if

World War II had not supervened, the considerable expenditure on the house by Lord Rothschild in the 1930s might have saved it for posterity. Tendring Hall at Stoke-by-Nayland, designed by Sir John Soane for Sir Joshua Rowley, Rear Admiral of the White, was a good example of the architect's work and might have survived if the plans of the architect Raymond Erith in the 1950s to reorder and restore it had come to fruition. Flixton, rebuilt by Anthony Salvin in a restrained Jacobean style in the 1840s, became a more extravagant creation when it was altered and extended later in the nineteenth century.

In terms of historic interest three stand out as particularly noteworthy. Brome Hall was one of the seats of the Cornwallis family from early in the fifteenth century until the 1820s, when it was sold to the Bungay grain trader Matthias Kerrison. Redgrave was built by Lord Keeper Bacon in Tudor times and added to by 'Capability' Brown for the Holt family in the 1760s. Hardwick House was the home of the Cullum family from the 1730s until it was sold in the 1920s when the family line expired.

Suffolk country houses which were demolished or destroyed had in their heyday played an important role in the villages where they and the estates of which they were the centrepiece provided much of the employment. The decline in agricultural incomes after the middle of the nineteenth century has already been noted as have the changes in the power and influence of the nobility and gentry as successive Reform Acts widened the franchise. Paradoxically, the second half of the century saw the enlargement of many houses to meet the social aspirations of their owners. However, with the changes in the social structure of the country in the twentieth century the sheer size of many of the houses may often have hastened their end. The shortage of labour and its rising cost after the Great War made servicing such large properties more difficult. Their use during World War II for military and institutional purposes did considerable, if not irreparable, damage to their fabrics. That there should have been so many losses is not perhaps surprising.

It should not, however, be forgotten that many Suffolk country houses survived. Ickworth House and Melford Hall passed into the ownership of The National Trust. Heveningham Hall, which faced an uncertain future in the last quarter of the twentieth century after acceptance by H. M. Treasury in lieu of estate duty, sale to an overseas buyer who neglected it and then damage by fire, has a new owner who is undertaking its restoration. Euston Hall, Helmingham Hall, Kentwell Hall, Little Glemham Hall, Shrubland Hall and Somerleyton Hall are among the other important houses that have survived as have the 'big houses' in many other Suffolk villages. Further losses of Suffolk country houses may be unlikely because of the protection provided by statute, but the proper maintenance of these old buildings may become more difficult in the straitened economic circumstances in which the United Kingdom finds itself at the end of the first decade of the twenty-first century.

ACTON PLACE

DEMOLISHED 1825 AND 1960

ACTON PLACE, SITUATED FOUR MILES NORTH-EAST OF SUDBURY, is best remembered for its connection with the Jennens family for whom in the 1720s a substantial house was built but never completed. In 1708 Robert Jennens had acquired Acton Place with an estate of 200 acres from the Daniel family, which had owned two manors in the parish since the first part of the sixteenth century but of whose house no record now remains.[1]

Jennens, who died in 1725/6, was a member of a Midlands family, his father being, reputedly, Humphrey Jennens, a very prosperous Birmingham ironmaker, of Erdington Hall in Warwickshire. Robert Jennens was succeeded by his son, William, who was baptised in 1701 and was a godson of King William III. He lived until 1798. William had an Exchequer annuity of £3,000 a year but lived as if penurious, reputedly occupying three rooms in the basement although the family apartments in the house had been furnished before he succeeded to the estate.[2] It is said that he left £2.5 million, with £19,000 in notes being found in the house on his death and a bank balance of £50,000.[3] Allegedly the richest commoner in England, he died intestate without leaving any record of his family, giving rise to speculation that the Robert Jennens who built Acton Place was neither the son of Humphrey Jennens nor the father of William. Litigation ensued as to the rightful heirs to his estate, but eventually in 1816 Acton Place passed to the Hon. Richard William Penn Curzon who was created Earl Howe in 1821.

'THE LARGE dwelling house with offices built by Mr Jennings [sic] near Stowmarket' was designed by James Gibbs but had not been finished by the time of Robert Jennens's death.[4] His son never completed it, the staircase and one wing, which was to have been a ballroom, being left unfinished. The house has been described as 'magnificent country seat, which for the grandeur of its hall, and the massive elegance of its marble chimney pieces, as well as the beauty of its stables and other offices was totally unrivalled in that part of the country'.[5]

It is depicted in the painting of the entrance front (illustration 1) as having a central block of eleven bays with the two outer sections of two bays each divided by pilasters and the central three bays pedimented. The central doorway was approached by flights of curved steps from lower

ground floor level to the piano nobile. The house is shown as having four storeys, with string courses at first and second floor levels. The roofs appear to have been hipped in three sections but the detail is unclear. The pavilions, which were connected to the central block by quadrant arcades, were of nine bays on the entrance front, with each section of three bays being flanked by pilasters and the central three bays pedimented. There was an entrance on the inner flank wall, which was also pedimented. Screen walls pierced with arches extended from the pavilions outwards into the pleasure grounds.

Internally the house is said to have had fifty-four rooms of which sixteen were never completed.[6] 'The hall was adorned with alto relievos, and the ceiling with paintings from the heathen mythology. At each corner was also a figure of the fabled divinities. At the end and on each side were paintings of fruit and animals by Lynders [sic].[7] Some circular recesses also contained six busts, of admirable workmanship. In the panels over the fireplaces were portraits of the late proprietor and his parents.'[8]

FOLLOWING William Jennens's death the house degenerated; lived in by two old servants, the rich tapestries were torn away and the gardens were allowed to become overgrown.[9] In 1825 Earl Howe ordered its demolition. The materials from the house were sold at auctions held in March and May 1825, the advertisements highlighting: 'excellent brickwork, stone copings, steps, paving, chimney-pieces, about 400 feet of Portland paving with black dots, very superior marble chimney-pieces', deal and oak floorboards, '16,000 feet of wall framings and wainscots, numerous deal and wainscot-moulded doors with superior dressings', doors, sashes and lead.[10]

The pavilions survived the demolition of the central block although one of these was pulled down later in the nineteenth century.[11] The Tithe Map of 1839 still shows them both.[12] However, five years later it was stated that the house had been taken down except for the servants' wing and a few outhouses.[13]

In 1874 it was reported that the surviving wing 'of the old structure has been improved and renovated of late years and laid out with pleasure grounds'.[14] The house which was formed from what remained of Jennens's mansion was L-shaped, with a wing added to the west side of the original building. On the nine-bay entrance front canted bays were added to the two bays at each end of the frontage at ground floor level. The rear wing consisted of three bays and two storeys with a single-storey extension at the intersection of the old and new buildings. The original pavilion showed three bays facing the garden together with a single-storey portico.

Further improvements made in the 1890s included alterations to the house, the creation of a partly walled kitchen garden and the building of two cottages, one by the stables and the other for use as an entrance lodge.[15] In 1907, when it was occupied by Mrs Braithwaite, the house was described as 'a fine mansion in an extensive park with many fine trees'.[16]

DIRECTORIES of Suffolk for the middle years of the nineteenth century do not list anyone residing at Acton Place, which remained in the ownership of Earl Howe's family. In the 1870s Major-General Edward Darvall was living there and the house continued to be occupied tenants during the rest of the nineteenth century and in the early years of the twentieth.

During World War II the estate was requisitioned and initially served as a base for the 12th Lancers. Subsequently it was used as a US military hospital. At the end of the war it was a home for refugees. In the late 1940s the property, which had belonged to a Mrs Pearson before the war, was sold to a Mr Baldwin who occupied part of the house with the remainder being converted into flats. In 1958 demolition of the house was mooted by a potential purchaser with a view to it being replaced by a farmhouse but nothing became of this proposal.[17]

By August 1960 the demolition contractors had moved in, and photographs of the house, now nearly completely pulled down, were published in the local press together with an advertisement for the sale of 'Clean Old Red Bricks, Peg Tiles, Portland Stone, Timber and floorboards, Oak and other doors, Floor boards, Antique Fireplaces, Oak Window Frames, Georgian staircase, Brick Rubble, Rockery Stones'.[18]

The last remaining part of Robert Jennens's palatial house had gone 135 years after the demolition contractors first came on the site. Its site and part of the surrounding parkland became the Acton Place industrial estate.

ASSINGTON HALL

DESTROYED BY FIRE 1957

A SSINGTON HALL STOOD SOME FOUR MILES SOUTH-EAST OF SUDBURY, south of the road to Colchester, in an estate which by the twentieth century had extended to over 2,000 acres. A mainly Tudor house with later additions, it was one of the few lost country houses of Suffolk to meet its end in a fire that gutted most of the building.

From the early years of the fourteenth century to the middle of the sixteenth the manor of Assington was owned by the Corbet family by whom it was sold in 1555/6 to Robert Gurdon of Lavenham.[1] Early in the next century his son, John, married the heiress of the Brampton family's estate at Letton in Norfolk. The Gurdons, who also acquired Grundisburgh Hall near Woodbridge to add to their portfolio of landed interests, were to remain at Assington until shortly before World War II.

Legend has it that Assington Hall was built on the site of an old monastery 'in which priests prayed for the souls of those slain in the battle' of Assandun.[2] However, the location of that battle is the subject of speculation, also being attributed to Ashdon, near Saffron Walden and to Ashingdon between Chelmsford and Southend near the River Crouch.[3] Originally the village of Assington was centred on the house and the nearby church, but it is believed that in the eighteenth century the village community was moved, probably to improve the Gurdon family's privacy. This clearance of the cottages and other properties near the house left it in a more isolated position in its own parkland.

IT IS THOUGHT that the first house on the site was of fourteenth-century origin when the manor was acquired by the Corbets, but what survived until the fire was mainly a late Tudor timbered house built on the foundations of the earlier house and arranged on three sides of a quadrangle.[4] The entrance front was recased in red brick by John Gurdon in the second decade of the nineteenth century, and it seems likely that the projecting side wings of the original house were pulled down at this time. Subsequent additions included a wing at the rear of the older building.

The house that survived into the twentieth century had five gables on the entrance front, the central one having a two-storeyed entrance porch which projected forward and had battlemented turrets. At each end of the

TOP RIGHT:
3 Assington Hall: the entrance front.

RIGHT:
4 Assington Hall: the rear of the house showing the nineteenth-century addition.

building there were polygonal turrets with minarets, also said to date from the time of John Gurdon. The fenestration was varied, with the windows in ten of the bays on the first floor being sashed whereas on the ground floor only five bays had sash windows, with three large mullioned and transomed windows surviving in the other bays. The entrance porch had a mullioned and transomed window on the upper floor. The windows in the gables serving the garret bedrooms were casements. The rear, plastered elevation had windows of various styles, and it was from the centre of this elevation that the nineteenth-century wing projected.

The house had five reception rooms – lounge hall, drawing room, dining room, study and library.[5] Many of the rooms were panelled. There were fifteen bedrooms (served by three staircases to the first floor and two from the first to the top floor), two dressing rooms and three bathrooms and two lavatories. Many of the rooms were panelled. The substantial domestic offices were situated in the rear wing (which was single-storeyed at ground level abutting the house, with further rooms at a lower level where the ground fell away at the back of the house).

AT THE END of the nineteenth century Assington was occupied by Sir William Brampton Gurdon, who was MP for North Norfolk and Lord Lieutenant of Suffolk from 1907 to 1910. In the latter year he died without children and the estate reverted to his nephew, Lord Cranworth. In July 1938 the whole of the Assington estate, the house in eighty-nine acres of parkland with 200 acres of woodlands, fifteen mixed farms, virtually the whole of the village, including the school and fifty-five cottages (some 2,100 acres in all), was put on the market.[6]

Subsequently the house became a training college for Roman Catholic priests.

In December 1956 the house, shorn of its estate, was bought by James Arnold Frere, Chester Herald of Arms, whose family was distantly connected to the Gurdons. Frere was in the process of restoring and refurnishing the house when in August 1957 most of it was destroyed by fire.[7] Thirty-foot high chimneys, the entrance porch, the minareted turrets and the facade of the left-hand gable remained standing, the rest of the Tudor house having collapsed. The rear wing, which survived, has been converted into residential accommodation.

BARKING HALL

Barking Hall, situated one and half miles south-west of Needham Market, became one of the seats of the Earls of Ashburnham in the eighteenth century. Standing next to the parish church, it was the 'big house' of a small village but of a substantial estate.

In the early medieval period the manor of Barking (otherwise Barking cum Needham) was apparently a possession of the monastery of Ely.[1] Before the end of the Middle Ages, however, it had passed to the Bishop of Ely from whom it was taken in 1562/3 by the Crown, the bishop being compensated by payment of a pension of £135 a year. Half a century later it was sold to Sir Francis Needham and John Yeomans. On Sir Francis's death in 1637 his son Thomas inherited the property, but it was then sold to Sir Francis Theobald whose son Robert left it to his sister Anne, the wife of Reverend Joseph Gascoyne, vicar of Enfield. It then passed to the Gascoyne's daughter Theodosia, who married John

5 Barking Hall: the entrance front.

Crowley of Greenwich, a merchant and alderman of London with substantial interests in shipping, iron trades and property in the London area, the Midlands and the North-East of England.[2] Crowley's sons died without male heirs and the estate passed to his four daughters, the youngest of whom, Elizabeth, married the second Earl of Ashburnham in 1756.[3] Barking then passed into the Ashburnham family.[4] It was to remain in their ownership until the end of the Great War.

BARKING HALL dated from the early years of the eighteenth century but replaced an earlier house lived in by the Theobald family in the late seventeenth century. Parts of this building, which, having twenty-two hearths in 1674, must have been of significant size, appear to have survived as 'the old wing', which was used as service quarters.[5] The centre block of the plain sash-windowed house was of nine bays and three storeys, the two outer bays at each end projecting forward and having pediments. Two-storey wings each of two bays were added later in the eighteenth century.[6] Both the central block and the wings had hipped roofs and plain brick balustrades. The windows were set in the brickwork without any ornamentation except in the case of the windows in the central bay where, on the upper floors, they had stone surrounds, with the first floor window also having a shallow segmental pediment.

The prominence given to the windows in the centre bay suggests that the house may originally have had a central entrance door but a plan dated 1832 shows that the entrance was then in the second bay from the left in the recessed central section of five bays which had a verandah.[7] The plan shows a housekeeper's room, a butler's pantry and a plate room on the ground floor but no other domestic offices on that floor, from which it may be assumed that the kitchen was in the basement or in the 'old wing'. Undated pencil amendments to the plan show the outline of where a conservatory was subsequently built on the east end of the house and an outline of a wing to the rear of the existing service rooms in the north-west corner. The rear extension was subsequently built and the house took its final form.[8]

BARKING was a secondary residence of the Ashburnhams whose principal seat was at Ashburnham Place near Battle in Sussex, a house which was itself partially demolished in 1959. From 1836 for about twenty years Barking was divided into tenements occupied 'by poor families' but later came into its own again when the widow of the fourth Earl lived there in the last quarter of the nineteenth century. In 1926 H. R. Lingwood, who had been Lord Ashburnham's agent at Barking, wrote that it had only been lived in occasionally by the family and had been let out to tenants.[9] A report at the time of the sale of the contents in 1918 stated that the tenants had had to provide their own 'modern necessaries' because there remained in the house only the 'antique furniture, together with a collection of family portraits and the library'.[10]

The fifth Earl died in 1913 and the estate was subsequently sold to what was described at the time as 'a local syndicate'. In December 1917 the syndicate, which had reputedly paid about £60,000 for the estate of 3,450 acres, put it up for sale by auction in over forty lots.[11] The house, the late eighteenth-century stables comprising four loose boxes, harness room, six stalls and a carriage house with the coachman's quarters above and forty acres, were offered as a single lot. The house, which appears to have been furnished at the time, was described as having an entrance hall, library, dining and two drawing rooms (one on the first floor), conservatory, nine bedrooms on the first floor and eight further bedrooms on the top floor. In fact it had more rooms on the ground floor than the auctioneers listed – the rooms described on the 1832 plan as the school room, the gentleman's room, the gun room and the housekeeper's and butler's rooms. Bids for the house reached only £2,800 and it was withdrawn from the sale, but subsequently it and five other unsold lots were disposed of privately.[12]

The house survived a further nine years. In April 1926 the building was sold for demolition, marble chimney-pieces fetching up to £10, the drawing room doors and panelling £40, the conservatory £17, the lead on the roof £330, the shell of the servants' wing £145 and that of the main house £325.[13] The house was then pulled down.

The stable block survived and, having been enlarged, has become a nursing home under the name of Barking Hall.

BARTON HALL

DESTROYED BY FIRE 1914

BARTON HALL, SITUATED FOUR MILES NORTH-EAST OF BURY ST EDMUNDS in the village of Great Barton, was one of the six country houses in Suffolk which were destroyed by fire in the twentieth century and not rebuilt.

The manor of Great Barton belonged to the Abbey of Bury St Edmunds in medieval times and at the Dissolution of the Monasteries was granted to Sir Thomas Kytson. In 1553 it was in the hands of John, Duke of Northumberland, Lord President of the Council in King Edward VI's reign, who exchanged it for the manor of Drayton Bassett, a Staffordshire property of Sir Thomas Aud(e)ley.[1]

Barton belonged to the Audley family until 1706 when it was sold to Thomas Folkes, a lawyer from Bury St Edmunds. Through the marriage in 1724 of Folkes's daughter and heiress, Elizabeth, to Sir Thomas Hanmer (she was his second wife) Barton Hall and its estate passed in 1746 to the Bunbury family.[2] Sir Thomas Hanmer, Speaker of the House of Commons in the reigns of Queen Anne and King George I, had no children and left his estates at Mildenhall, which he had inherited from his mother, and Barton to his nephew the Reverend Sir William Bunbury.[3] It remained one of the Bunbury family seats until its destruction in 1914.

Sir William's son Charles bred the horse Diomed, winner of the first Derby Race in 1780.[4] His brother was the celebrated painter and caricaturist Henry William Bunbury many of whose drawings adorned the walls of Barton before the fire and whose son, Lieutenant General Sir Edward Henry Bunbury, inherited the house on Sir Charles's death in 1821. Sir Edward married a member of the family of the famous eighteenth-century radical politician Charles James Fox and, in the course of a distinguished army career, was charged with accompanying Napoleon to St Helena. The Bunbury family were considerable collectors of paintings, the artists represented in the collection including Reynolds, Van Dyck, Veronese, Correggio, Rubens, Lely, Kneller and Rembrandt. Its library had a valuable collection of books including those inherited from Sir Thomas Hanmer.[5]

ROBERT AUDLEY, who died in 1624, is thought to have built the original house either in late Elizabethan or early Jacobean times. It was presumably similar to other Suffolk houses of this era but underwent considerable

TOP RIGHT:
6 *Barton Hall: the entrance front in 1819 (from T. Cromwell's* Excursions through the county of Suffolk).

RIGHT:
7 *Barton Hall: the entrance front in the early twentieth century.*

alterations in the eighteenth and nineteenth centuries. John Kirby, writing in 1735, said that the house 'has been lately built in a beautiful manner by _____ Fowke esq [*sic*]; whose Daughter and Heiress being married to Sir Thomas Hanmer carry'd it into his family'.[6] Whether the work Thomas Folkes carried out was a major rebuilding of the house or simply updating is not known. Sir William Bunbury is reputed to have modernised the house after he inherited it and his son was responsible for the building in the late 1760s of a library designed by Sir William Chambers, the architect of Somerset House.[7] This library, with its fine plasterwork to walls and ceilings, handsome bookcases and magnificent marble chimneypiece, became the most important architectural feature of the house.[8]

An engraving from the time of Sir Charles Bunbury (who died in 1821), shows a plain Georgian-style house.[9] The original house had been encased and fitted with sash windows, and on the entrance front a pillared portico had been added. This part of the house, a 'long narrow building of brickwork facing the south east, though modernised, (was) part of the original building'.[10] It contained what became the drawing room, which was described as part of the old house with low ceilings and divided into three with folding doors, presumably being three smaller rooms converted into one.[11]

The house had nine bays on the south-east (original entrance) front and was three-storeyed. In the engraving (illustration 6) it is shown with small sashed windows on the second floor, with the hipped roof partly hidden by a low parapet. These windows appear to have served garret rooms within the roof space. The north-west front had, at the southern end, a full-height canted bay, then a recessed section without windows to the left of which was another matching canted bay. In the eighteenth century a two-bay section completed this front: this had a double-storey semi-circular bay with three windows. The second floor windows on the north-west front were at a lower level than those on the entrance front, making it difficult to ascertain how the floor levels were set on this floor of the building.

The nineteenth century saw further alterations to the house. The south-east front, previously the entrance front, became the garden front with the pillared portico being replaced by a conservatory and the entrance moved to the north-east side of the house where a large extension was added. The small windows on the top floor of the garden front were replaced by larger sashes, suggesting that what had been garret rooms were converted into more commodious accommodation. The low parapet was replaced by a balustrade, obscuring the roof from view. The north-west front was similarly balustraded and the semi-circular bay was replaced by a full-height bay with canted sides and polygonal turrets. While the house retained its sash windows drip mouldings were fitted and the balustrade supplemented by polygonal turrets on the corners and between each set of three bays on the garden front and also at intervals on the north-west front. These additions restored an Elizabethan/Jacobean aspect to a building which otherwise appeared to be of Georgian origin.

Changes to the house continued to be made almost to the end of its existence: these included the building of a billiard room. The Bunbury family based itself at Mildenhall after 1901 and the property was then let.[12] Structural alterations were carried out for Sir Henry Bunbury when Frank Riley-Smith was the tenant in the early 1900s, and when Sir John Smiley took a lease of the house in 1912 further extensions were made to the building.

THE END of Barton Hall came suddenly on the night of 9/10 January 1914. Sir John and Lady Smiley were entertaining a large party of guests when fire broke out at about half-past midnight. The fire and its aftermath were vividly described in the local newspaper, with an extensive account of the efforts to salvage the furniture, pictures, clocks, silver and books. The local police and fire brigade together with the house guests and estate staff repeatedly entered the burning house to bring out valuable artefacts, which were then stacked under trees and in outhouses.

Attempts to put out the fire, which had quickly taken hold, were thwarted: the water pumping apparatus operated by electricity failed and the nearest water supply was half a mile away. By two o'clock the house was completely ablaze and floors started to collapse. As the local newspaper reporter wrote:

> In three hours there was hardly a room intact. A pitiable scene met the eye. ... The rescuers were still at their work transferring the property from the building on to the lawn, and amidst all this bustle a number of ladies, still in their evening dress with overcoats over them, were sitting here and there on a sofa or standing and despondently watching the destruction of the fine old mansion.

By half-past four the stone staircase had collapsed and the water tanks at the top of the building fell through the floor. A little later the south wall cracked. The house had been destroyed, and 'instead of there being a magnificent mansion, all that [could] be seen [was] a mass of blackened ruins and twisted girders, presenting a striking scene of devastation'.[13]

Barton Hall was never rebuilt and Sir Henry Bunbury sold the whole estate of 2,136 acres. The buyer, George Grant Stevenson, purchased it with a view to selling on and in July 1915 the estate, divided into 104 lots, was put up for auction.[14] Sixty-three lots were sold for a total of £27,000, the site of the house with its remaining buildings, the gardens and parkland of 139 acres was bought in at £9,500 and the remaining lots were withdrawn, the aggregate of the bids for these coming to nearly £24,000.

In the following October another sale of fifty lots took place, with the site of the house being withdrawn when bidding reached £875.[15] The next year the sale of materials from the 'dismantling of Barton Hall' was advertised: '20 tons of lead, 50 tons of iron, 1 ton of brass and copper, quantity of zinc, 200,000 good clean bricks, 2,000 yards of iron pallisading, fine old oak boards, old oak fireplaces and porch with antique old doors'.[16] Trees and shrubs were included in the sale. Seven acres of land with the courtyard and outbuildings (the servants' bedroom wing, the dairy, knife and boot houses and a range of larders) were also put up for sale again, but having been withdrawn at £140 were later sold privately to a buyer from Wickham Market.[17]

A small part of the house remains as a ruin but the rest of its site and other land in Great Barton which formed part of its parkland and estate have since been the subject of residential development.

BOULGE HALL

BOULGE HALL, TWO MILES NORTH-WEST OF WOODBRIDGE, is best known for its association with the FitzGerald family who came to live here in 1835. Edward FitzGerald, the poet and translator of the *Rubaiyat of Omar Khayyam*, who was born in 1809 at nearby Bredfield House, was its most renowned member.

The house was owned in the first half of the nineteenth century by Mary Frances, daughter of John FitzGerald of Kilkenny. She married Dr John Purcell who changed his name to FitzGerald after the death of his father-in-law. Edward FitzGerald, their third son, was educated at King Edward VI School, Bury St Edmunds and Trinity College, Cambridge, and from 1835 to 1853 lived on the estate at Boulge Cottage. Mrs Fitzgerald died in 1855 and the Hall and its estate passed to her eldest son, John. After his death in 1879 the estate was retained

8 Boulge Hall: the entrance front.

by his executors until it was sold in 1890 to Robert Holmes White, a London solicitor, whose father John Meadows White was a member of a long-established East Anglian family. John White had established himself with his cousin Thomas Borrett in London in legal practice in the 1820s, becoming a Parliamentary solicitor and also solicitor to the Ecclesiastical Commission. Following its purchase by Robert White, Boulge became the home of his son, Robert Eaton White, who became prominent in the affairs of Suffolk and was created a baronet in 1937.[1]

THE HOUSE was built for William Whitby about 1794 but appears to have been substantially recast in the nineteenth century.[2] In 1866 the architects W. G. Habershon and A. R. Pite undertook work to the house said to have cost £800, but what alterations were made is not known.[3] Externally the house had a very Victorian look to it with the windows of the rooms on the garden front being sashed and some of the windows on the entrance front being mullioned and transomed with sashes. The large bay on the garden front and many of the chimneys were typical of the second half of the nineteenth century but other features such as crow-stepped gables may have reflected earlier origins. It was built of white brick with plain tiles and a modillion cornice and was of two principal storeys with dormer-windowed attics.

It is clear that the White family were responsible for substantive renewal of the house and the development of the estate in the twenty years after they acquired the property. Their correspondence and other papers covering the work they undertook survive.[4] That work included the installation of electric lighting in 1906 and parquet flooring, the erection of outbuildings, development of the gardens and the erection of a gardener's cottage and of horticultural buildings and vineries (the latter constructed by Boulton & Paul).

SIR ROBERT WHITE died in 1940 and five years later Boulge Hall with sixteen acres and its estate were placed on the market for sale by auction. The sale catalogue describes the house as being 'comfortable', of brick with a slate roof and in good repair.[5] It comprised a lounge hall, drawing room, dining room and study and eight principal bedrooms, two bathrooms and ten secondary and servants' bedrooms. The stable block had three loose boxes, a harness room and double garage. There was a chauffeur's cottage. The estate of 850 acres included three farms, two in Bredfield and one in Hasketon, and woodland and was sold to Corpus Christi College, Cambridge.[6]

In July 1955 it was reported that the East Suffolk Planning Committee had been informed that Boulge Hall was to be demolished because of the repair costs, which were estimated at £7,000.[7] Although the house had been provisionally listed Grade II, the Ministry of Housing and Local Government had raised no objection as it was of local rather than national interest. The department had suggested that interesting features of the interior should be preserved and the stable clock and gate piers should be retained for reuse in any later development, and the Planning Committee recommended that a photographic record and plans should be made for the National Buildings Record.

The house was said to have Adam fire baskets, exquisite figured brass finger plates and door knobs, carved mantels and cut glass chandeliers. Outside there were wrought iron gates and a sundial said to tell the time in Constantinople, Rome and the Canary Isles. No record of a sale of the valuable fittings and fixtures has been located, but it may be assumed that the usual practice of selling these off prior to demolition was followed in the case of Boulge Hall. In any event early in September 1955 demolition of what was described as the 'seventeenth century mansion' began with only the stable block being retained.[8] An auction sale of salvaged materials took place the following November.

BRAMFORD HALL

DEMOLISHED 1956

BRAMFORD HALL STOOD ON HIGH GROUND ON THE WEST SIDE OF THE GIPPING VALLEY four miles north-west of Ipswich. It stood in an estate of 1,235 acres and was one of the numerous properties which in the absence of male heirs passed through marriage to the family of Broke of Nacton. Sir Percy Loraine whose mother was a daughter of Captain Charles Acton Broke, was the last member of the family to own Bramford.[1]

In 1595 William Acton, a clothier from Ipswich, acquired Beverlies and other manors in the parish of Bramford and in 1612 the manor of Bramford itself.[2] His son John (who was born in 1587 and was High Sheriff of Suffolk in 1631) purchased further lands in the parish.[3] John

*9 Bramford Hall:
the entrance front.*

Acton is said to have erected the original house in the 1630s and it became the seat of his family whose last male heir was Nathaniel Lee Acton, who inherited Livermere Hall near Bury St Edmunds in 1768.[4] On the death of Nathaniel Lee Acton in 1836 Bramford Hall and its estate passed in turn to his two sisters, the second of whom was the widow of Sir William Fowle Middleton Bt of Shrubland. After the death of their son, Sir William Fowle Fowle Middleton, in 1860 the property passed to his nephew, Sir George Nathaniel Broke Bt, and thereafter to Sir George's niece who married Rear-Admiral Sir Lampton Loraine Bt. Family papers indicate that in Victorian times the house was mainly let to tenants.[5] At the turn of the nineteenth and twentieth centuries, one of these tenants, Major-General J. C. Russell, commissioned a series of photographs of the house and estate. These survive and provide a fascinating insight into life on the estate at that time.[6]

Sir Lampton Loraine died in 1917 and his widow became a tenant of her son Sir Percy, a distinguished diplomat who was British Ambassador in Turkey and later in Rome and on whose behalf the estate was managed, the Hon. John Henniker (of Thornham) being the agent.[7] After Lady Loraine's death in 1933 her daughter, Isaura, remained at Bramford until 1937. It appears that she was the last member of the family to live in the house.

THE ORIGINAL HOUSE was probably built on four sides around a central courtyard but it was substantially altered either in the middle of the eighteenth century by Nathaniel Acton or by his son Nathaniel Lee Acton, who was also responsible for substantial alterations to Livermere. The house that resulted was of brick rendered with stucco c. 1780 and consisted of a main block of seven bays on three storeys under a hipped roof with a parapet, which originally had battlements, these being removed in 1857.[8] Below the parapet was a cornice and below the second floor windows a band or string course. The main block facing east was one room deep with three chimneys built on the rear wall and exposed to view in a manner similar to the chimneys on the entrance front at Livermere. Behind the main block was a brick-faced service wing of two storeys. The roof of the glazed entrance portico provided a balcony with a wrought iron balustrade at first floor level in the three central bays. There was a two-bay wing of two storeys to the right of the entrance front. When this was added is not known but it may be the enlargement of the house (estimated to cost at least £2,000) referred to in papers relating to the

1857 renovation scheme. As part of this scheme a semi-circular bay of two storeys was erected on the south elevation to the designs of Morgan and Phipson architects.[9] At a later date this bay had a canopy fitted at ground floor level to form a verandah. To the left of the south front were a conservatory and glass houses. Internally the house had a drawing room, dining room and library with five principal bedrooms and attic rooms.

The house was the subject of substantial renovation and modernisation shortly before World War II, the work being supervised by Professor A. E. (later Sir Albert) Richardson. The extent of the work suggests that by 1937 the house was in poor repair and lacking in modern facilities. In total some £8,000 was spent on electric lighting, plumbing and general building works.[10] The costs were considerably in excess of original estimates and Sir Percy, who was based in Ankara while the work was in progress, sought and obtained a substantial reduction in the architect's fees as a result.

IT APPEARS that it was intended to let the house after the renovations were completed, and the agent estimated that a rent of £750–800 a year might be achieved if the shooting rights were included. In the event the house does not appear to have been let before it was taken over by the War Department for use as officers' quarters during the war.

Bramford was in the class of houses for which, in the post-war period, the family appears to have had no further use and for which there was no market demand. Moreover, its condition is unlikely to have been improved by its use by the Army. Sir Percy Loraine had another seat in Northumberland and also a London residence. He had no children, his brother had been killed in an aircraft accident in 1912 and neither of his sisters married. In 1953 the contents of the house were sold by auction, the sale including a pair of wrought iron gates forming part of the fence between the park and the garden. The catalogue photograph of these gates shows the unoccupied house behind them.[11] The demolition of most of the house took place early in 1956, a sale of materials taking place in March that year.[12] Sir Percy Loraine died in 1962 and the major part of the estate of 1,235 acres was sold by his trustees in 1972.[13] The remainder, including the site of the house, was sold two years later.[14]

Part of the house survived and has been incorporated in a modern dwelling. Most of the housing developments in Bramford were built on former estate land.

BRANCHES PARK

DEMOLISHED 1957

Branches Park mansion stood a mile west of the Church of St Margaret of Antioch in Cowlinge in the west of the county. Its estate lay in both the parishes of Cowlinge and Little Bradley. The original manor house of Cowlinge, a manor in which the Drury family of Rougham, east of Bury St Edmunds, had an interest, stood on a different site from the later Georgian house.[1] The lordship passed through various families until, on the death in 1709 of Sir Stephen Soame, whose father had been Lord Mayor of London, it was sold to Francis Dickins, a bencher of the Middle Temple. At the time he made his will Dickins lived in Hampshire, but there is a memorial to him in Cowlinge Church where in 1733 he rebuilt the tower and provided two bells.[2]

Dickins had been assembling land holdings in Cowlinge and Lidgate since 1705 when he purchased Hardhouse Field, an acquisition which was

10 *Branches Park: the entrance front about 1820.*

followed by others until his death in 1747.[3] Around 1730 he built a new house on the estate he had assembled. He was succeeded by his nephew, Ambrose, who employed Lancelot 'Capability' Brown to landscape the 190-acre park.[4] On Ambrose's death the property passed to Francis and Diana Dickins of Wollaston, Northamptonshire who sold the mansion house and the bulk of the estate in 1806/7 to John Kemp, a maltster from Sible Hedingham in Essex, for £28,000. It is clear that Kemp financed his acquisition of the estate by mortgaging it, and his ownership ended with his bankruptcy and the sale of the property by his assignees in 1817. By this time the estate consisted of 942 acres together with the great and small tithes extending over 3,000 acres.[5] Kemp had also acquired from Dickins the lease of the rectory of Cowlinge owned by Trinity Hall, Cambridge.[6]

The estate was acquired by Henry Usborne of Manchester Square, London, being financed through his marriage settlement.[7] He was High Sheriff of Suffolk in 1823 and died in 1840. In that year the estate extended to 1,602 acres and was valued at £63,920.[8] Following Usborne's death the estate was put up for sale but it remained unsold.[9] In 1844 the house alone was let for three years to the rector of nearby Depden.[10] The granting of this lease was followed in 1845 by the sale of the estate for £60,500 to James Simpson, described at the time as a 'gentleman from Manchester': in fact, Simpson came from Oswaldtwistle, near Accrington.[11] He died in 1847, leaving his Branches and other estates (with the exception of his estate at Methven in Perthshire) to his second son, also James, on whose death it passed to trustees for his grandson, James Alfred Simpson, who was born in 1853.[12]

The three-generation ownership by the Simpsons ended in 1889 when the house and a substantial part of the estate were sold to Major General James Dundas Cockburn for £30,000.[13] Following his death some ten years later the property was sold in 1902 to Gilbert Augustus Tonge. Tonge was one of the principals in the provision merchants Kearley & Tonge of Mitre Square, London, originally founded by Hudson Kearley (later Viscount Davenport). Their business empire included the International Tea Company with retail branches in many parts of the country, a jam-making enterprise in Southall and a biscuit factory. The financial success of Kearley & Tonge no doubt provided Gilbert Tonge with the means to purchase the Branches Park estate and shortly afterwards to undertake substantial additions and improvements to the house.

TOP LEFT:
11 Branches Park: the garden front in the late nineteenth century.

LEFT:
12 Branches Park: the entrance front after the additions made in the early twentieth century.

THE DESIGNER of Francis Dickins's house has not been identified. It was a three-storey brick building of five bays on each front the entrance (north) and garden fronts being 140 feet in length. The three central bays at first and second floor level on the entrance front were framed by pairs of pilasters and divided by single pilasters all of which supported a central pediment. The three central windows on this front had round-arched tops. The majority of the windows were pedimented. Later in the eighteenth century single-storey pavilions projecting forward on both the entrance and garden fronts were added on each side of the original building. On the entrance front these had canted bays with sashed windows set in blind arches and on the garden front had tripartite windows in the 'Venetian' style, with massive ornamented arches. After these additions the building appears to have remained largely unaltered until the beginning of the twentieth century, although service buildings may have been added on the west side of the building in the nineteenth century.[14]

The sale particulars in 1817 give a description of the accommodation at that time: a large paved entrance hall from which opened a 'breakfast parlor', a library, a music room, a 'noble eating room' and a drawing room (both of these being thirty-six feet by twenty-four feet), a 'gentleman's parlor' and domestic offices. On the first floor were a morning room and boudoir, five bedrooms, two dressing rooms, a 'water closet', an 'elegant gallery with a domed skylight, enriched ornaments, and pilasters' and two staircases, and on the top storey seven bedrooms, a dressing room and closets. There were six staff sleeping rooms.[15]

The additions and alterations made by Gilbert Tonge were substantial, and the house, after enlargement, has been described as an eighteenth-century house altered into a 'late Renaissance house'.[16] The architect employed by Tonge was George Hornblower (1858–1940), who is said to have been in partnership with Tonge but the nature of their professional relationship (if any) is unclear.[17] The builders were F. B. Thackray of Huntingdon.

The single-storey pavilions were retained but extended in width and built over to provide additional bedrooms. Further extensions and a water tower were also added, resulting in a house of eleven bays, being almost doubled in size.[18] This is demonstrated by comparing the description of the house in 1817 with that when it was put on the market in 1929. The ground floor now had, in addition to the vestibule and entrance hall, a dining room, two drawing rooms, a boudoir, two sitting rooms, a morning room, a billiard room, a study and a library and, at the west end of the house, 'well shut off', the substantial domestic offices. On the first floor, reached by two staircases, there were eleven principal bed and dressing rooms, with a further twelve on the second floor. In all there were eight bathrooms and fifteen servants' bedrooms. The stable block with six loose boxes and three stalls contained accommodation for up to four grooms. There was a range of garages and other buildings including an indoor swimming pool.[19]

GILBERT TONGE died in 1927, and in July 1929 the house and its estate of nearly 2,700 acres was put on the market. The outcome of that sale generally is not known but it seems that the house and much of the estate remained unsold, with Mrs Tonge remaining there during the 1930s. In 1935 further alterations were made to the house by the architects J. Burlison and W. Turner Lord.[20] By 1939, however, Mrs Tonge was living elsewhere, and in the early 1940s Mrs Violet Fitzgerald was the owner and occupier of the house and also owned a considerable part of the estate.[21]

In 1947 Miss Rachel Parsons, the wealthy daughter of Sir Charles Parsons, the inventor of the steam turbine, and herself a notable society hostess in the 1930s, bought the house. She spent part of her considerable fortune – £840,000 inherited from her father – on thoroughbred horses and became well known in the Newmarket area for her eccentricities. It was reported that, after she encountered difficulties engaging staff, she occupied only two rooms of the large house, with many rooms turned over to the storage of fodder and potatoes.[22] In 1955 Miss Parsons moved to Newmarket and it was there on 3 July 1956 that she was found dead. Four months later a local stableman, Dennis Pratt, was convicted of her manslaughter.[23]

Rachel Parsons died intestate and in December 1956 the house with over 700 acres was sold by auction by her personal representatives.[24] The purchaser was a company, Thomas Oakley (Luton) Limited, which then sold it to another company, E. Longhurst & Sons Limited of Epsom. In March 1957 the fixtures and fittings 'from the seventy room mansion' were sold by auction in over 400 lots – 6,300 feet of mahogany and pine panelling, wrought iron balustrading, mahogany-panelled doors, marble and wood chimneypieces, and wrought iron grates, wood and marble flooring, pavings, lead urns and figurines. 'Another Big House Doomed', a local paper reported.[25] In April 1957 the Georgian pedimented stable block, other outbuildings and twenty-seven acres of land were put up for sale, reserving to the vendors until the end of December that year a right of way for the removal of the structure and fabric of the mansion.[26] Demolition of the house then took place.

The fate of Branches Park mansion, for the first century and a half of its existence a compact and elegant house, was perhaps sealed by its conversion during Gilbert Tonge's ownership into a very large and less architecturally attractive building. It is possible that without the extensions built by Tonge the house might have survived into the period when such houses became statutorily protected and new uses for them were found. The stable block has survived and been converted into a dwelling, and a new house has been built on part of the site of the demolished mansion.

BREDFIELD HOUSE

DEMOLISHED 1950

Bredfield House, occasionally referred to as Bredfield Hall and as Bredfield White House, stood three miles north-west of Woodbridge. It was built by Robert Marryott, a lawyer from Woodbridge, in about 1655 but was the reshaping of an earlier house.[1] Forty years later it passed into the ownership of the Jenney family, two of whose forebears had been prominent lawyers in the fifteenth and sixteenth centuries and who were lords of the manor.[2] In 1765 it formed part of the marriage settlement of Edmund Jenney and Anne, daughter of Philip Broke of Nacton.[3]

During the Jenneys' ownership the house was tenanted by the Purcell family and Edward, the third son of Dr John Purcell, who changed his name to FitzGerald. This Edward was the translator of the *Rubaiyat of*

13 Bredfield House: the entrance and garden fronts.

Omar Khayyam (see page 27). He was born at Bredfield in 1809 before the family moved to Boulge Hall in the next village. In 1859 Stewart William and Arthur Henry Jenney sold the property to Joseph White, and it remained in the ownership of the White family until the middle of the twentieth century.

MARRYOTT'S house was built of brick on an H-plan.[4] It had a kitchen and dairy at the rear of the right-hand wing in what survived of the earlier timber-framed house dating from the late fifteenth or early sixteenth century.[5] It had Dutch gables on the projecting wings of the entrance front and one at the rear of the left-hand wing. It was of two storeys with attics and two segmentally pedimented dormers at the front. Considerable changes, including a new staircase, were made to the house in the eighteenth century when an orangery was added to the rear of the left-hand wing and other works, including the creation of a canal in the garden, were undertaken.[6] In the middle of the nineteenth century the space between the rear wings was partially infilled. An inventory of the house in 1852 refers to the old and new drawing rooms, the kitchen and the new kitchen, and the scullery and the new scullery, suggesting recent changes to the old house.[7]

Substantial alterations to the appearance of the house were also made. These included the building of two-storey canted bays with balustrades on the entrance front, the erection of Tudor-style barley-twist chimneys, new windows and entrance doors and the overlaying of the original brick with stucco. Internally the house retained to the end its eighteenth-century staircase with slender fluted balusters and its mantelpieces with enriched friezes and ducks-nest cast iron grates. The panelling in one room also remained.[8]

Latterly before it was taken down the house had a vestibule, lounge hall, staircase hall, dining room, study, library and domestic offices on the ground floor, a drawing room on the half-landing, eight principal bedrooms, a dressing room and two bathrooms on the first floor and six rooms in the attic. The stable block, which survived the demolition of most of the house, was contemporaneous with the house built by Marryott and has similar Dutch gables.

DURING World War II the house was requisitioned by the War Department and, following the death of Captain J. H. Lachlan White, his executors put on the market in 1946 the house and stable block with its walled garden, twenty-three acre park, a further 175 acres of land (including the Home Farm) and eighteen cottages.[9] The roof of the house had suffered considerable damage and the entrance lodge had been completely destroyed by enemy action. The agents also noted that 'a considerable claim for Dilapidations was pending' to cover damage done during the property's wartime occupation.[10]

The house was bought by Group Captain and Mrs Hyde. In 1948 its demolition was mooted and this took place two years later.[11] Part of the timber-framed service wing of the house dating from before Robert Marryott's time was retained and has been enlarged to create what is now known as Fitzgerald House. The handsome stable block and walled garden have survived, and the early eighteenth-century garden house, which also escaped demolition, has been extended to form the present Bredfield House.

A plaque designed in 1938 by Sir Frank Brangwyn marking Bredfield as the birthplace of Edward FitzGerald was also retained. Two verses of a poem by FitzGerald quoted in a letter by a member of the Omar Khayyam Club, published in 1948, are particularly apposite.[12]

Lo an English mansion founded
In the elder James's reign
Quaint and stately and surrounded
With a pastoral domain.

Yet the secret worm ne'er ceases
Nor the mouse behind the wall;
Hearts of oak will come to pieces
And farewell to Bredfield Hall.

BROME HALL

DEMOLISHED c. 1958

Brome Hall, for four centuries one of the seats of the Cornwallis family, stood near the Suffolk/Norfolk boundary between Eye and Diss. The family inherited the manor of Ling in the parish of Brome early in the fifteenth century following the marriage of Philippa, heiress of Robert Buckton, to John, son of Thomas Cornwallis, a London merchant. His descendant Sir Thomas was Comptroller of the Household in the reign of Queen Mary.[1] After her death, he was suspected of being a Catholic recusant and is said to have retired to Brome, where he rebuilt the hall, which remained in his family until 1823.[2]

The Cornwallis family was prominent in public life through the seventeenth and eighteenth centuries, providing an ambassador to Spain in the reign of King James I, a Treasurer of the Royal Household and Surveyor of Customs in the reign of King Charles II and a Paymaster General in that of King George I. Frederick Cornwallis was raised to the peerage by King Charles II, and the fifth Baron was created Viscount Brome and Earl Cornwallis in 1753. His son Charles served in the American War of Independence where his involvement in the surrender of Yorktown in 1781 does not appear to have affected his prospects. Five years later he became Governor General of Bengal where he served until 1793 and again in 1805. He died in India soon after his return there in 1805 and was buried at Ghazipore near Varanasi (Benares), having been promoted to the rank of General, made a Knight of the Garter and created a Marquess.

The Cornwallis family inherited the Culford estate near Bury St Edmunds in the seventeenth century, and in the early 1790s the first Marquess commissioned the remodelling by James Wyatt of his Tudor house there.[3] Brome became the family's secondary seat and rebuilding there did not take place for another twenty years until after the second Marquess had inherited the estate. He, however, died without children in 1823 and the Cornwallis family's ownership of Brome came to an end with its sale.

The purchaser was Matthias Kerrison, the son of a Norfolk clergyman, who had made a substantial fortune in the grain trade in Bungay, where he also had other business interests including the development of the navigations on the Ouse and Waveney rivers. His purchase of Brome Hall

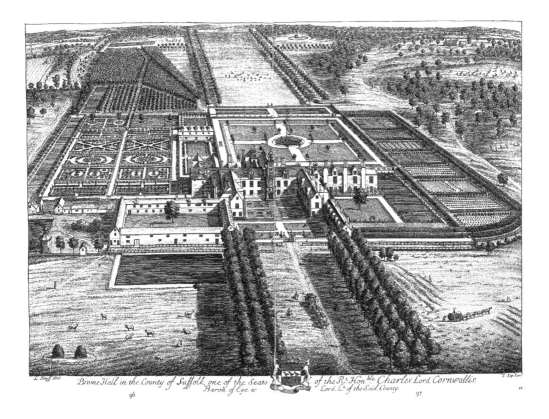

L. Knyff Del.   Brome Hall in the County of Suffolk, one of the Seats   of the Rt.Honble. Charles Lord Cornwallis.
96   Baron of Eye &c   Lord. Lt. of the Said County.   97   J. Kip Inv.

followed on from his acquisition from Viscount Maynard of the adjacent Hoxne Hall estate (Oakley Park as it was shortly to be renamed). Matthias Kerrison died in 1827 leaving the estate to his son, General Sir Edward Kerrison. Brome remained in the ownership of the Kerrison family for nearly a century until after the death of Sir Edward's grand-daughter, Lady Bateman.

THE HOUSE built by Sir Thomas Cornwallis was, as can be seen from Knyff and Kip's engraving (illustration 14), a large house. The central block of seven bays with its entrance porch surmounted by a slender polygonal tower capped by a cupola had two forward-projecting wings forming a open courtyard. To the rear and to both left and right of the main block stood what appear to be later extensions to the original U-shaped building, and there were substantial service buildings and outhouses. The house had mullioned and transomed windows.[4] Around it were developed large formal gardens with plantations and formal avenues of trees.

14 Brome Hall: bird's-eye view about 1700 (from Knyff & Kip's Britannia Illustrata*).*

By the early years of the nineteenth century Brome Hall, as a secondary residence, must have been much larger than needed and no doubt old-fashioned by the standards of Regency England. The author of *Excursions through the County of Suffolk*, published in 1819, wrote:

> The building is of brick and the chimneys are curiously ornamented. The great hall is very lofty, and without a ceiling, the timbers being finished like those in some of our ancient churches; but it is wainscoted to the height of about ten feet. At one end a large window is embellished with the arms of the family, in painted glass, at the other, over the entrance is a gallery: below this is the butler's pantry, separated from the room with a flight of stairs on each side.

Evidently that part of the account of Brome had been written some years before publication because the author continues:

> A great part of the hall was taken down a few years ago ... and among other changes it has been observed that several of the out-offices of Brome Hall have been converted into residences for cottagers.[5]

In 1815 the second Marquess Cornwallis had employed the architect George Wyatt to make radical alterations.[6] These involved the construction of rooms within the Great Hall, the changes being so substantial that a century later it was said that it was difficult to determine within the reconstructed building exactly what had been the hall's precise position.[7] The outer wings of the old house were demolished and a much smaller house created. The survival of Tudor brickwork, crow-stepped gables and some ornamented chimneys evidenced the origins of the house but its lack of symmetry, its battlemented towers and two-storey bays demonstrated that in the nineteenth century it had gone through a transformation from its Tudor origins. It had been converted from an Elizabethan palace into a country house. Two letters of June 1815 from George Wyatt have survived, one of which, addressed to Lewis Wyatt, reveals that the cost of rebuilding was some £2,000, excluding materials many of which came from the old buildings and were recycled.[8] In the other, presumably addressed to the builder at Brome (no Clerk of Works having been engaged), Wyatt writes that he had been urging the Marquess to approve the reuse of the wainscoting removed from the Great Hall to 'line' the new dining room – 'I write therefore at his Lordship's request to

beg of you, by no means, to suffer the old wainscoting to be <u>destroyed</u> or cut up for anything.'[9] Lewis Wyatt subsequently added a bay window to the new dining room.[10]

After the second Marquess's alterations the house had five reception rooms, eight principal bedrooms, six secondary and staff bedrooms, and extensive domestic offices comprising eleven rooms (kitchens, servants' quarters and storerooms). In addition there were four maids' bedrooms and (in an adjoining building) four men's rooms. The stabling with its clock tower comprised eight stalls and three loose boxes, two coach houses, a harness room, lofts and four grooms' bedrooms.[11]

LADY BATEMAN died in 1918. In November the following year the Brome and Oakley estates were sold by her son, the third Lord Bateman, to Rowland Hodge, a Tyneside shipbuilder.[12] Hodge did not retain Oakley Park for long, selling it in 1920, and before 1924 he had also sold Brome. In that year the house with a hundred acres, together with the Home Farm, another farm and cottages and land in Brome and nearby villages (in all 475 acres), was sold at auction on behalf of an unnamed vendor. The gardens extended to seven acres with terracing, a conservatory, a topiary garden and a Dutch garden dating from the middle of the previous century. The purchaser for £9,000 was Miss Maude Tacon whose father, Sir Thomas Henry Tacon, had been a solicitor in Eye and prominent in public affairs in Suffolk.[13] She retained the Brome estate for nearly thirty years, but it appears that she did not live in the house after the beginning of World War II during which it was used by the Army. Miss Tacon died in 1952, and in June the following year the contents of the house were sold.[14] In October the estate was put on the market.[15]

The hall was purchased for £3,200 by Mr C. A. West, the tenant of the Home Farm (which he also bought for £5,800).[16] Mr West died in 1957, and the following year his son, Oliver West, confirmed that as the house was in such a dilapidated state the only thing to do was to pull it down. He hoped to use the bricks to build a new house on the site, and that did indeed happen.[17]

The house demolished in 1958 was only a pale shadow of Sir Thomas Cornwallis's great house, but with it departed a piece of not only of Suffolk history, but also of the history of England in which the Cornwallis family had played a distinguished role.

CAMPSEA ASHE HIGH HOUSE

DEMOLISHED 1953

CAMPSEA ASHE LIES TWO MILES EAST OF WICKHAM MARKET and Ashe Common and provided the site for High House (so called, apparently, on account of its four storeys), which William Glover, a servant of Thomas Howard, Earl of Suffolk, built there in the early seventeenth century. This was on the estate that William's father, John Glover, a servant of Thomas Howard, third Duke of Norfolk, had acquired from Thomas Goodwyn and others in the reign of Elizabeth I. The Glover family did not remain long at the house as William Glover was killed in 1641 at the White Hart in Wickham Market, and in 1652 his son sold the property to John Sheppard whose family came from Mendlesham, some miles to the west of Campsea Ashe.[1] The Sheppard family retained the estate for almost 250 years, enlarging the original brick built house and, in the early nineteenth century, building the stable block.[2]

The Sheppards were a prominent gentry family, and various members served the office of High Sheriff of Suffolk. In addition to the Campsea Ashe estate they also owned the nearby Bawdsey estate. John George Sheppard, the last of the family to own High House, was a member of the jury at the first trial for perjury of the impostor Arthur Orton, who claimed

16 Campsea Ashe High House: the entrance front in 1905.

to have succeeded to the Tichborne baronetcy. Indeed, the strain imposed on Sheppard by his attendance at the year-long trial is said to have broken his health.[3] Following his death in 1882, leaving a widow but no children, High House and its estate were sold. The property was auctioned in London in July 1883 and, the bidding having started at £50,000, it was sold to the Hon. William Lowther of Lowther Lodge, Hyde Park, a brother of the third Earl of Lonsdale, for £105,000 (the equivalent of over £5,000,000 today).[4]

THE HOUSE that William Lowther purchased in 1883 was materially different from that which William Glover had built in the seventeenth century. A fire in 1864 had severely damaged the original house and its later additions. John George Sheppard had employed the architect Anthony Salvin to rebuild the house after the fire. The house, which was created from the remains of the old house, was in the Jacobean style of its predecessor, a style for which Salvin was renowned (his other Suffolk rebuilding at Flixton also replaced an early seventeenth-century house that had been severely damaged by fire). The reconstructed house was on the same E-shaped 'footprint' as the old house, with a four-storeyed central section but without the cupola which had graced its predecessor. The polygonal turrets on the corners of the sections of the entrance front were retained but changes were made to the fenestration. The gables were crow-stepped. Internally Salvin incorporated some surviving elements of the old house. notably two fine ceilings which were suspended and supported while rebuilding took place.[5] One of these was a panelled and embossed ceiling of early seventeenth-century style and the other a fine rococo one with classic mythological figures in bas relief.

The house that resulted from the 1860s' rebuilding was a substantial property. The Particulars of Sale in 1949 state that it had six reception rooms, thirty-one bed and dressing rooms and the extensive household offices needed to service a mansion of this size – kitchen, scullery, pantries, larders, brushing, flower and boot rooms, a servants' hall and sitting room and boiler houses for domestic hot water and central heating. The garaging, stabling and other outside premises were also extensive – two garages and a covered washdown, eleven loose boxes, four living rooms, a harness room, fodder stores, fire engine house, game larder and gun room. There was also a squash court.[6]

The house stood in what the selling agents described as a 'delightful pleasure ground', three features of which were particularly noteworthy.[7] The bowling green, possibly dating from William Glover's time, and the long canal dating from the late seventeenth century (probably one of a pair the second of which was partly filled in) were bordered by massive yew hedges of considerable antiquity.[8] The yews were extraordinarily shaped, probably a consequence of neglect in the period of the Sheppard family's ownership when they became overgrown and covered with ivy, which is said to have taken William Lowther fifteen years to eliminate. The eight cedar trees had been described in the 1883 Particulars of Sale as 'the first to be introduced into England', although the writer of handwritten extracts from those Particulars, presumably either the Hon. William Lowther or his son, added the note 'This is a doubtful statement'.[9] Nonetheless the trees, believed to have been planted around 1750, were clearly handsome specimens. The gardens also included sunken and Japanese gardens, a walled garden with a vinery, peach and plant houses and a cucumber pit.

On William Lowther's death in 1912 the property passed to his son, James Lowther, who was Speaker of the House of Commons from 1905 to 1921 and was created Viscount Ullswater when he retired from the Speakership. Both Ullswater's eldest son and his grandson predeceased him, and on his death in March 1949 the viscountcy was inherited by his great-grandson. Ullswater's death signalled the end of the Lowther family's ownership of the house.

FOLLOWING the sale of the contents of High House at auction for (according to newspaper reports at the time) £36,000, High House and the Campsea Ashe estate of 2,700 acres together with the village school in nearby Blaxhall, and the Green Man public house and the police house both in Tunstall, were sold in November 1949. The agricultural property with a rent roll of £3,700, which included thirteen dairy and mixed farms and twenty-five other houses and cottages, was bought before auction by the Public Trustee for the Desborough Settlement Trust as part of an estate duty mitigation scheme.[10] At the auction High House, with sixteen acres of gardens and grounds, was 'knocked down' to Mr F. C. Fisher, an Ipswich estate agent, for £4,600.[11]

Fisher appears to have been acting for Lady Delaney, but she died shortly after her purchase of the house and over the next three years the building fell into a ruinous state. In 1952 the property was sold to Richard Schreiber and the house was demolished. The squash court, the gardener's cottage and the coach house and stable block survived as private dwellings together with parts of the historic gardens.[12]

CARLTON HALL

CARLTON HALL STOOD IN A LARGE PARK BETWEEN SAXMUNDHAM AND KELSALE, facing across a low valley to Carlton Parish Church. The main block was destroyed by fire on Christmas Day 1941, the service wing being converted into a house after the war. At the beginning of the twenty-first century the remaining wing and its environs were developed with new housing including a new mansion.

The original Carlton Hall appears to have been on a different site from the building burnt down in 1941.[1] Its owner in 1655 bore the name Osborne, described as 'a Kentish man his estate between £200 and £300 p. annum'.[2] This hall may have been the seat of the lord of the manor of Carlton but the manor belonged to the Bence family of Thorington and was held separately from the estate from the early eighteenth century.[3]

In the middle of that century Carlton was owned by Osborn Fuller of Tottenham High Cross in Middlesex who acquired it in 1753 from the mortgagees of William Fuller of Saxmundham and his wife.[4] Whether Osborn and William Fuller were related and whether Osborn's name reflects relationship with the Osborne who owned Carlton Hall in the previous century are matters for speculation. Osborn Fuller died in 1794, having increased the size of the estate by a number of purchases both in his own name and that of his son Edward, who was born about 1782. Edward Fuller also made a number of purchases to increase the size of the estate, but it was subject to mortgages and various parts were sold off in 1837 to Lionel Dove.[5] In 1850 the estate was purchased by Edward Walter Bonham, who lived in France, and was transferred to the marriage settlement of his son Henry, who married Augusta Musgrave.[6] Following Henry Bonham's death in 1856 his widow, who in the following year married the second Earl of Stradbroke, became the effective owner of Carlton until it formed part of the marriage settlement of her son, Henry Walter Musgrave Bonham, in 1875.[7]

During most of the time when the house belonged to the Countess of Stradbroke and the Bonhams it was a tenanted property being occupied by Richard Garrett III, who, on taking over the engineering business in Leiston founded by his grandfather in 1778, built it into one of the leading developers and manufacturers of agricultural equipment in the country with a world-wide export business.[8] After Richard Garrett's death his widow remained at Carlton, and it was later occupied by their son. In addition to renting Carlton Hall the Garretts in 1868 bought the adjoining Carlton Rookery estate, which subsequently became part of the main estate. The Garretts were succeeded as tenants at Carlton by Captain George Price, a Member of Parliament.[9] In 1905 Major-General Sir Ronald Lane took a tenancy with an option to purchase, which he exercised two years later. His wife, Augusta, became the owner, paying £20,000 for the estate.[10] The property remained in the Lane family until, in 1937, following the death of Sir Ronald Lane whose wife had predeceased him, the estate of 586 acres was put on the market.[11]

THERE APPEARS to be no record of when the house was built or by whom, but it seems likely that it was built by Osborn Fuller in the middle of the eighteenth century.[12] It was added to in the nineteenth century. Of three storeys, it had five bays, the central three having a portico with four Ionic columns and the outer ones having canted bays to full height. To the left

17 Carlton Hall: the entrance front.

AXMUNDHAM. CARLTON HALL.

54109

of the main block there was a long two-storey wing terminating with a canted bay, again to full height.[13] This was originally a single-storey extension to which the upper floor was a later addition. Behind both this part of the house and to the rear of the right-hand end of the main block there were further wings. The date these additions to the house were made is not known.

The various additions to what was probably a modest Georgian house made Carlton into a substantial mansion with a large entrance hall, small and large drawing rooms with intercommunicating double doors, dining room, small and large libraries, a study and staircase hall lit by a lantern. The principal rooms had moulded cornices and some had ornamental ceilings. The chimneypieces were of marble some with carved wood surrounds. On the first floor there were twelve bedrooms, three dressing rooms, three bathrooms and two staff bedrooms, and on the second floor a further five staff bedrooms. As was customary in houses of this size there were extensive domestic offices with a housekeeper's room, a butler's bedroom with sinks and two plate safes and a staff bathroom. The basement provided cellarage and boiler rooms and further domestic offices.[14]

AT THE BEGINNING of World War II the house was requisitioned by the government, but on Christmas Day 1941 the main block was destroyed by fire. After 1945 the long service wing was converted into a house with two reception rooms and four bedrooms. This was sold in 1948 together with two cottages and the lodge and 117 acres of gardens and parkland, including the walled garden and stables, garages, barns and other outbuildings.[15] Subsequently it was lived in by Sir Maurice Batho.

At the beginning of the twenty-first century the house and adjoining buildings were sold for redevelopment. The 1948 house was converted into two dwellings and a further nine houses were built on adjoining land. A new hall was built adjacent to the site of the original hall.

CAVENHAM HALL

DEMOLISHED 1949

AVENHAM HALL, SEVEN MILES NORTH-EAST OF BURY ST EDMUNDS, was the mansion house of an estate renowned in the late nineteenth century for its shooting. The manor was held in medieval times by a number of noble families: Fitzgilbert; de Clare, the Earls of Hereford; de Stafford, the Earls of Stafford and the Dukes of Buckingham. In 1590 it was held by Thomas Bedingfield and later by Sir Edmund Lewknor.[1] In the first half of the eighteenth century Cavenham belonged to Richard Long and then to Robert Johnson. After a short period of ownership by Joseph Watkin, the property was sold in 1767 to Thomas le Blanc.[2] In 1794 it was bought by the first Marquess Cornwallis, and fifteen years later sold to Henry Spencer Waddington.[3] The cost was £35,000.[4]

The Waddington family owned Cavenham for ninety years. On the death of Henry Spencer Waddington in 1864 it passed to his son of the

18 Cavenham Hall: the garden front of the house designed by Andrew Noble Prentice.

same name, who was a Member of Parliament and was High Sheriff of Suffolk in 1876. Spencer, the son of his marriage to Caroline, a daughter of Vice-Admiral Sir William Proctor Beauchamp, third baronet, inherited the estate in 1895, and three years later sold it to Herbert Ernest Matthew Davies.

THE OLD HOUSE, a rectangular U-shaped house with its courtyard facing the road through the village and with outbuildings located between it and the road, did not long survive its acquisition by Herbert Davies.[5] In 1898 it was replaced by a new house positioned further from the road than its predecessor and surrounded by parkland. The new stable buildings and coachman's cottage occupied 'the position of an old range of stable buildings' and were described as 'charmingly situated between the present house and the garden', with 'only the gate piers retained from the previous building'.[6] As frequently occurred when a new house was being built the old house served as lodgings for the builders. The architect of the new house was Andrew Noble Prentice and the contractors were Waring & Gillow Limited.[7]

The house was designed in a late Renaissance style in 'a strikingly free and opulent plan', and was built of dark red narrow bricks (laid five courses to the foot) with Casterton stone facings.[8] Some walls on the entrance front had figured plasterwork. The main part of the house was of three storeys, with the top floor being lit by dormer windows and by windows in the gables. Tall chimneys rose from the steeply pitched roof. Two wings on the entrance front had Dutch gables. To the left of the entrance porch a two-storeyed wing in a style reminiscent of East Anglian vernacular buildings projected forward to form a partly enclosed entrance court.

Between 1899 and 1901 Cavenham featured in three articles written by Prentice and published in the journal *The Builder* with plans of the house, photographs of the drawing room and of the stable block, which he also designed.[9] The house, Prentice's largest domestic building, commanded the attention of the German writer H. Muthesius in his book *Das Englische Haus* as an example of contemporary English house design.[10]

The house was large, the plans showing a loggia, hall and inner hall, dining, morning, drawing and billiard rooms, conservatory and winter garden with an extensive range of domestic offices on the ground floor and master bedroom, boudoir, nine further bedrooms, four dressing rooms and three bathrooms on the first floor. The second floor had a maidservants' wing of eight bedrooms and a manservants' wing of three bedrooms. In one of his articles Prentice described the drawing room as thirty-one feet by seventeen feet by twelve feet six inches high. It had a large bay window and was mahogany-panelled, the larger panels being filled with rich green silk material. The mouldings and enrichments were gilded 'old gold'. The ceiling had bold fruit enrichments and the fireplace had modelled figures and other ornaments. The stable block contained six stalls and a loose box, the walls being lined with green tiles and brown salt-glazed bricks.[11] Prentice also designed the lodges and a three-bedroomed coachman's house with reed-thatched roof. Clearly this was a house commissioned by a man of considerable means.

HERBERT DAVIES did not live to enjoy his new house as he died in 1899 when it can hardly have been finished. Subsequently it was owned by Adolph Goldschmidt, the father of Sir James Goldsmith, the financier. In 1918 the house and estate were put up for sale.[12] It failed to sell at auction and was subsequently purchased by Brigadier-General Sir Archibald Home who lived there until it was placed on the market again in June 1946. The estate consisted on 2,627 acres and the property to be sold included Cavenham Mill, three farms, a market garden, the Plough Inn on Cavenham Heath, cottages and village properties, a shop and post office.[13] In September that year the remaining contents, consisting of 400 lots, were sold by direction of Sir Archibald and Lt.-Col. D. A. F. Home.[14]

Three years later, in August 1949, it was reported that Cavenham, 'unwanted for any purpose and falling into disrepair for lack of an occupant is being demolished'.[15] The house was described as a 'white elephant' after Sir Archibald Home left owing to high taxation, dwindling incomes and staff problems – nobody would rent it and plans to convert it to flats had fallen through. The Cavenham Hall designed by Prentice had existed for barely half a century.

CHEDISTON HALL

DEMOLISHED 1955

CHEDISTON HALL WAS LOCATED ON HIGH GROUND TO THE NORTH OF THE ROAD FROM THE VILLAGE OF CHEDISTON TO HALESWORTH. In the middle of the nineteenth century its estate extended to over 2,000 acres.[1]

The house was originally a Tudor house, probably built by the Norton family, who had acquired Chediston in the late sixteenth century. An archaeological survey has not revealed any evidence of medieval remains on the site, suggesting that it was a new house on a fresh site.[2] In the following century it was owned by Sir John Pettus and then by the Fleetwood family, from whom it was bought in 1722 by Walter Plumer. Plumer is said to have 'lately rebuilt the Hall in a beautiful Manner and made it his seat', but it is not known what work he undertook.[3] His family remained the owners until 1833 when the estate was purchased by George Parkyns. In 1819 the house was described as 'now a farmhouse'.[4]

George Parkyns bought Chediston from Robert Plumer Ward who had inherited it from his wife, the widow of the last Plumer in the male line. It is recounted that Plumer Ward had mortgaged the property to a chartered company with limited powers to hold land, and these having been exceeded the estate was forfeited to the Crown. The Crown regranted the property and the sale to Parkyns was completed. However, after Parkyns' death it was discovered that his title was defective as he was the son of his father's second marriage in France, where he was born. Under English law as it then was he was an alien and, as such, incapable of holding land in England. In 1846 the Crown regranted the property to Parkyns' daughter, Madame Marie Claire Leguen de Lacroix.[5] It then descended through her family.

GEORGE PARKYNS rebuilt the house, commissioning Edward Blore to prepare the designs, but the work actually executed was at variance with his plans.[6] The basic rebuilding was in 'Jacobean' style, the footprint of the house remaining a traditional East Anglian rectangular U. The entrance was through a projecting porch, which rose to the full height of the building. According to an estate map of 1722, prepared when the house was acquired by Walter Plumer, 'the projecting wings of the mansion extended further from the body of the building, and the area in front was shut in by a high wall, having large gates opposite the hall door'.[7] If this was the case it seems likely that it was during the 1830s that the wings

Chediston Hall

19 *Chediston Hall: the entrance front.*

were reduced in length and the wall creating the front enclosure was taken down. The parapet had battlements and there were string courses above and below the first floor windows. The projecting porch and the wings had polygonal turrets surmounted by pinnacles. The cross-wing had two bays on each side of the entrance with sash windows and the building, which was timber framed, was encased in white bricks.[8]

The estate map of 1845 shows the house with an extension at the rear joining up with the stable and other service buildings, which were set back to the left of the house and arranged around two interconnecting courtyards.[9] The garden contained a long rectangular canal running parallel to the north front of the house. This has been attributed to the eighteenth century, although the suggestion has also been made that it might be the remains of a moat.[10]

CHEDISTON seems to have been a tenanted property for most of the last 170 years of its existence. A memorial in Chediston Church records that the Beale and Baas families resided at Chediston Hall from 1787 to 1875, although a lease of 1801 contains a provision that the Plumer family could occupy the house 'if they shall think proper to come and reside there'.[11] In the twentieth century Eugene Jean Louis Leguen de Lacroix lived at Chediston until his death in 1936.

During World War II the house was requisitioned by the War Department and apparently suffered fire damage towards the end of the Army's occupation. The estate is said to have been acquired by the Metropolitan Railway Company after the war, but the house was not lived in again, and in 1955 it was demolished.

DOWNHAM HALL

DEMOLISHED 1925

DOWNHAM HALL STOOD ON LOW GROUND ON THE SOUTH SIDE OF THE LITTLE OUSE RIVER, three miles from Brandon in the village of Santon Downham, a parish created by the merger of Santon across the river in Norfolk and Downham in Suffolk. In 1668 the village was subject to what was described as a 'sand-flood', when a wave of sand (believed to have originated near Lakenheath) overwhelmed the village where 'many houses were overthrown and buried, and their pastures and meadows which for so small a town were considerable were over-run and destroyed'.[1]

In the late Middle Ages the village was held partly by the Abbey of Bury St Edmunds and partly by the Priory of Ixworth. After the Dissolution of the Monasteries the manor was granted to Sir Thomas Kytson. From the middle of the seventeenth century Downham Hall was owned by the Wright family.[2] Thomas Wright's house had twelve hearths in 1674. The last member of his family to own it was Ann Wright from whom the estate was acquired in 1778 by Charles Sloane, first Earl Cadogan (of the second creation).[3] He died in 1807 and the estate subsequently, in 1830, was bought by Lord William John Frederick Powlett, later Duke of Cleveland. On his death in 1864 the estate was left for the use of his widow, Caroline, a daughter of the first Earl of Lonsdale, but it was put on the market in 1870.[4]

The purchaser was Edward Mackenzie of Fawley Court near Henley on Thames, Oxfordshire. Edward Mackenzie's father was a Scottish-born engineer and the family had been heavily involved in canal and railway ventures.[5] It was, no doubt, from these that their wealth derived. Downham became the residence of Edward Mackenzie's second son Edward Phillipe who also had property in Kirkcudbright. Edward Mackenzie bought the Downham estate (which included the Home and three other farms) of 5,921 acres for £81,500.[6] His elder son William inherited the property with Edward Phillipe having the right to live there as long as he wished.

THE WRIGHT family's original house was replaced by, or remodelled as, a Georgian building in the late eighteenth century either by the last Wright owner or more probably after Earl Cadogan's acquisition of what was then the 3,134-acre estate.[7] In 1836 it was altered by Lewis Vulliamy for Lord William Powlett when a portico with two pairs of pillars was built on the entrance front and a new staircase installed.[8] Vulliamy may also have been responsible for the addition of apses in the dining room.[9]

TOP RIGHT:
20 Downham Hall: the entrance front.

RIGHT:
21 Downham Hall: the garden front.

The entrance front consisted of a central block with a small pediment over three arched windows lighting a shallow second floor. On the first floor beneath the arched windows were three sashed windows below which projected the pillared portico. To each side of the pedimented section of the front there were wide single bays with windows reaching the full height of the floors, those on the first floor being taller than those on the ground floor. To each side of the central block there were two-storey wings each of two bays, but that on the right (to which was attached a conservatory) was wider than that on the left. These wings had sashed windows. To the left there were further buildings (including one with a pantiled roof), which provided the house's service quarters.

On the garden front the central block had seven bays, the central three being in a bow whose height was greater than that of the flanking wings. The top floor of the bow had arched windows. There was also a two-storey bow on the wall to which the conservatory was attached. At the service end of the house there was also a substantial wing on the garden front.

The differing widths of the wings flanking the central block have already been noted. The internal layout of the house also appears to have been lacking in symmetry. That this was the case supports the view that the late eighteenth-century work was the remodelling of an earlier house. However, it is also possible the alterations made in the nineteenth century were executed without regard to maintaining the symmetry of the building.

The house stood in a well-wooded park with two mile-long carriage drives, one leading to the Thetford and the other to the Brandon road. The estate provided extensive game reserves, and the house was set in gardens described as being in the Italian style.[10]

COL. EDWARD Phillipe Mackenzie gave up possession of the estate in 1917.[11] In the following year it was sold to Frederick William Wateridge for £75,000.[12] Within a few years most of the estate had passed to the Forestry Commission and was extensively planted, principally with coniferous trees, to form part of the Brandon and Thetford afforestation scheme.

Downham Hall was demolished in 1925. What had been a typical estate village, described by a former rector of the parish as 'feudal', had become a base for forestry workers.[13] The vestiges of the old village survived, but much of it now consists of modern housing developments. Only a small part of the mansion house survives as The Old Billiard Room and linked icehouse together with the coach house and tack room.

DRINKSTONE PARK

DEMOLISHED 1951

THE MANSION HOUSE OF DRINKSTONE PARK STOOD MIDWAY BETWEEN BURY ST EDMUNDS AND STOWMARKET south of what is now the A14 trunk road and on the edge of the village from which it took its name. There is no evidence that it was built on the site of any earlier house, but it is likely that its parkland predates the building of the house and was possibly the area of a medieval deer park.[1] The house and its park stood in an estate comprising Links Farm and other land in the parishes of Drinkstone and Hessett, which the second Joshua Grigby assembled in the middle of the eighteenth century.[2] After additions in the years following his death in 1771 the estate extended to some 250 acres, and the park around the house was laid out with plantations and a sheet of water.

Joshua Grigby II, whose father, son and grandson all bore the same name, came from a family of some means but he greatly augmented his inheritance in the course of his career as a lawyer. He acted as steward of

22 Drinkstone Park: the entrance front.

various manors held by landed gentry in Suffolk and as Town Clerk of Bury St Edmunds and prospered from his property and commercial dealings. The writer of a letter contemporaneous with his death in 1771 speculates that his estate might have amounted to £100,000 (equivalent to some £6 million), but this appears to have been an over-estimate and a later appraisal of Grigby's wealth suggests a figure of £58,000.[3]

On Joshua Grigby II's death the estate passed to his son Joshua Grigby III, a barrister and Member of Parliament and then in 1798 to his grandson, another Joshua. Joshua Grigby IV was a local magistrate, a deputy lieutenant of Suffolk and in 1810 High Sheriff of the county. After his death in 1829 without children the house was lived in by his second wife, Anna, until her death in 1853, but the estate had been left to John Harcourt Powell, the son of Grigby's niece, Lucy. For much of the second half of the nineteenth century Thomas Harcourt Powell lived at Drinkstone, where he created a very fine garden with specialised hot houses, greenhouses and a fernery and planted many specimen trees in the park.[4] Thomas Harcourt Powell died in 1892, and the house ceased to be occupied by members of the family who built it.

DRINKSTONE PARK mansion was built in 1760, being described in *The Suffolk Traveller* in 1764 as 'new erected'.[5] Whether it was erected for John Grigby II or for his son is not known. It was a plain, unadorned building of white brick, probably from nearby Woolpit, with stone quoins and a hipped slate roof. It was of five bays on the entrance front and five bays on the sides of the main block, which had three storeys. At the rear there was a two-storey wing with a bay extending to both floors, which is likely to have been a later addition. A porch was also added in the nineteenth century. In its final form the house provided 'a Lounge hall partly panelled, 4 reception rooms, 10 best bedrooms, 6 servants rooms and 3 bathrooms'.[6]

IT SEEMS that during the nine years following after Thomas Harcourt Powell's death the house was let to tenants including the Hodgson-Roberts family and John Reginald Hargreaves, who was to buy the property in 1901. It remained in his family until after World War II, although they do not appear to have lived in it after his death in 1934 when Drinkstone was inherited by his son, John Carne Hargreaves, an Army officer.

During the war the house was requisitioned by the War Department and was used first as a Divisional Headquarters and later occupied by United States troops and German prisoners of war.[7] Occupation by the forces resulted in considerable damage, a fate to which many other houses fell victim. After the war Hargreaves did not return to the house, and in 1949 sold all his property in Drinkstone and Hessett.

The purchaser in 1949 was a speculative buyer, John Wilfred Russell of Crowborough, and in January 1951 the house's fixtures and fittings were sold in 150 lots, including oak panelling, sixty sash windows and sixty panelled and glazed doors, chimneypieces, roof and floor joists, slates and roofing lead.[8] The shell of the house was reported to have been sold to Mr O. H. Churston of Eye, who said at the time that he had no specific plans for what remained of the property. However, shortly afterwards the house was demolished. The stable block was converted into two dwellings, and the Garden Cottage survived, while a new house was built in the old walled garden and another was built in the grounds.

EASTON PARK

DEMOLISHED 1923

ASTON PARK, ALSO KNOWN AS THE WHITE HOUSE, LOCATED BETWEEN FRAMLINGHAM AND WICKHAM MARKET, belonged in medieval times to the Charles family of nearby Kettleburgh and passed in the sixteenth century to the Wingfield family of Letheringham.[1] Sir Anthony Wingfield Bt is said to have begun building a new house in 150 acres of parkland near Easton church in 1627 to replace a medieval house, but it is not clear whether Wingfield's house was on the same site as its predecessor or was on the site where the White House was subsequently erected. Later in the seventeenth century changes in the family's fortunes led to its sale to an illegitimate descendant of one of the Princes of Orange, William Henry Nassau, who came to England with William of Orange by whom he was created Earl of Rochford.

In the second half of the eighteenth century Easton Park was the residence of the Hon. Richard Nassau, son of the third Earl of Rochford, who married as her second husband Anne, co-heiress of Edward Spencer of Rendlesham and widow of the fifth Duke of Hamilton who was also second Duke of Brandon.[2] On the death of the last Earl of Rochford in 1830 Easton passed to the Dukes of Hamilton and Brandon. It was during the tenure in the second half of the nineteenth century of the twelfth Duke, who spent much of his time in Suffolk, that the estate was considerably extended and the house enlarged.[3]

THE ROCHFORDS' house, probably dating from the middle years of the eighteenth century, was a plain classical brick built building of two storeys. There were fifteen bays on what was in the later years the house's garden front, the central three bays projecting forward with a pediment supported by pilasters.[4] The house was described in 1833 as

a very comfortable residence, but contains no rooms of large size and they want light. The hall, which is in the centre, was floored by the late Rochford with stucco, but it did not succeed; the stucco has cracked and dried very unevenly. In the hall is a chimney piece carved by Grinling Gibbon [*sic*] supported by two caryatids, and in the centre a female face very beautifully carved, with flowers and fruits.[5]

In the park, with its crinkle-crankle wall built during the fifth Earl's time, there was a fine octagonal summer house with a cupola dating from the

1780s. This stood at the north-east corner of part of a ditched enclosure called 'The Wilderness', which contained a cockpit dating from the eighteenth century and which may have been a moated enclosure and the site of the medieval house.[6]

The twelfth Duke's enlargement of the house in 1875 was in a totally different style, with typically Victorian timbered gables with oriel windows and with an extension at one end of the original building incorporating an octagonal tower. The house as enlarged had six reception rooms and a smoking room, twelve principal and two bachelors' bedrooms, two bathrooms, a school room and three bedrooms in a separate wing, eleven bedrooms for female staff and, with their own staircase, seven menservants' rooms. There were extensive domestic offices.[7]

In addition to extending the house the duke built a model farm on the estate, adopting the same style of architecture, the dairy having 'Early English' windows and the walls decorated with ornamental tiles. There was extensive stabling (with nine staff bedrooms), bothies for four men and the garden buildings with vineries, peach houses, melon, cucumber and plant houses needed to support a large establishment.

WRITERS on the history of the country house have noted that the late nineteenth century saw substantial borrowings by many of their owners, and the twelfth Duke was no exception. His lifestyle coupled with expansion of the estate and the costs associated with the additions to the house and the erection of the model farm left him heavily indebted. In 1892, three years before his death, the debts secured on his Suffolk properties (which included the Great Glemham estate) amounted to £138,500, including £30,000 charged on the Easton estate and dating back to the days of the Earls of Rochford. The rest had been incurred in the previous twenty-five years.[8] The twelfth Duke had only one child, a daughter, who in 1906 married the Marquis of Graham, son of the fifth Duke of Montrose, and on his death his Suffolk estates were left in trust for her. His Hamilton estates passed for the benefit of the Dukes of Hamilton and Brandon. The first task appears to have been clearing the debts on the estate, and this was accomplished by 1898. The Great Glemham estate was sold in 1912. This was followed by the division of the trusteeships of the Suffolk and Scottish estates by Act of Parliament in 1918.[9] In April 1919 the Easton estate of 4,833 acres was put up for sale by the trustees.[10]

Much of the property was sold to Harry Capon of Kenton Hall who bought a number of lots for a total of over £60,000 with a view to resale, but the house was withdrawn when bidding reached £10,300.[11] The Marchioness of Graham was reported as having bought the house and other property after the auction, 'retaining possession of the home of her childhood'. Her ownership was not to last long and in 1922 the house with 783 acres was on the market again.[12] At this sale the house was sold for £5,000 to Mr Percy Dudding of Martley Hall, another property which the Marchioness bought after auction in 1919 but which she subsequently sold.[13]

The house did not long survive the second auction, and in 1923 it was demolished, some of the materials from it being used to improve Martley Hall. The fifth Earl of Rochford's crinkle-crankle wall remains substantially intact and the stables, coach house and estate office survived. The twelfth Duke's model farm, probably the most architecturally important element in the Easton estate properties, also survived and is the focal point of a farm park bearing the name Easton Farm Park.

EDWARDSTONE HALL

DEMOLISHED 1952

EDWARDSTONE HALL STOOD NORTH OF THE ROAD FROM SUDBURY TO HADLEIGH two miles north-west of Boxford. It was located in parkland near Edwardstone Church and was approached through a massive arched gatehouse which survived the demolition of the major part of the house.[1]

In the early Middle Ages the manor of Edwardstone belonged to the Montchesney family but it passed in the fifteenth century to the Waldegraves.[2] At the end of the sixteenth century it was purchased by John Brand, a clothier, whose family' ownership lasted for over a century. In 1662 Susanna Brand married Sir John Morden, a Levant merchant and the founder of Morden College in Blackheath, originally a home for merchants who 'were down on their luck'. The connection between Edwardstone and Morden College has survived for more than three centuries. By the marriage of the heiress of the Brand family to Sir Robert Kemp the estate passed into his family, but it was sold in 1714 to William French, a draper of London.

In 1794 Edwardstone was sold by French's eventual heir, William Sheldon, to Thomas Dawson of Easington in Co. Durham from whom it descended to the family of the Earls Belmore, passing to the third Earl's fourth son, the Hon. Henry William Lowry-Corry.[3] The family increased their landholdings in the vicinity of Edwardstone by the purchase in 1897 of the Dawson family's Groton estate.[4] The house was to remain the seat of this branch of the family until it was pulled down.

THE HOUSE demolished in 1952 was the successor to an earlier house, which, when it was owned by John Brand in 1674, was recorded as having fourteen hearths.[5] The later house appears to date from the time of Charles Dawson, who lived from 1777 to 1853. It has been described as being in Victorian Mock Tudor style.[6] At the entrance to the park in which it stood is a red-brick archway and lodge of two storeys also in 'Tudor' style known as Temple Bar.[7] This is believed to date from 1840 and the rebuilt house may be of the same date. To what extent the house was a complete replacement or incorporated elements of its predecessor is not known.

On the entrance (west) front the brick-built house was a four-bay two-storeyed building with the entrance door in the second bay from the left, which projected forward slightly, as did the fourth bay. Both the projecting

TOP RIGHT:
25 Edwardstone Hall: the entrance front about 1850, engraved by G. C. Finden.

RIGHT:
26 Edwardstone Hall: the north front.

The Hall Edwardstone.

bays had crow-stepped gables, the others having plain parapets. Above the entrance porch there was an oriel window. The north front of two central bays flanked by projecting wings, again with crow-stepped gables, had a large projecting square bay in the central section. The windows were mullioned and transomed with sashes: all had drip mouldings.

The east (garden) front was less regular than the north and west elevations, suggesting either the incorporation of parts of the old house or later additions. The projecting wing at the eastern end of the north front extended only a short way southwards, having a crow-stepped gable on the south side matching that on the north. This gable end looked out on to a small courtyard to the south of which was a large building, which appears to have been built in two stages: one of two bays was flanked by polygonal turrets of the style associated with many East Anglian Tudor houses and had a battlemented balustrade, while the other of three bays had a plain balustrade. This section of the house had sashed windows on the ground floor. The configuration of the house on the south side is not known but must have contained the domestic offices. The only architectural feature of this part of the house evident in both an engraving made in Charles Dawson's time and later photographs is a bell turret.

When the house was on the market in 1951 it was described as having, on the ground floor, a lounge hall, drawing room, dining room, library, boudoir and morning room, together with the extensive range of domestic offices associated with Victorian country houses. Three staircases led to the first floor, which had nine bedrooms, a dressing room, and four staff bedrooms. In addition there were three attic rooms. The brick-built stables and outbuildings provided seven stalls and a loose box, a harness room and brew house, garaging for four cars and two men's bedrooms and other service rooms.[8]

COL. THE HON. HENRY William Lowry-Corry died in 1927, and his son, Major H. C. Lowry-Corry (later Lt Col. Sir Henry), succeeded to the property. He served in both the Great War (during which he was awarded the Military Cross) and World War II (during which he was a prisoner of war). He was High Sheriff of Suffolk in 1946 and subsequently Vice-Lieutenant of the county. After World War II he took up residence in a smaller house on the estate, and in June 1951 the hall was offered for sale by auction. In the following year it was pulled down except for a small section of the building which was converted into a house.

FLIXTON HALL

DEMOLISHED 1952/3

LIXTON HALL STOOD FOUR MILES SOUTH-WEST OF BUNGAY near the River Waveney on the border with Norfolk. It was the seat of the Tasburgh family until the estate was sold in the middle of the eighteenth century to the Adairs for whom the house was rebuilt a hundred years later and subsequently extended.

The Tasburgh family originated in Norwich but first acquired, probably by marriage, property in South Elmham St Peter near Flixton in the late fourteenth or early fifteenth century.[1] They enlarged their estates over the succeeding two hundred years and, in 1544, after the Dissolution of the Monasteries, acquired Flixton Priory, having previously leased land from the Priory. It is not certain whether the house was built by John Tasburgh (1533–97) or by his son Sir John (1576–1629). Nor is it certain whether Flixton Hall stood on the site of the Priory or on that of a 'capital mansion' in 500 acres purchased in 1607 by Sir John from his cousin Thomas Bateman. The latter, of course, could only be the case if Sir John was the builder. However, Sir John's 'newe parke' is referred to in 1611, and a nineteenth-century account states that the hall was built about 1615. The probability is therefore that Sir John's acquisition of the Bateman property was followed by the rebuilding of the house there on

27 Flixton Hall: the entrance front, engraved by W. Angus for Seats of the nobility and gentry, of Great Britain and Wales *(1787), from a watercolour by T. Sandby (1752), showing the old house before the moat was filled in.*

what was a moated site. The extent to which it may have incorporated elements of an earlier building on the site is not known.

The Tasburgh family's tenure of Flixton lasted until the last male member died in 1719. The wealth and influence of the family had reached its peak in the time of Sir John, and the decline in the family fortunes in the years after his death has been attributed to his marriage to Lettice Creasy, a member of a Roman Catholic family. Fines for recusancy and sequestration of the estate took their toll. On the death of a later John Tasburgh in 1719 the estate passed to the Wyborne family into which his sister, another Lettice, had married. On the failure of the Wyborne male line the estate was sold around 1750 to Alexander Adair whose family originated in Scotland but which had settled in Ireland in the first half of the seventeenth century.[2] The house remained the Adair family's Suffolk seat until shortly before its demolition.

SIR JOHN Tasburgh's Flixton Hall has been described as being in 'the style called Inigo Jones' Gothic', and was said to have been one of his designs, but there does not appear to be any documentary evidence to support this contention. The house was similar in design to many other East Anglian houses of its period, being rectangular U-shaped with a central projecting entranceway. The forward projecting wings terminated in five-sided bays extending to the full height of the three-storey building. The entrance was similarly constructed with a pedimented doorway flanked by pairs of columns. The windows were also pedimented. The battlemented balustrade on the entrance front was surmounted by barley-twist pinnacles, those on the corners being the upward extensions of polygonal turrets. An extension to the building at the rear of the right-hand wing, which had a large round arched window on the ground floor, appears to have been of later date than the rest of the house.

It is probable that during the second half of the eighteenth century an open colonnade on the south front was closed up and converted to separate rooms, but whether any other additions or alterations were made to the house before the 1830s is not known.[3] The external aspect was, however, changed by the filling in of the moat shown in the view of the house painted in the time of the Wyborne family's ownership (illustration 27).[4] It is suggested in one account that in 1832 the house was damaged by fire, but whether this was the case is not clear.[5] There is, however, reason to think that around 1837 Anthony Salvin, the prolific mid-

Victorian architect whose career of country house and church building spanned nearly sixty years, was consulted by Sir Robert Shafto Adair.[6] Sir Robert had not by then succeeded to the estate and it is not known whether Salvin was consulted about improvements to the house or only to other buildings on the estate. Salvin's work on restoring the hall commenced in 1844 but before this, in 1842/3, he had designed the Priest's House in Flixton village for Sir Robert. Work on the house was interrupted by a fire in 1846, which destroyed about half of the building, a contemporary account stating that the roof had fallen in and the south walls had fallen outwards.[7]

The extent to which Salvin was able to incorporate elements of the old house is not now clear, but his own drawing of the house after the fire shows that the damage was severe, although probably not as extensive as some contemporaneous accounts suggested. The reconstructed house stood on the foundations of its predecessor, and photographs taken some fifteen years after the rebuilding show a house very similar in appearance to the former house.[8] Salvin's rebuilt house was in Elizabethan and Jacobean style, with tall chimneys, battlemented parapets, pinnacles, weather vanes and a cupola. It has been said that it was in the rebuilding of Flixton that Salvin gained his intimate knowledge of East Anglian buildings of the late sixteenth and early seventeenth centuries, incorporating stepped gables, polygonal shafts at the angles and mullioned and transomed windows, the style he was later to use in the rebuilding of Campsea Ashe High House for John Sheppard and at Stoke Holy Cross in Norfolk built for Henry Birkbeck.[9] The interior has been described as a 'meticulous Jacobean reproduction' – 'here Salvin created one of his most lavish interiors'.[10] The service wing to the left and rear of the house may have pre-dated the 1846 fire. It was in a different style from the main building, having two gables and looked similar to a traditional Suffolk village house. Of the old house's service buildings the dovehouse survived, but the extent to which Salvin may have incorporated other service areas from the old house is not clear.[11] The cost of the rebuilding was £29,000.[12]

Other Victorian architects were also involved at Flixton. Sir George Gilbert Scott was responsible for terracing on the south side of the house.[13] In the late 1880s the building was enlarged for Sir Hugh Adair by the architect Fairfax Bloomfield Wade who made extensive alterations and additions resulting in a house of sixty rooms.[14] Wade's work changed what, at least externally, had been a relatively restrained Jacobean reconstruction into an 'extravaganza' of a house. He replaced Salvin's modest cupola on top of a square clock tower with an ornate octagonal tower surmounted by what has been described as 'a wedding cake', added a florid entrance porch, embellished the exterior of the south side of the house with polygonal shafts and stepped parapets and refenestrated the Georgian colonnade to match more closely the rest of the building. Wade's work also included replacement of Salvin's service wing with a much larger building that stylistically matched the rest of the house and provided extra accommodation.

FLIXTON HALL remained the Suffolk seat of the Adairs until after World War II. Major General Sir Allan Adair succeeded his father in 1949, and in November 1950 the hall and its contents were sold over a period of five days. A contemporary report stated that the sale marked 'the break-up of another of the stately homes of England' and attributed this to the burden of death duties and the costs of maintaining the property.[15] The main estate, which had extended to 850 acres and included the villages of Flixton and Homersfield, was also sold. There were reported to be fears that the house would be demolished but at the time of the contents sale this was said to 'be unlikely'.

In the early months of 1951 proposals were put forward for the use of the house as an agricultural institute for Suffolk, the establishment of which had been planned for nearly half a century.[16] Rushbrooke Hall near Bury St Edmunds was also offered for this purpose. The building was said to be structurally sound and would accommodate between sixty and eighty students and staff. The proposal was approved by the County Council in March 1951 but vetoed by the Ministry of Agriculture in April.[17]

No other use for the house was found and a year later, in June 1952, it was reported that demolition had begun.[18] Its new owner, Mr R. G. Lawrence, was reported as saying that he 'intended to have the demolition carried out with every care having regard to the valuable material which will become available'. He expected that the work would last a year and that there would be three or four auctions on site.

By the end of 1953 Salvin's lavishly decorated house, a house which epitomised the revival of older styles in the mid-nineteenth century, had largely gone, all that remained being the main block reduced to a single-storey building roofed in corrugated metal and used with some of the service buildings for agricultural and storage purposes.

FORNHAM HALL

DEMOLISHED 1951

ORNHAM HALL STOOD IN THE PARISH OF FORNHAM ST GENEVIEVE
SOME THREE MILES NORTH-WEST OF BURY ST EDMUNDS, and the
manor belonged, prior to the Dissolution of the Monasteries, to the
Abbey there. In 1539/40 Fornham passed with nearby Hengrave to Sir
Thomas Kytson and later, following the death of his son Thomas, to Sir
William Gage.[1] It then belonged to the Gipps family before the estate was
purchased in 1731 by Samuel Kent, a London distiller, who left it to his
son-in-law, Sir Charles Egleton, a London goldsmith, who had already
acquired land at neighbouring Fornham St Martin. On Egleton's death in
1769 the estate passed to his son Charles, who changed his name to Kent
and was knighted in 1782. It was he who was responsible for the building
of the house, but he did not retain the estate for many years after its
completion, selling it in 1789 to Bernard Edward Howard who became
the twelfth Duke of Norfolk in 1815.

During the Duke's time substantial alterations to the house were
undertaken but, after his death in 1842, the estate was sold to Lord
Manners, a kinsman of the Duke of Rutland, for a reputed figure of
£75,500.[2] The next owner, from 1862 until his death in 1896, was Sir

*30 Fornham Hall:
the garden front
about 1825.*

William Gilstrap, a Nottinghamshire brewer, who paid £85,000 for the property and enlarged the estate by purchasing land in the adjoining parish of Fornham All Saints.[3] From him the estate passed to George Espec John Manners, whose wife was a Gilstrap and who himself was a descendant of both the thirteenth Duke of Norfolk and the fifth Duke of Rutland. When George Manners, who was knighted in 1920, died in 1939 Captain Duncan MacRae of Dunoon became life tenant under Sir William Gilstrap's will. It was during his tenure of the estate that the house was sold, with demolition following shortly thereafter.

WHEN CHARLES KENT decided to improve the existing house at the beginning of the 1780s he initially consulted Lancelot 'Capability' Brown who visited Fornham in February 1782 and again in September that year.[4] It seems that it was originally intended that Brown would undertake work to the existing house, to the church (which had been damaged by fire in 1780 reputedly owing to the negligence of a man shooting magpies) and to the surrounding park. His proposals were, however, not adopted. Instead James Wyatt was engaged to design a new house which was built about 1785.[5] The church was never restored but its tower was retained as a garden feature.

The garden front of Wyatt's house is depicted with thirteen bays, the outer three bays on each side projecting forward with windows in blind arches.[6] The middle three of the central seven bays had a semi-circular pillared portico, which provided a balcony on the first floor over which was a canopy. The house was two bays deep and of three storeys with a plain parapet and hipped roofs.

The alterations for the twelfth Duke of Norfolk were undertaken about 1828 by Robert Abraham, a London architect who had close connections with the Norfolk and other Roman Catholic families.[7] Alterations to Wyatt's house have also been attributed to Samuel Acton.[8]

A view of the entrance front of the house in the twelfth Duke's time shows the main block with nine bays, the five central bays brought forward with pilasters at each end and pairs of pilasters between the bays.[9] There was a plain parapet over the outer bays with the central section heightened with six pilasters and containing five windows, three square and two circular: whether these provided light to attic rooms or were simply a decorative feature is not clear. To the right of the main block was a two-storeyed wing of six bays. The rectangular entrance porch was supported on fluted columns with plinths. Later photographs show the two-storey wing raised to three storeys. Late nineteenth/early twentieth-century photographs of the garden front show Wyatt's building with the later wing having a large, full-height canted bay. Clearly, there had been a number of additions and alterations to the house in Victorian times, and it had developed into a substantial mansion of the size needed for the lavish living and entertainment customary in the late nineteenth century.

The accommodation it provided is revealed in the description when the house was sold in 1950: hall, drawing room with Adam fireplaces, dining room with a service room, library, morning room, billiards room, eight principal bedrooms and dressing rooms, eighteen secondary and seven staff bedrooms, together with extensive domestic offices (servants' hall, housekeepers' rooms, kitchen, scullery, pantry, still-room, five larders and a lamp room). In the yard were extensive offices, a bakery, a laundry and fuel sheds.

SIR GEORGE MANNERS had other property and does not appear to have lived at Fornham, the house being let in the years preceding World War II, during which it was requisitioned by the War Department. The property suffered 'some damage during its requisition ... but the Adam decorations' were 'substantially complete'.[10] It appears to have been unused after the war, and its demise was heralded by the sale of its contents in March 1950 when a thousand lots were put up for auction: period furniture (including pieces by Sheraton, Hepplewhite and Chippendale), books, pictures, sculptures, carpets, linen, china and glass and the 'bedroom appointments', all 'as assembled by the late Sir William Gilstrap Bart'.[11]

31 Fornham Hall: the entrance front.

The following October the whole estate was put up for sale by auction.[12] In addition to the house and 224 acres of park, the estate consisted of seven farms, the Old Rectory, school and school house and the Woolpack Inn in Fornham St Martin, cottages, allotment land and meadows and two entrance lodges. The total area of the estate was 2,400 acres. Ominously for the future of the house, the sale catalogue pointed out that while a private buyer was hoped for or the house could be used as a school, institution or for a commercial purpose, if it was purchased for demolition it would provide an immense quantity of timber, slate, period fittings and other building materials.

On 20 October it was reported that the estate had been bought 'by a well known local man for the purpose in due course of realising the timber which includes oaks planted by the eleventh [sic] Duke of Norfolk 150 years ago'.[13] It was surmised that the mansion would probably go back on the market with a view to it being sold for use as an 'institution or some such purpose. At any rate demolition is not to be its present fate.'

However, the end of Fornham Hall was near. In June 1951 it was reported that the purchaser at the previous October's sale had been 'Mr Hurlock of Brooke [sic] Hall, Nacton'. There had been proposals for institutional use but when these had come to nothing there had been suggestions that a preservation order would be made. However, demolition had been authorised and the house was in the hands of a syndicate. It was proposed to hold sales of ornamental fixtures and fittings and demolition material.[14] Within three months the local press reported that 'another big house comes down', and published a photograph of the entrance front in course of demolition.[15] This was followed by a report of the sale of a 20,000-foot run of timber from the house, stating that at a previous sale doors and windows had been sold.[16] The bricks and rubble were being sold privately. 'Quite a large portion of the Hall has now been razed to the ground and before long there will be no trace of the mansion.'

Fornham Hall was another example of a house for which its owners had no use, which had suffered damage while requisitioned during World War II and for which no institutional purpose could be found. The stable block and estate cottages survived and have been converted to dwellings. The parkland was subject to gravel extraction, but at the end of the twentieth century this ceased, 'and the landscape is recovering'.[17]

HARDWICK HOUSE

DEMOLISHED 1926/7

Hardwick and its neighbour Hencote were manors held by the Abbey of Bury St Edmunds from 945 until the Dissolution of the Monasteries, when Hardwick was granted to Sir Thomas Darcy, Lord Darcy of Chiche, and Hencote to the Drury family of nearby Hawstead. Hardwick was owned by a number of families in the latter part of the sixteenth century, until in 1610 it was purchased by Sir Robert Drury, thus bringing into common ownership the Hardwick, Hencote and Hawstead estates. In 1656 Sir Robert's wife's nephew, Sir Christopher Wray of Ashby, Lincolnshire, sold the property to Sir Thomas Cullum, first baronet (who had been Sheriff of London in 1646) for £17,787.[1] The Cullum family owned Hardwick House for the remainder of its existence.

The Drury and Cullum families were associated with a number of other Suffolk houses which have been lost. Sir Robert Drury's wife was a daughter of Sir Nicholas Bacon of Redgrave. The second Cullum baronet, also Sir Thomas, married Dudley, daughter of Sir Henry North of the Manor House, Mildenhall. Her sister, Peregrine, married William Hanmer whose son Thomas's marriage to Elizabeth Folkes brought Barton Hall into his family. Hawstead Place was abandoned as the Cullum residence in the 1730s, and was gradually reduced in size over the next ninety years until it was finally demolished. Redgrave, Mildenhall and Barton have also disappeared.

Hardwick House, which stood some one and a half miles south of Bury, was a Jacobean house of about 1612 thought to have incorporated the medieval Abbey Lodge. The portico surmounted with the Drury arms in stonework survived until the demolition of the house. Sir Robert Drury was, it is said, responsible for the installation in 1612 of panelling with sixty-eight painted panels which were removed from Hawstead. These were included in the sale of the contents of the house in 1924, when they were described as having been in the Painted Closet, which was 'probably the Oratory of the last Lady Drury'.[2]

The Cullum family was distinguished for its historical and scientific interests: plants and gardening particularly were a continuing passion over many generations. Sir Thomas Cullum, the second baronet, was the noted gardener who built a greenhouse fifty-eight feet by fourteen feet (very large for its time) at Hawstead. The Reverend Sir John Cullum, the sixth

TOP RIGHT:
32 Hardwick House: the entrance front.

RIGHT:
33 Hardwick House: the garden front.

baronet, was a Fellow of both the Royal Society and the Society of Antiquaries and the author of *The History and Antiquities of Hawstead*, published in 1784 the year before his death. His son, Sir Thomas Gery Cullum, was also a clergyman and in addition to being a Fellow of the Royal Society and of the Society of Antiquaries was a Fellow of the Linnaean Society. The large library reflected the varied interests of members of the family and many books from it are now housed in the Suffolk Record Office at Bury St Edmunds.

THE CULLUM family was responsible for the enlargement of the house and alterations to it at various times in the late seventeenth and the following two centuries. In 1681, the second baronet altered Hardwick by building a new roof with three gables on the south front and adding matching gables to the old roof on the north front. He also embellished the house with pyramids and balls. The Georgian additions and alterations to the house dating from the time of the sixth and seventh baronets may have included the refenestration of the south front with small-paned sash windows.

Further additions to the property in early Victorian times included a two-storeyed library with a decorated ceiling built in 1839 and turrets in a French chateau style and bay windows added to the south front. Matthew Habershon, an architect who designed in the Gothic revival style but was also an enthusiast for timber-framed buildings, was responsible for the 1839 additions to the house and for embellishments that distinctly altered its Jacobean character.[3] He was also responsible for substantial architectural features in the extravagant garden, which was laid out with parterres in 1845. The north front appears to have been less affected by later work to the house, retaining the three gables and mullioned and transomed windows dating from the seventeenth century. The additions made during the period of Cullum ownership created a substantial house with a very long facade.

When the house and its estate were sold in December 1924 the house was described as having a large entrance hall, two libraries (with two annexes), two drawing rooms with interconnecting folding doors and an overall length of forty-four feet and nearly twenty feet wide, dining room, China room, statue gallery and billiard room. There was an upstairs morning room, seven principal bedrooms and dressing rooms, nine bachelors' and secondary bedrooms and twelve servants' bedrooms. In addition to the domestic offices there was a winter garden, orangery, peach house and palm house, a range of glasshouses, stabling, a chauffeur's cottage and a riding school.[4] The clock tower, dating from 1851, housed a clock made by W. Nelson Last, a noted Bury St Edmunds clock and sundial maker.[5]

THE REVEREND Sir Thomas Cullum was the eighth and last baronet, and on his death in 1855 the Hardwick estate passed to his second wife, Anne Flood, who died in 1875 without any children or any direct heir. Sir Thomas's first wife, Mary Anne Eggers, had died in 1830.[6] Their daughter, Arethusa, married Thomas Milner Gibson, and it was the son of this marriage, George Gery Milner-Gibson-Cullum, who was the last member of the family to live at Hardwick.[7]

Milner-Gibson-Cullum died in 1921 and the contents of Hardwick House passed to his residuary legatee, Mrs Reginald Gurney, on whose instructions they were sold by auction in June 1924.[8] The sale, held over four days, comprising some 1,750 lots of old English furniture, old china and pottery, statuary in Carrara marble, oil paintings, the painted panelling originally from Hawstead, over two thousand books, 'objets de vertue' and general furnishings.[9] The Hardwick and Hawstead estates had, however, reverted to the executors of Milner-Gibson-Cullum's step-grandmother Lady (Anne) Cullum, who had died forty-five years earlier. Given 'the failure of certain limitations' in her will the property became subject to the Intestate Estates Act 1884 and a Royal Warrant was issued appointing trustees for the sale of the property on behalf of the Crown. Over the next two years the whole estate of over 1,400 acres became the subject of a series of sales and purchases, which culminated in the demolition of the house.

The trustees arranged for the whole estate to be sold by auction December 1924.[10] However, it was sold beforehand to a Mr Towler who, having offered sitting tenants their holdings (Hawstead Place Farm was bought by William Orbell), proceeded with the sale of the remaining property.[11] This included, as a single lot, the house, its grounds and park and the Home, Stonebridge and Horsecroft Farms totalling some 726 acres together with the Manors of the Grange and Hawstead. The grounds, with their Lodge Cottage and 700-yard drive, included an Italian garden with a fountain, rose and flower gardens, shrubberies and a two-acre kitchen garden. These were situated in a park of cedars, oaks, elms,

Scots firs and beeches with a sycamore and lime avenue at the end of which stood a figure of Hercules brought from Hawstead Place where it had been the the centre piece of the Inner Court. The house and grounds and the adjoining farms attracted a top bid of £19,000 but were withdrawn from the auction and sold subsequently to John W. Greene, a Bury solicitor.[12] Other lots comprised Hawstead Lodge, Babworth Priory and the maltings at Fornham All Saints, a large number of cottages and accommodation and building land.

Five months later there was a further sale on the instructions of John William Mitcham of Littleport (for whom Greene may have been acting at the earlier sale) when the house and grounds of 140 acres and the three farms (Home, Stonebridge and Horsecroft) came on the market as individual units.[13] The reserve on the house itself is stated to have been fixed at 'what is practically a nominal reserve price' to reflect the fact that there would be costs associated with reducing the size of the house, suggesting that the house was recognised as being too large for continued use in its then state. The purchaser was Alderman George C. Gooday of Sudbury, a retired builder with substantial property interests, who is quoted as saying that as a boy he had enjoyed attending fetes at Hardwick but had never thought he would purchase it. He said that he had not formulated detailed plans for the future of the property but intended to renovate the house and demolish the riding school, as 'the late Mr Cullum' had planned before his death.[14]

Gooday's purchase did not save the house: perhaps that was not his intention and he had, in reality only been a speculative buyer. On three days in November 1926 a fixtures and fittings sale was held consisting of some 750 lots including 11,000 square feet of oak and pine boarding, a handsome oak staircase, forty-nine carved marble and wood mantelpieces, sixty-seven carved stone vases and figures, six wrought iron gates, eleven greenhouses and the 'very rare turret clock chiming on 3 bells and fitted with a wind indicator'.[15] The sale catalogue ends with the statement that 'After the Sale of the Fixtures and Fittings, The Fabric of the Mansion will be sold for demolition', the fabric consisting of tiles, slates, roofing timbers, lead, valuable brick and stonework, shaped and moulded cornices, valuable old brickwork forming an Octagon chimney, three staircases and 'many other lots of building materials'.[16] Everything was to be cleared from the site by the middle of August 1927. What he described as 'everything he could rescue worthy of being retained' was used by Mr A. W. Hewitt (who had acquired part of the gardens) to incorporate in a new Elizabethan-style house known as Hardwick Manor House.[17] At the same time seventeen plots of building land in Hardwick Lane were also sold.

Thus Hardwick House ceased to exist. The lack of heirs to the estate and the size of the house at a time when many large houses were available on the market no doubt contributed to bringing its long existence to an end. It had not been a 'great' house in architectural terms but one with an interesting history whose development reflected the interests of its successive owners and their expectations of a comfortable lifestyle in a country house with a large estate.

Part of the grounds of Hardwick House with its magnificent cedars and other ornamental trees is open to the public, and many of the estate buildings remain on the periphery of the park and in the locality. The lane leading to the Home Farm now provides access to a modern development principally of executive houses in the midst of which still stand, somewhat incongruously, the Home Farmhouse and Dairy Cottage, a cottage ornée. The main lodge still stands in Hardwick Lane and part of the estate became the site of the West Suffolk Hospital.

HENHAM HALL
DEMOLISHED 1953/4

HENHAM HALL, SOME FOUR MILES INLAND FROM SOUTHWOLD, replaced an earlier house on the estate which in late medieval times had belonged to the de la Poles, Earls of Suffolk. After the execution of Edmund de la Pole in 1513 the property passed to Charles Brandon, Earl of Suffolk and after his death was granted to the Hoptons from whom the Rous family, previously living at Dennington, acquired it in 1545.[1]

THE ELIZABETHAN house, with its walled entrance courtyard and frontage embellished with towers at each corner and a central towered entrance, was destroyed by fire in 1773 (apparently through the carelessness of a drunken butler), but it was not until 1792 that the building of the new house commenced. Shortly after the fire James Byres had produced plans for a new house but these were never executed.[2] Instead Sir John Rous (later the first Earl of Stradbroke) employed James Wyatt as his architect.[3] Wyatt had previously designed houses for Sir Charles Kent at Fornham and the Marquess of Hertford at Sudbourne and interiors for Sir Gerard Vanneck's house at Heveningham. To redesign the landscape Rous employed Humphrey Repton whose Red Book survives.

Wyatt's house was built on a site adjacent to that of its predecessor. It was a plain three-storeyed building of seven bays on the entrance front and five bays on the flank. The central three bays on the entrance front projected forward and were surmounted by a pediment. The portico with two columns provided a balcony at first floor level. At the rear was a courtyard in which the domestic offices were situated. The principal rooms – drawing room, eating room, library and Sir John and Lady Rous's private rooms – were on the first floor together with the saloon in the centre of the entrance front between the drawing and eating rooms. The saloon had a central window flanked externally by pilasters and with a pediment. The house was described in the nineteenth century as having been designed without any pretensions to architectural effect.[4] It took eight years to build and cost a little over £21,000.[5]

Wyatt's house was remodelled by Edward Middleton Barry who converted it into an Italianate building in 1858 and subsequent years.[6] Barry's alterations included removal of the pediment on the entrance front, the erection of a balustrade around the roof on which a tower was erected and the building of a colonnade across the front from which the main

TOP RIGHT:
*34 Henham Hall:
the house in 1824
(from H. Davy,
Views of the
Seats of the
Noblemen and
Gentlemen of
Suffolk).*

RIGHT:
*35 Henham Hall:
the house viewed
along the terrace.*

entrance was removed to the side. Terraces were added in front of the house. Internally Barry embellished the house, but some parts of Wyatt's work remained, including the staircase, which Barry 'dressed up' to create a richer style.[7] In 1867 a report of a fire at Henham referred to the 'apartments' being spacious and the principal rooms being handsome and stately and having been recently redecorated at great expense.[8] The fire clearly did considerable damage but was confined to the south-east corner of the house, containing the billiard room, the state drawing room and a few bedrooms which were destroyed. The reporter expressed the hope that 'the main walls of the house will prove to have sustained no serious injury'.

Later the house was considerably enlarged. Wyatt's house of four reception rooms and seven bedrooms with dressing rooms became a house with eight reception and fifty-three bedrooms. This massive increase must have been occasioned by the important place that the Earls of Stradbroke held in the political and social life of the county of which three successive earls were Lords Lieutenant in the nineteenth and twentieth centuries.

DURING the Great War the house was used as a military hospital with Lady Stradbroke as matron and during the 1939–45 War was again requisitioned for military use.[9] In 1946 there was a fire in the house, but this was not serious and the main damage was to the dining room. By 1953 the fate of Henham was sealed: complications over the succession to the estate coupled with the deterioration of the fabric during the war left the family with no alternative but to demolish the house. When seeking a licence to demolish Lord Stradbroke's agents reported to the local planning authority that

> the house is far too large for modern use and internally is very badly planned for occupation, even for industrial or institutional purposes; further it has suffered considerable damage during requisition. The Hall contains vast reserves of building material which can now serve a better purpose through demolition than to remain standing at constant maintenance expense.[10]

Authority to demolish was given.

On 21 April 1953 furniture, books and paintings returned to the house by the trustees of the third Earl's estate together with garden ornaments were sold. The following day the fixtures and fittings – chimneypieces, 'the superb mahogany suite of doors to the State Apartments and principal bedrooms', 'the fine wrot iron staircase

balustrade', bookcases, panelling, flooring and windows – were put under the hammer. Finally, 'the shell of the mansion' was sold for demolition, with a year being allowed for removal.[11]

The next day the sale was reported in the press under the heading 'Henham Hall is coming down soon', stating that Lord Stradbroke had tried to sell the house for scholastic or institutional use but without success.[12] Two London Livery Companies both engaged in replacing their bomb-damaged halls had bought fittings, the Mercers Company acquiring the sixteen mahogany doors for £1,000 and the marble chimneypiece in the saloon being bought for the Butchers Company for £80. The shell, including 100,000 feet of timber, thirty-five tons of lead and a million bricks, had been bought by a firm of Ipswich building contractors, George A. Kenney & Sons Limited, for £3,100.[13]

Following the demolition of the house the estate buildings, some of which are attributed to James Wyatt, survived and the estate remains in the ownership of the Rous family. Henham Hall was one of the many houses designed in the eighteenth century as a comparatively small country seat, which was later enlarged to the extent that in the changed circumstances of the middle of the twentieth century its continued existence could not be sustained.

HOBLAND HALL

DAMAGED BY FIRE 1961, THE REINSTATED
GROUND FLOOR DEMOLISHED 2002

HOBLAND HALL (IN EARLIER TIMES HOBBELOND'S) WAS NINE MILES
NORTH OF LOWESTOFT on the narrow piece of land between the
North Sea and the River Waveney, an area now in Norfolk but being
south and east of the Waveney was historically part of Suffolk. Much of
the house was destroyed by fire in 1961.

In the fifteenth century Hobland was owned by Sir John Fastolf, who
died in 1459, and it was one of the properties that William Waynflete
arranged should become the property of Magdalen College, Oxford. It
remained in the college's ownership as an investment property let to a
succession of tenants over the intervening centuries until 1938 when it
was sold. There is no archival evidence that the college played any part in
the building of Hobland Hall or of any previous house on the site, such
works normally being the responsibility of tenants whose leases ran for
periods of about six years.[1] In 1801 when leased to Thomas Fowler the
property was described as 'all that site of the Manor of Hobland Hall, in
the County of Suffolk, with all lands, closures, &c., thereto belonging in
Gorleston, Bradwell, South Town, Hopton, and Belton, and formerly in
the tenure of John Pitcairn, clerk, Gerrard Trotter, &c'. Twenty years later,
when the then tenant John Thirkill became insolvent, the estate extended
to about 630 acres.[2]

THE HOUSE was of late eighteenth-century date although there was
evidence of what was probably an earlier building at the rear.[3] A brick
dated 1793 might provide evidence of the date it was constructed, but the
accompanying initials 'CT' shed no light on who might have been
responsible for erecting the house, the known names of lessees in the late
eighteenth century being Schutz, Pitcarne (or Pitcairn), Trotter, Urquhart
and Fowler. John Thirkill, who before getting into financial difficulties
was clearly a man of considerable means, might be a candidate for the
building of the house but he did not become the lessee until 1808, which
is later than the house can reasonably be dated on architectural grounds.[4]

Built of red brick with a hipped slate roof, the house was of two
principal storeys and an attic floor with two pedimented dormer
windows. On the entrance front it had five bays, the central bay breaking
forward and surmounted by a pediment under which was a round arched

window. The front was flanked by brick pilasters and had a string course. The doorway had Roman Doric pilasters and a pediment with broken entablature, the door having a semi-elliptical fanlight with curved glazing bars. On the left flank of the house was a two-storey elliptical bay and as a later addition an open-fronted garden room with pillars. The house was enlarged in Victorian times by the addition of domestic offices and outbuildings for which the Barber family, tenants between the 1840s and 1880s, was presumably responsible.

The principal internal features of the house were a fine hall and staircase with three turned balusters on each tread and the drawing and dining rooms with Adam-style chimneypieces. One of these fine rooms had an elliptical recess flanked by Ionic columns. In addition on the ground floor there was a study and small billiards room and domestic offices, the principal upper floor having five bedrooms, dressing rooms and two bathrooms.[5]

Latterly, the house stood in grounds of three acres with stabling, garages and a walled garden, but in the latter part of the nineteenth century it stood in a well-wooded park of thirty-six acres.[6]

37 Hobland Hall: the entrance front; the ground floor survived the fire in 1961.

THE LONG succession of tenants came to an end in 1938 when Magdalen College disposed of the property to Tom Cook, a well-known figure in the coursing world, who sold the house in the following year. The next owner, Christopher E. Kevill-Davies, retained the property for fourteen years after which it ceased to be occupied as a residence. It became the Yarmouth district headquarters of the building contractors R. G. Carter of Drayton, Middlesex, and was used as offices and storage space.

In January 1961 Hobland Hall caught fire, and what had been an attractive house with some fine detailing both externally and internally was largely destroyed.[7] The shell of the ground floor was converted into a single-storey building retaining some of the original architectural features, and this became offices used by Birds Eye Foods.[8] It survived until 2002 when it was demolished to make way for a large red brick house in an undistinguished 'Georgian' style.

HOLTON HALL, HOLTON ST PETER

DEMOLISHED 1957

OLTON HALL WAS SITUATED SOME DISTANCE NORTH OF THE PARISH CHURCH IN THE VILLAGE OF HOLTON ST PETER, east of Halesworth. It stood in parkland of nearly ninety acres, the whole estate extending in the late nineteenth century to over 450 acres.

Holton's medieval manor house is thought to have been at a different site from that on which Holton Hall was built in the eighteenth century. The date when the house was built is not known, but it has been suggested that the survival of woodland with intersecting 'rides' indicates that it was erected in the early part of the century when this was a fashionable mode of landscaping.[1] No picture of this house appears to have survived nor has any record been located giving the names of those who owned it in the first century of its existence. By 1832 the estate had come into the possession of the Reverend John Brewster Wilkinson, a parson with substantial property interests.[2] The house was not his principal residence,

*38 Holton Hall:
the garden front.*

and in 1841 was occupied by Mrs Harriett Lloyd, the rest of the estate being let separately.[3] By 1844 the house was let to the Reverend Richard Day, Vicar of Wenhaston.[4]

Nine years later the property was sold to Andrew Johnson, who was Agent for the Halesworth Bank (which later became part of Barclays Bank).[5] On his death in 1862 Holton passed to his son of the same name and became a tenanted property again.[6] By 1874 Charles Easton was living in the house, which in that year was 'being enlarged and improved'.[7] Easton is stated to have bought Holton in 1871.[8] However, the nature of his initial interest in the property is unclear as the estate was put on the market in 1886 by order of the mortgagee and the house was not conveyed to Charles Easton until 1887.[9] His family was to live there until the late 1930s.

In 1882 the original Georgian house was badly damaged by fire. Easton employed the architect Charles Smith of Reading to rebuild the house.[10] The new house was built on the foundations of its predecessor, but how much of the old house survived the fire and was retained is not known. The new building has been described as a Georgian house dressed up and made to look slightly ridiculous with a Frenchified roof and oddly placed balconies.[11]

The house was of three storeys and five bays. On the entrance front the three centre bays projected forward, with the central bay projecting further forward. The central bay had pilasters at the corners and was surmounted by a pediment, but this did not rest on the top of the pilasters, there being three or four courses of brickwork in between. The entrance portico had two pairs of pillars. The windows on the upper floors were sashed without ornamentation, except the first floor window in the centre bay, which was tripartite with stone mullions and a low segmental pediment. Those on the ground floor were round arched with drip mouldings. At the left-hand corner of the building there was a turret. To the right, detached from the entrance front and adjoining the service wing, there was a tower built in the style of a campanile.

On the garden front the projecting central bay had pilasters at the corners. The ground floor had canted bays, the larger central one supporting a pillared balcony with an arched canopy on the first floor and an open balcony on the second. Above this was a parapet behind which rose the mansard roof covered with ornamental slates. The remainder of the roof was covered with plain slates. The windows in the outer bays on the first floor had segmental pediments. To the left of the garden front there was a conservatory or winter garden. To the right of the garden front there was a single-storey room but this was a later addition to the building.

The house was described in 1886 as having a 'Noble Central Hall enriched with fluted columns and well lighted by stained glass clear-storey windows, leading to the principal Rooms, and by an easy and ornamental Staircase to the Chamber Gallery or landing and the principal bedrooms'.[12] The frieze in the hall was stated in 1937 to have come from St James's Chapel, York Street, London.[13] Folding doors 'from Westminster Hall Law Courts' led to the library, small business room, drawing room and dining room out of which opened a conservatory leading to a 'comfortable and well lighted billiard room'. The drawing and dining rooms had bay windows. The house had nine principal bedrooms, ladies' boudoir, dressing rooms and bathrooms and five staff bedrooms. The domestic offices were 'compact and suitable for a well ordered Establishment', and the house was heated with 'well planned hot water pipes'.

The house, with its stabling, carriage house and harness rooms, fruit and game stores, gardener's cottage, barn, kitchen and fruit gardens, vinery, greenhouse and peach house, came with 450 acres of which eighty acres was parkland.

CHARLES EASTON died around 1890. He was succeeded by his son, Major Charles John Easton, who died in 1909 and whose own son Charles was killed in the Great War.[14] Charles John Easton's widow remained at Holton until 1937 when the house and estate (the income of which was £296 a year) were put on the market.[15] It is not clear whether the house was in fact sold at that time as Mrs Easton's furniture 'removed from Holton Hall' was not included in an auction sale until early in 1947.[16]

The house was requisitioned during World War II and was occupied by American airmen based at the fighter station at Upper Holton and by girls in the Land Army. After the war the house, which had, no doubt, suffered from the depredations of service occupancy, was redundant. It survived a few more years until it was pulled down in 1957. The area where the house stood has became a static caravan park and the park is now a recognised County Wildlife site.[17]

HUNSTON HALL

DESTROYED BY FIRE 1917

Hunston Hall stood some two miles to the east of the road from Ixworth to Stowmarket. This small country house, unoccupied at the time, was destroyed by fire in 1917.

It appears that the manor of Hunston belonged in the later Middle Ages to the Priory of St Mary at Ixworth before passing at the Dissolution of the Monasteries into lay hands and, it seems, becoming merged with the manor of Hunston Hall.[1] The original Hunston Hall was on a different site from the house destroyed in 1917. It lay to the west of the parish church near to the parish boundary, but there is now no trace of that house and its moats are so mutilated that their plan can no longer be traced.[2]

39 Hunston Hall: the entrance and garden fronts.

The Heigham family from Rougham owned Hunston from the eighteenth century when it came to them through marriage.[3] Their house

was situated nearer the centre of the parish to the east of the church. Whether there was a house on this site when they inherited is not clear, but the presence of four tall brick chimneys serving the rear (presumably service) wing suggests that this part of the house may have survived from an earlier building.

THE HEIGHAMS' house was a plain Georgian building of six bays on the entrance front and three bays on the flank. The windows on the ground floor were arched, and the entrance portico consisted of a canted bay supported at ground level on two pillars with accommodation above. The height of the open portico was less than that of the ground floor of the house and the upper floor height correspondingly greater than that of the rest of the upper floor. The windows were sashed. On the garden flank there was a canopy stretching the whole width of the house.

THE HEIGHAM family's residence at Hunston Hall seems to have been somewhat sporadic in the nineteenth century. John Henry Heigham was living there in 1844 but eleven years later he was resident at another property on the estate, Hunston Cottage, a seventeenth-century building, and the hall was let. In 1885 Clement Henry John Heigham, who was Chief Constable of Suffolk, lived in the hall, but three years later he was living in Ipswich and two other members of the family were at the hall. In 1900 the house was let again with members of the family living at Hunston Cottage.[4]

In July 1917 the house was vacant when on the 30th of that month it was destroyed by fire.[5] The Heigham family did not rebuild it, and two years later the whole of the estate was put on the market.[6] It extended to 668 acres, and the site of the house (the outbuildings of which had survived the fire) and Hunston Cottage, thirteen other cottages and accommodation land were included in the sale.

LIVERMERE HALL

DEMOLISHED 1923

LIVERMERE HALL STOOD SOME EIGHT MILES NORTH-EAST OF BURY ST EDMUNDS in Little Livermere, with its parkland extending into Great Livermere. The manor of Murrells (alias Little Livermere) was held by a succession of families from medieval times through to the end of the sixteenth century when, in 1597, it was acquired by William Cooke of Barrow and William Chapman, who were brothers-in-law.[1] Six years later they acquired the 'site of the manor of Great Livermere alias Broom Hall with the mansion house, gatehouse and closes'.[2]

The Cooke family's ownership of property in Great and Little Livermere lasted a little over a century during which time additions were made to the estate.[3] After the deaths of Cooke and Chapman, who in 1617 had partitioned their joint estate by allocating Broom Hall to Cooke and Murrells to Chapman, both properties passed to Cooke's son, Richard. On his death in 1688 his son, also Richard (who appears to have adopted the spelling Coke for his surname), inherited the estate but he died later in the same year. In 1692 trustees appointed by Act of Parliament assigned Richard Coke the younger's lands to the trustees of his son Arundell's marriage settlement. In 1699 they appear to have been transferred to Arundell Coke himself.

In 1709 the estate, which by then extended to more than 2,000 acres, was sold by Coke to Thomas Lee of Kensington who paid £7,500 for the manors of Murrells and Broom Hall, fifteen messuages, two dove houses, six gardens, six orchards, 600 acres of land (presumably arable), 100 acres of meadow, 250 acres of pasture, 1,200 acres of heath and the advowson of Little Livermere Church.[4] Lee's family had owned Lawshall, south of Bury St Edmunds, since the manor there was acquired by Sir Robert Lee, Lord Mayor of London, who died in 1605. The acquisition of the Cokes' property was followed by the purchase of further property in Great Livermere in 1715.

There are some accounts of the history of the Livermere estate which do not accord with the account given above. These relate to the ownership of Livermere Hall after 1688. It is stated that either Richard Cooke the elder or his son was responsible for building the house and that it was left to the second Duke of Grafton from whom it was purchased by Baptist Lee (Thomas Lee's son) in 1722 or 1724. However it has also been suggested that the house was not built until after Baptist Lee inherited the

estate from his father about 1720. In regard to these conflicting accounts it is to be noted that the only surviving picture of Livermere Hall before the alterations made to it by Nathaniel Lee Acton at the end of the eighteenth century (illustration 40) shows the central core of the house to be of late seventeenth-century date, and surviving documents provide no evidence that the title to the Livermere estate acquired by the Lee family derived from the dukes of Grafton.[5] Nevertheless, the circumstances in which the house was built and came into the possession of the Lee family are not definitively known.

Baptist Lee's ownership of Livermere lasted from the early 1720s until he died in 1768, having won £30,000 (equivalent to £2.5 million) in the state lottery in 1733. After his death in 1768 the estate passed to his nephew, Nathaniel Lee Acton, of Bramford, who lived until 1836 when he was succeeded by his elder sister who outlived him by only a few months. It was then inherited by his younger sister, Hariott, the widow of Sir William Fowle Middleton, first baronet. The estate then passed to the second baronet, Sir William Fowle Fowle Middleton, who died without children in 1860. From him it descended to his nephew, Sir George Nathaniel Broke, who assumed the name of Middleton and on whose death it passed to his brother Charles's daughter, Jane Anna. She married the fourth Baron de Saumarez in whose family's ownership Livermere remained until shortly before its demolition. Wilson and Mackley have pointed out in their book *Creating Paradise* that over two centuries the estates of the Lee, Acton, Fowle, Middleton and Broke families were united by marriage and descent to the Barons de Saumarez.[6] In addition to Livermere these Suffolk estates included Bramford, Broke, Crowfield, Lawshall and Shrubland, which was the de Saumarez family's principal residence.

LIVERMERE HALL does not seem to have replaced any earlier house on the site but has been seen as a replacement for the manor house of Broom Hall, a moated house in Great Livermere, which was abandoned and whose site on the south side of the stream between Great and Little Livermere became the kitchen garden for Livermere Hall.[7]

The picture of the house (illustration 40) was painted after the additions of substantial wings and is of the north (entrance) front. As has already been stated, it shows the house's nucleus to have been a building in the style associated with the second half of the seventeenth century. It had seven bays, the three central bays being recessed and providing the principal entrance. It was of two storeys, with five dormer windows in the hipped roofs (three over the central section and one over each wing). The additions to this central block made in Baptist Lee's time consisted of projecting wings joined to the original building by curved sections, which created a courtyard divided from the parkland by a ha-ha surmounted by wrought iron work with a central entrance gate. The wings provided stabling, carriage houses and grooms' accommodation, and to the north opened directly on to the parkland outside the enclosed entrance courtyard.

Further alterations in the last decade of the eighteenth century for Nathaniel Lee Acton (some of which are attributed to Samuel Wyatt) resulted in a much less attractive building.[8] The two-storeyed curved sections on the entrance front were replaced by single-storey colonnades. The original central block of seven bays was stuccoed or refaced with stone and mathematical tiles, the recessed three bays being brought

42 Livermere Hall: the garden front about 1900.

forward with four pilasters and a plain pediment and the gable windows in the original roof replaced by a third storey. A single-storey entrance porch of three bays providing a balcony to the first floor was added, although this may have post-dated the other alterations to this face of the house. The south front was extended by the addition of two wings of three bays and two storeys and a bowed bay in the central section, where the building was raised to three storeys (as on the entrance front) and stuccoed. The rear walls of the south front wings, which rose behind the colonnades on the entrance front, were without windows and without stucco, giving an unattractive aspect to the entrance front and the appearance of work which was never completed. The house was altered internally although the original staircase was retained.[9]

The projecting wings were refenestrated and surmounted by open cupolas with ogee roofs. The wages book of De Carle, stonemasons of Honey Hill, Bury St Edmunds (who also worked on other houses in the area and notably at Culford for Marquess Cornwallis), provides details of work done to the wings between 1790 and 1797, including the building of a plinth, a 'new Ketton fasia' and pilasters. The ha-ha dividing the courtyard from the park was also removed and replaced by plain ring fencing with gates.[10]

The park surrounding the house was largely created in the Baptist Lee's time and involved exchanges of land (including glebe) with other owners in both Little Livermere and Great Livermere. The village of Little Livermere was demolished and its population dispersed.[11] The church was retained and its tower heightened to make it visible from the house so that it formed a feature of the view across the park. It still stands, a roofless ruin. By 1765 the park included two stretches of water, the Broad and Long Waters extending to thirty-seven and a half acres, which the house overlooked.[12] The Long Water ran through both Livermere and the adjoining Ampton Park, the property of James Calthorpe. In the 1790s Humphrey Repton prepared a Red Book proposing substantial changes to the park but although he was working on making the landscape at Livermere at the same time as he was working at Henham the extent to which his plans were executed is not known.[13] In 1815 Lewis Kennedy also produced proposals for alterations to the park, and it appears that some at least of these were executed.[14]

Nathaniel Lee Acton lived until 1836.[15] After his death few changes appear to have been made to the house. Its accommodation consisted of a drawing room, dining room, boudoir, morning room, study, sitting room, extensive household offices and five principal and ten secondary and servants' bedrooms. It was not, therefore, a very large house suitable for the extensive entertaining common in the period before the Great War.

THE LACK of the substantial additions often made to houses in the late nineteenth century may be attributed to the fact that Livermere was a secondary property superfluous to its owners' domestic requirements and usually tenanted. However, tenants were not always easy to find and the rents contributed to costs rather than produced spendable income.[16] Nevertheless, Livermere remained a tenanted house for some eighty years until, after the Great War, the de Saumarez family decided to sell the estate.

The house and its estate of 2,738 acres were put up for sale by auction by Knight, Frank & Rutley in October 1919.[17] At auction the property was withdrawn from sale at £40,000, a higher figure having been offered before the auction.[18] The estate was subsequently sold for £43,300 to Pierce Lacy, a Birmingham businessman who was created a baronet in 1921, who then owned Ampton.[19]

Following the sale of the estate in 1919 the hall was unoccupied. A story that the hall was burnt down rather than demolished was refuted by a local author writing in 2001 who stated that no-one could actually recall there being a fire and that the house was pulled down in 1923 as Sir Pierce did not want the upkeep of two mansions.[20] Some of the fireplaces are reported to have been removed to Shrubland, the seat of the former owners.[21] The lodges in the villages of Great Livermere and Ampton survive, and the foundations of the house remained visible at the end of the twentieth century.

THE MANOR HOUSE, MILDENHALL

DEMOLISHED 1934

THE MANOR HOUSE, MILDENHALL, STOOD TO THE NORTH OF THE PARISH CHURCH OF ST MARY, near the centre of the town. In the medieval period the manor of Mildenhall was, like many other manors in Suffolk, held by the Abbey of St Edmunds. After the Dissolution of the Monasteries it passed through a number of hands, including those of Sir Nicholas Bacon, Lord Keeper of the Great Seal, until it was acquired by Henry, son of Roger, second Lord North, in 1586. Thereafter it passed by descent until the final sale of the estate in 1933.

The date when the house was built is uncertain. One account of its history suggests that it was built about 1570 before its acquisition by the North family.[1] However there is no record of Sir Nicholas Bacon (a prolific builder of large houses) erecting a house at Mildenhall, and in 1608 'the King Majesty's manor house called Mildenhall Hall' was described as 'ruined and in decay'.[2] The Norths' tenure of Mildenhall appears originally to have been in the nature of a lease, and it was not until 1614 that Sir Henry North obtained a grant of the 'site of the Manor and Grange of Mildenhall' from the Crown.[3] It seems likely that the house was built shortly after Sir Henry North secured his tenure of the property.[4] On the death of his son, the second baronet, the property passed to his sister, the wife of William Hanmer whose son, Sir Thomas

43 The Manor House Mildenhall: the garden front in 1898, when the house was occupied by the Society of the Sacred Mission.

Hanmer, was Speaker of the House of Commons. From him it passed to the Bunbury family whose other Suffolk seat was Barton Hall but who also had landed interests in Cheshire.

THE NORTHS' original house was the subject of considerable alteration and extension over succeeding centuries. On what was originally its entrance front there were three gables, the right-hand one projecting forward of the other two and having a lower roof height and retaining its mullioned and transomed window on the first floor. This appears to have been the original building to which the other two gable-ended wings were added, probably later in the seventeenth century. The fenestration of these wings was subsequently changed to sashed windows and a gable was added to the flank of the left-hand wing. All three of these wings were of two principal storeys with garrets in the gabled roofs. To the rear a three-storey extension containing the library was added early in the eighteenth century.

In the 1819 edition of *The Suffolk Traveller* it is stated that the house 'contains numerous apartments and a gallery the whole length of the front, but the rooms are in general of small dimensions'.[5] Schoberl, writing a year earlier, said of Sir Thomas Hanmer that 'contiguous to his house he had a very fine bowling green; and was one of the last gentlemen of any fashion in this county who amused themselves with this diversion'.[6]

The house had, on the ground floor, a double-height dining hall, ante-drawing (tea) room, drawing room and library and the domestic offices. The first floor had a billiard room, a suite of two bedrooms, two further bedrooms (one with a dressing room), the bathroom and two servants' rooms. The second floor contained the long gallery, two further bedrooms and servants' quarters.[7] By the standards of Victorian times this was not a large house, which no doubt explains why the Bunbury family resided at their much larger house at Great Barton, which became their principal Suffolk seat.

IN 1844 it was reported that the house was occupied by a gardener.[8] In the middle of the 1860s Sir John Lister Kaye lived in it, and during his short incumbency as Vicar of Mildenhall in the 1870s the Reverend Hemming Robeson occupied the house.[9] Following the death of Sir Charles James Fox Bunbury in 1886, his widow moved from Barton to live in the Manor House where she remained until her death in 1894.[10] At the end of the nineteenth century the house was leased to the Society of the Sacred Mission as a training college for missionaries, but its use for this purpose was not allowed to interfere with the running of the girls' school, which had been started in the north wing of the house in the 1860s and was then located in the Great Hall.[11]

Barton Hall being let the family moved back into the house by 1904, the then baronet, Sir Henry Charles John Bunbury, having previously lived at Woodlands, another property on the 8,000-acre estate.[12] At that time the estate included Wamil Hall (in earlier times the seat of the Warner family), but this was sold in 1911 together with a number of farms, reducing the family's land holding by 2,900 acres.[13] This sale marked the beginning of the disengagement of the Bunbury family from the Mildenhall area. There were to be further sales in 1919, but Sir Henry remained at the Manor House until his death in 1930, and during his time the house was the subject of considerable refurbishment and the gardens were renewed and relaid.[14]

Following Sir Henry's death the family ceased to occupy the house, and in March 1932 the contents of the house were sold: the 800 lots included the oak refectory table, which formed part of 'the equipment of the Banquetting Hall when it was refurnished during the Jacobean era'.[15] In July the following year the house and the remainder of the estate was put up for sale in fifty-seven lots.[16] Although the house and service buildings adjacent to it were offered for sale as a whole, parts of the fabric were also lotted separately. These lots included the panelling in the dining room, 'ante-drawing or tea' room, drawing room, library, the bedroom passage and the bathroom, together with an oak staircase, doors and shutters. Also lotted separately was an Early Tudor Mural Painting with heraldic figures and another lot included six 'Early English Oil Paintings in panels'. The fine wrought iron gateway was also put up for sale. The house, garden and service buildings were withdrawn at £2,700, and the house and garden sold separately for £500.[17]

The way in which the house was lotted for the 1933 sale suggests that the property was not expected to attract a buyer for continued use as a dwelling. Its site close to the centre of the town made the property a target for redevelopment, and the next year saw the end of the Manor House, when it was demolished and the site turned into building plots. Panelling from the house is reputed to have been exported to the United States, and the Tudor mural was transferred to the Victoria and Albert Museum for preservation.[18] Mildenhall's connection with the Bunbury family and those from whom they had inherited the Manor House, a connection that had extended over three centuries, had come to an end.

MOULTON PADDOCKS

DEMOLISHED 1950

OULTON PADDOCKS, UNLIKE MOST OF THE LOST COUNTRY HOUSES OF SUFFOLK, WAS NOT ORIGINALLY THE HOUSE AT THE HUB OF A LARGE COUNTRY ESTATE. Situated between the village of Moulton and Newmarket, it was, in the middle of the nineteenth century, a small house with only a small acreage of land. Its expansion into an estate with a substantial country house in over 1,000 acres arose from its proximity to Newmarket and its development as a racing establishment.

At the time of the enclosure of Moulton in 1841 the property, then known as Fidget Hall, with sixty-four acres was owned by George Samuel Ford.[1] A year later at redemption of the tithes the property, now with a further eight acres, was owned by William Webber.[2] By 1850 it had passed into the hands of Sir Robert Pigot, was known as Moulton Paddocks and was described as his 'occasional seat'.[3] In 1868, when Col. Frederick Daniel Fryer occupied the house, it was again described as Fidget Hall, but by the early 1870s the old name finally seems to have been dropped in favour of Moulton Paddocks, presumably reflecting the owner's interest in racing.[4] The next thirty years saw a number of owners; by 1879 Col. Fryer's son, by 1888 Lord Gerard and then George Alexander Baird

44 Moulton Paddocks: the garden front.

following whose death the property was put up for sale by auction in 1895. Having failed to sell in 1895 the estate was marketed again in 1898, and in the next year was bought by Sir Ernest Cassel.

Cassel was born in Cologne in 1852, the son of a banker. His initial training in his home city was followed by periods with banking businesses in Liverpool and Paris. Moving to a London financial house in 1870 at the outbreak of the Franco-Prussian War, he established the foundations of what was to become an immense fortune. Alongside his work for his employers, Bischoffsheim and Goldschmidt, he engaged in ventures on his own account and in 1884 became wholly independent. He became one of the wealthiest and most powerful figures in the City of London, and at his death left over £7 million, having reputedly given over £2 million to charities during his lifetime. Cassel was a confidant of King Edward VII who was a frequent visitor to Moulton Paddocks. He married in 1878, but his wife died young leaving him with a daughter who married Wilfred Ashley, later Lord Mount Temple. Lord and Lady Mount Temple's elder daughter, Edwina, married Lord Louis Mountbatten, later Earl Mountbatten of Burma.[5]

During the second half of the nineteenth century both the house and its estate were enlarged. Webber's seventy-two acres increased to 757 acres and his small house became a substantial mansion. As far as the estate was concerned its expansion dated at least from the Fryer family's time for in 1885 Frederick Fryer, the son, was named as one of the owners to whom 'a great part of the soil [in Moulton] belongs'.[6] Lord Gerard also added to the estate when he bought a hundred acres from Trinity Hall, Cambridge.[7]

The development of Moulton Paddocks as a major racing establishment has been attributed to Cassel but even before his purchase of the estate it had 'two sets of stud farm premises with accommodation for Thoroughbred Sires and a large number of Brood Mares and Foals'. Cassel added to the estate in 1908, 1914 and 1920 so that by the time of his death in 1921 the estate had been further enlarged to over 1,300 acres.[8] The property's access to Newmarket was improved by the construction in 1901 of a new estate road. The extent to which the estate was devoted to racing and breeding activities is demonstrated by the fact that in 1922, when it was on the market, half of the total acreage comprised the residence, its home farms, the stud farm with accommodation for sixty horses and the training establishment with stabling for a further forty horses.

WHICH OF THE various owners were responsible for the development of the house in the nineteenth century is not clear. The house at the time of the 1895 sale gives the appearance of having had numerous extensions added to a smaller neo-Georgian house. On the garden front the two-storeyed central block had five bays, the three central bays being surmounted with a pediment. The outer bays projected forward with canted sides, and along the pedimented central section of the frontage there was a canopy. To this wings were added: those abutting the centre did not match, being differently aligned and of different heights. That on the left of the garden front had a further extension added and a tall building (probably the water tower) to its rear. No attempt had been made to create a harmonious design, and its description as 'a long dull neo-Georgian mansion' was fully merited.[9]

When Cassel bought the house it had six principal and four secondary bedrooms and twelve servants' rooms.[10] By the time of his death it had been extended so that it had twenty 'excellent' bedrooms and eleven servants' rooms. The house had two dining rooms, a drawing room opening into a winter garden, billiard room, library and study, the 'usual offices' and the range of outbuildings necessary for the running of a substantial establishment.[11]

A YEAR AFTER Cassel's death, Moulton Paddocks was sold to the racehorse owner Solly Joel on whose death ten years later his son Dudley inherited the estate. When Dudley Joel lost his life on active service in 1941 the estate passed to his brother and sister, and in October that year the furnishings of the house were sold.[12]

In June 1950 it was reported that Moulton Paddocks had almost gone, the housebreakers had almost completed their task, little now remained and as it had been demolished it had been sold bit by bit as building material. Even the gardens were to be removed, and 'the mansion will merge back into the landscape'.[13]

Fidget Hall's location near Newmarket made it a prime site for the development of a racing establishment in the latter half of the nineteenth century and the early years of the twentieth. However, the way of life which required a house of such size was short lived: Moulton Paddocks' existence as a large country house lasted for only three-quarters of a century but its estate survives as a racing establishment.

OAKLEY PARK, otherwise HOXNE HALL

DEMOLISHED 1923

Oakley Park, as Hoxne Hall was renamed in the nineteenth century, because its estate lay largely in the parish of Oakley, was a remodelling of an older house, and stood some three miles north-east of Eye near the Norfolk border. There was a monastery here before the Norman Conquest but in the early Middle Ages the property passed to the Bishops of Norwich whose palace it became. The palace was a large complex of buildings with a road running through them, and it has been suggested that this was the site of the Roman Villa Faustina, subsequently taken over by the Anglo-Saxons and adapted to other uses.[1]

After the Dissolution of the Monasteries it was leased to Charles Brandon, Duke of Suffolk but in 1543 the manor was granted to Sir Robert Southwell, Master of the Rolls. From the Southwell family it passed in 1621 to the Prescotts, and is said to have been acquired in 1642 by the Maynard family of Great Easton in Essex.[2] The lordship of the manor and the property appear to have been in separate hands at this stage in their history. It seems that the estate passed from the Prescotts to the Style family, a member of which had married a Prescott. Subsequently it was acquired, possibly through marriage, by the Maynard family whose ownership lasted until 1820, when the estate was sold to Matthias Kerrison, a niece of whom had married Henry Maynard. Kerrison was a wealthy grain merchant from Bungay, who also bought nearby Brome Hall from the Cornwallis family. It was during its tenure by Matthias Kerrison's son, General Sir Edward Kerrison Bt, that the house became known as Oakley Park. The estate remained in the family until shortly before the house was demolished.

To what extent the episcopal palace survived once it came into the hands of lay owners is not clear. A map of the Hoxne estate in 1619 shows a six-bay rectangular U-shaped house with the projecting full-height entrance porch placed in the second bay from the left of the recessed cross-wing.[3] In front of the house was a gatehouse flanked by substantial service buildings. The gatehouse tower is depicted as a more ornate structure than the house itself, suggesting that it may have been a survival from episcopal times and that a new house was built in the late Tudor or early Stuart period. In 1654 the house was rebuilt by Robert Style, a younger brother of Sir Humphrey Style, but the extent of that rebuilding

TOP RIGHT:
45 Oakley Park: the Hon. Henry Maynard's house in 1819 (from T. Cromwell, Excursions through the county of Suffolk).

RIGHT:
46 Oakley Park: the entrance front after Sydney Smirke's remodelling in the 1830s.

is not known. It appears that by the end of the seventeenth century Style's house had fallen into disrepair, with only two or three bays standing in 1700. A map of that date depicts the house but not the gatehouse and ancillary buildings shown on the 1619 map: these had presumably been demolished by that time.[4]

In the first half of the eighteenth century the Maynards built a new house. This Palladian building (of which neither the exact date nor the architect have been identified) had seven bays on the garden front and eight on the sides. The outer bays projected forward and were flanked by double pilasters on which rested a parapet; above this were Venetian windows lighting garret rooms on the second floor. The parapet continued between the wings and was surmounted by a balustrade behind which rose the house's pitched roofs. The windows on the ground floor were pedimented. The configuration of the entrance front is not known. However, it seems likely that there was a courtyard either on the entrance front or in the centre of the building and that this was roofed over at a later stage of the

47 Oakley Park: the south portico after Sydney Smirke's remodelling in the 1830s.

house's development. A photograph dating from 1908 shows that the glass-roofed salon had internal windows at first floor level on the side walls, suggesting that these may originally have been external walls.[5]

General Sir Edward Kerrison commissioned the architect Sir Jeffry Wyatville to propose improvements to the house, but his designs were not executed, and the house as remodelled in the 1830s was the work of Sydney Smirke.[6] Smirke is perhaps better known for his public buildings in London, such as the Reading Room at the British Museum and the Oxford and Cambridge and Conservative Clubs, where he demonstrated what has been described as his 'penchant for the Renaissance'.[7] That style was also evident in his work at Oakley, of which it has been written 'Oakley Park seemed almost a Pall Mall palazzo which had strayed into the Suffolk countryside'.[8]

Smirke's remodelling of the eighteenth-century house of the Maynards converted it into a mansion in a bold neo-classical style with double-storeyed Corinthian porticos to the south and west fronts. Many of the plastered ceilings and chimneypieces from the Maynard's house with their caryatids supporting the mantels appear to have been reused, and, as J. Mordaunt Crook has commented, the incorporation of decorative elements from the eighteenth-century house must have encouraged Smirke to use Palladian rather than Grecian forms. As he has written,

> But the controlling order is a bold Corinthian, and an accumulation of minor details contribute to an overall sense of rich texture and bold projection – the scagliola columns raised on pedestals in the top-lit central hall, the paired columns of the grand portico, the balustrades and urns ranked up and down the terraces, the scrolly stable cupola, the bold keystones and massy brackets. ... Neo-classical proportions were combined with a decorative scheme which in all its strength and boldness of contour can only be described as early Victorian.[9]

Smirke's remodelling does not appear to have embraced the whole of the house: behind the grand frontages and the principal rooms there was a medley of single- and two-storey buildings on the north side of the house comprising the domestic offices and service buildings. Whether any other alterations were made to the house after Smirke's remodelling is not known.

The house that resulted from Smirke's work was a substantial mansion.[10] The entrance hall led to the salon, which served as the staircase hall and opened into the ballroom and the 'Fine Suite of Reception Rooms' – drawing room, ante room, dining room, boudoir, library and smoking room. As the selling agents in 1921 wrote:

> The Art Decorations ... are very fine, artistically and elaborately carved in the best manner of the period. The statuary marble, stone and carved wood mantelpieces are fine examples, and the ceilings, doorcases, architraves, each of individual character, are most artistic befitting a Mansion of this character.

On the first floor there were twelve principal bedrooms and two dressing rooms, and on the second floor ten secondary bedrooms, including day and night nurseries and valets' and maids' rooms. The servants' wing, 'quite shut off from the Principal Bedchambers', had five rooms for menservants and seven for maidservants and was said to be adequate for twenty-five servants. The domestic offices were extensive as with all houses of this size.

The house stood in large gardens within a seventy-acre park. The stables, set back beyond the entrance front of the house, were also designed by Sydney Smirke and replaced those which had stood in front of the house in the Maynards' time. They provided twelve stalls, five boxes, two coach houses, a washing stable and boxes for brood mares. There was a three-acre walled kitchen garden with ranges of glasshouses, a gardener's cottage, laundry and brickworks.

SIR EDWARD KERRISON lived until 1854, having been a Member of Parliament for most of his life after he gave up active military service after the Napoleonic Wars. In addition to managing his estates he was heavily engaged in public affairs in Suffolk, including the founding of Framlingham College. He was succeeded by his son, Sir Edward Clarence Kerrison, who followed his father as Member of Parliament for Eye. On his death in 1886 the Oakley and Brome estates passed to his daughter, Agnes, the wife of the second Lord Bateman whose family's seat, Shobdon Court, an early eighteenth-century house in Herefordshire, was also demolished in the inter-war years. The house was tenanted in the last years of the nineteenth century.

During the Great War the house and park were used as a cavalry depot. Lady Bateman died in 1918, and in November the following year both the Oakley and Brome estates were sold by her son, the third Lord Bateman, to Rowland Hodge of Chipstead Manor in Kent.[11] Hodge paid

£175,000 for the two estates.[12] Whatever may have been Hodge's plans for the estate when he purchased it, he did not retain it for long. In May 1920 the house and 7,400 acres were offered for sale, but the house and many other lots failed to sell at auction.[13] Subsequently in December the house, together with 1,296 acres, was purchased by Lord Bateman's brother and heir, the Hon. Charles Bateman-Hanbury.[14] The return of this part of the estate to the Bateman family was short-lived as in October 1921 the property was on the market again, this time by order of mortgagees.[15] The purchaser was Lord Terrington, but the conveyance was to his sub-purchaser, Lawrence Bernard Lister, an accountant from Stowmarket.[16] Before Lister completed his purchase for £28,500 on the last day of July 1923 he had already put the property excluding the house up for auction.[17] The particulars of sale stated that 'the Mansion known as Oakley Park, otherwise Hoxne Hall, and 10ft. surrounding same has been disposed of'. Clearly, the house was earmarked by Lister for demolition, and this must have followed shortly after his acquisition and onward sale of the building.

The stable block survives and has been converted to residential use. It is all that remains of a very grand property, one with a long history and in its final form the product of the wealth of a self-made merchant from Bungay and the ambitions of his soldier son.

48   Oakley Park:
the drawing room.

OUSDEN HALL

DEMOLISHED 1955

OUSDEN, OR OWSDEN AS IT WAS KNOWN FOR MANY CENTURIES, LIES SEVEN MILES SOUTH-EAST OF NEWMARKET and was owned by four principal families in the five and a half centuries before the Hall was demolished. The manor of Ousden was acquired by Richard Waldegrave at the beginning of the fifteenth century and held by that family until it was sold to the Moseley family in 1567. This family built the house in late Tudor times and extended it in the eighteenth century. They sold the estate in 1800 to John Smith of Staffordshire from whom it passed four years later to the Reverend James Thomas Hand.[1] In 1835 it was inherited by Hand's nephew, Thomas James Ireland, who is reported to have entertained King William IV during visits to Newmarket.

Following Thomas Ireland's death in 1863 the estate was bought by Bulkley John Mackworth-Praed, a member of the Praed banking family whose business became incorporated into Lloyds Bank. It seems that during the period of ownership by Mackworth-Praed, who died in 1876, and his son Sir Herbert, a banker and Member of Parliament for Ipswich, the family did not live at Ousden and the house was let. In 1908, three years after the death of Bulkley John Mackworth-Praed's widow Emily, Sir Herbert put the property on the market.[2] There was considerable interest in the property both from London agents and personal enquirers but no sale was achieved, and in the meantime the house continued to be let principally for the shooting rights.[3] This remained the position until 1913 when Sir Herbert's youngest half-brother, Algernon, bought the estate.

Sir Herbert's difficulties in selling Ousden appear to have stemmed from the fact that he sought an unrealistically high price for the property. In 1910 his agents, Biddell & Blencowe of Bury St Edmunds, wrote to Hamptons, the London property agents, stating that the price had been reduced to £55,000. Two years later professional valuations of £45,000 and £38,000 were made. This latter figure was compared with the £85,000 that the estate was said to have fetched at auction in 1863 when the market was at its highest, 'just three years before the failure of Overend & Gurney' (the most famous banking failure of the nineteenth century).[4] These figures exemplify the falling values of landed estates in the years of agricultural depression from the 1870s onwards, which caused problems for many landowners. Algernon Mackworth-Praed paid his half-brother £41,965.[5]

TOP RIGHT:
49 Ousden Hall: the house sketched by the Reverend E. Farrer from drawings of 1804 and 1807, showing the Elizabethan/ Jacobean front and the Georgian wings.

RIGHT:
50 Ousden Hall: the entrance front before the 1914 alterations, when the upper floor of the portico was removed and a two-storey extension added in the left corner of the frontage.

Ousden Hall in 1804
and also from a photo from the sketch in 1807

N.B. No wings to original house
Wings built 1760
Centre block pulled down and
rebuilt in front of 1833
47.

Eliz M Ireland
Feby 23 1853.

This rough sketch was taken from Miss Ireland's drawing, in possession of Mrs Praed. June 1924.

THE HOUSE WHICH Algernon Mackworth-Praed bought stood on the site of the late Tudor or Jacobean house that the Moseley family had built on a moated site and which may itself have been in part a remodelling of an earlier building.[6] The north (entrance) front of the Moseleys' house as depicted in 1734 had seven bays three of which, the second, the fourth (the central containing the entrance doorway) and the sixth, projected forward and had 'Dutch' gables. The mullioned and transomed windows on the ground floor were pedimented, as were the first floor windows in the projecting bays. These had mullioned garret windows. The central arched doorway had a classical surround, which is said to have survived later rebuilding. The house appears to have been a rectangular U-shaped building with the wings extending to the rear.

51 Ousden Hall: the garden front.

The house was enlarged in 1760 by the addition of wings at each end of the north front (illustration 49).[7] These projected forward to create an

entrance court and were of two bays on the front and two deep with sashed windows. They had two principal storeys with attics in the hipped roofs behind parapets. The late eighteenth century also saw landscaping of the pleasure grounds and parkland in which work the landscape gardener William Emes is believed to have played a part.[8]

In about 1820 the original building, which had been retained when the house was enlarged in the eighteenth century, was replaced when a new central block was built between and in the same style as the eighteenth-century wings. This had seven bays on the ground with pilasters between the bays and with a single-storey pillared portico. The upper floor had six bays and there were four garret windows in the roof. The rear of this new building formed the garden front of the house. Other alterations may also have been made at this time.

In 1835–6 Thomas Ireland engaged Thomas Rickman to make further alterations to the house.[9] These included the building of a square bay on the first floor over the north portico and the building of a pedimented portico on the west front of the house with a room above lit by a Venetian window. What further work Rickman may have undertaken is not known, but the large canted bays at the end of each wing with their large paned windows give the south (garden) front a predominantly Victorian appearance.

When, following Ireland's death the house, with its estate of 2,350 acres in Ousden and adjoining parishes, was put on the market in 1864, its accommodation consisted of 'a spacious hall', billiard room, drawing room 'with Marble Chimney Piece and richly Gilt Cornice', dining room, study, ante room and domestic offices on the ground floor. On the first floor, approached by the principal staircase of oak with an inlaid handrail (one of the more distinguished features of the house), were eight principal bedrooms, seven dressing rooms, night and day nurseries, and on the second floor there were nine secondary and servants' bedrooms. There were stables, loose boxes and two double coach houses, and the 'well enclosed' kitchen garden had a vinery and conservatory.[10] There is no record of any substantial work being done to the house in the next half-century.

Algernon Mackworth-Praed bought the house to live in, and soon after his purchase he employed Arthur Blomfield of Sir Arthur Blomfield & Sons to make alterations and additions.[11] These included the building of towers at both the eastern and western ends of the house, alterations to the front porch and the conversion of the study into a dining room – it appears that the situation of the original dining room had been inconvenient. The room above the entrance portico was removed and a room built in the angle between one of the wings and the main front. A new water installation was provided and the house was rewired and redecorated. These works cost a little over £4,000.[12]

ALGERNON lived at the house until the beginning of World War II, during which it was requisitioned and used by the Army and later occupied by German and Italian prisoners of war. After Algernon's death in 1952 his trustees held sales of the contents and of silver and books.[13] Two years later the house, which had passed to his great-nephew, Cyril Mackworth-Praed, was placed on the market.[14] Before the auction scheduled to take place in June 1954, the estate of 2,593 acres with a rent roll of £6,986 p.a., was sold to Lady Shelley-Rolls, but the house was said to be beyond economic restoration and in 1955 was pulled down.[15]

The clock tower survived through the endeavours of the vicar, who was reported as seeking funds to save the tower and asked the contractors to stop demolishing it.[16] Subsequently the clock, installed in 1868 by G. & F. Cope of Nottingham, was removed for safekeeping and installed in a museum in Bury St Edmunds.[17] The dovecote in the field opposite the stable block survived.[18] The stable block, described in 1908 as having 'superior stabling, with seven roomy boxes, four stalls, double coach house, harness room with chambers over, coachman's cottage, laundry etc, enclosing a courtyard', also survived. In the early 1970s part of it was converted into a house which incorporated the coachman's cottage.[19] In the last decade of the twentieth century the stable block was remodelled to form a substantial country house with the clock tower (fitted with a new clock) standing in the house's redesigned garden and grounds.

THE RED HOUSE, IPSWICH

DEMOLISHED 1937

THE RED HOUSE WAS SITUATED ONE AND A HALF MILES FROM THE CENTRE OF IPSWICH on land between the roads leading out of the town to Westerfield and Tuddenham. Its tree-lined entrance drive led northwards from the Tuddenham road. It was the seat of the branch of the Edgar family which traced its descent from William Edgar of Great Glemham.[1]

William Edgar's grandson, Lionel, acquired a newly built messuage and sixty-seven acres of land in the parish of St Margaret's Ipswich in 1641.[2] This purchase was the first in the parish by the Edgar family of which documentary evidence has survived. Over the succeeding two centuries the family acquired additional land in St Margaret's and substantial holdings in villages around Ipswich. Members of the family appear to have had a propensity for marrying heiresses, a fact that may account for the extent of the property they acquired.[3]

52 The Red House, Ipswich: the entrance front in 1840, which remained unchanged until the house was demolished (engraving by H. Davy).

Lionel Edgar's grandson Thomas, who died in 1692, was Recorder of Ipswich and Reader of Gray's Inn. His son, also Thomas, died in 1677, having married Agatha, heiress of Borodaile Mileson of Norton, the name Mileson being thereafter used as a Christian name in succeeding generations of the family.[4] Thomas and Agatha Edgar's son, Mileson, is the first described as being 'of Red House Park', although the house was almost certainly built before his time.[5]

The estate then passed in the direct line through two Mileson Edgars to Reverend Mileson Gery Edgar, who died childless in 1853, leaving the property to his widow, Elizabeth.[6] She outlived her husband by thirty-seven years, dying in 1890.

THE RED HOUSE'S central block (to which wings were added at a later date) is thought to have been built in 1658, although some sources have attributed it to the early eighteenth century.[7] Although no archaeological evidence of activity on the site prior to the eighteenth century has been found, the 1937 sale particulars stated that the hall contained 'a Jacobean Oak Staircase ... with twisted and carved balusters and tread spandrels'.[8] Moreover Thomas Edgar is recorded in 1674 as having a house with thirteen hearths in St Margaret's Parish, and the evidence therefore points to the house being of mid-seventeenth-century rather than eighteenth-century date.

The house's central block was of five bays with the outer bays projecting forward. It had three storeys (with a semi-basement containing the domestic offices) with string courses, a plain parapet and plaintile roofs. The entrance doorway was pedimented and approached by stone steps. The two-storey wings also with semi-basements are believed to have dated from the middle of the eighteenth century. They had 'Venetian' windows on the first floor, string courses, plain parapets and hipped roofs. Whether any further additions or alterations to the house were made is not known. Certainly the entrance front as depicted in 1840 remained unaltered until the house was demolished.[9]

When the estate was sold in 1937 the sale particulars gave only a brief description of the interior of the house, no doubt reflecting the fact that it was by then uninhabitable.[10] It had five reception rooms and eleven bedrooms with two bathrooms. The semi-basement contained the kitchens and domestic offices.

To the left of the house there was a separate building depicted by Davy in 1840 (illustration 52) as having Venetian windows at each end of its frontage similar to those in the eighteenth-century wings of the house. A photograph of the house (undated but probably taken in the late nineteenth century) shows this building without Venetian windows. This building was not referred to in the particulars of sale when the house was placed on the market in 1937, but may have been an orangery. The brick-built stable block with a plain tile roof was situated to the rear of the house on the right-hand side and had a clock tower. There was a gardener's cottage and a walled garden which extended to three-quarters of an acre and contained a vinery.

THE EDGAR ESTATES became considerably encumbered by debts in the nineteenth century, and remortgaging in 1866 appears to have resulted in mortgages to secure borrowings of £17,500. More than £15,000 was outstanding when Elizabeth Edgar died, and her will provided that the estate was not to pass to her husband's nephew, Captain Mileson Edgar, until the debts had been reduced to that figure. The will appears to have been drafted with a view to the retention of the Red House by the beneficiary and his use of it as his residence. In the event the will gave rise to litigation, Captain Edgar's elder brother declined to act as executor and Captain Edgar himself lived not at the Red House but at his other property, Sparrow's Nest.

In 1895 the house and twenty acres of land were let for ten years together with the shooting on the remainder of the Edgar estate.[11] In March 1900 the contents of the house were sold by Christies, but whether the tenancy continued after that sale is not known.[12] The house was lived in at various times during the first quarter of the twentieth century but was not occupied after 1925.[13]

The situation of the Red House so close to the centre of Ipswich and the town's expansion in the nineteenth and twentieth centuries made it vulnerable to housing and other development. As early as 1855 the Ipswich Burial Board had acquired land on the southern side of the estate from Elizabeth Edgar, although the rest of the estate remained intact until, following the Great War, the Ipswich ring road, Valley Road, was built, breaching the avenue of trees stretching from Tuddenham Road to the front of the house.[14] Clearly, the pressure of housing development together with the fact that Captain Edgar did not live in it placed the house at risk.

After Captain Mileson Edgar's death in 1935 his personal representatives sold the estate. Firstly, in July 1936, thirty acres of land on the southern side of the estate were sold for development, divided partly into blocks of housing land and partly into plots for individual houses.[15] Then, in the following April, 222 acres of land comprising 'the Mansion and Grounds, Park Lands and Dairy Farm' (Red House Farm) were put up for sale. A considerable area of the parkland, 'with belts of trees and studded with magnificent oaks offering attractive residential sites', was stated to be 'ripe for immediate development'. The house, having been unoccupied for a number of years, was described as 'not suitable for occupation but is capable of reconditioning'.[16] The buyer was William Pipe, who paid £17,500 for it.[17] It seems improbable, given the house's state of dereliction and with housing development proposed on land adjoining the eight acres of grounds sold with it, that there can have been any real possibility that it would be restored and, indeed, it did not long survive the sale by Captain Edgar's personal representatives.

The house, disused for some years, was demolished in 1937, when the site became part of a modern housing development. Two sections of the avenue of trees survive to the north and south of Valley Road.

REDGRAVE HALL

DEMOLISHED – THE GEORGIAN BUILDING 1947,
THE TUDOR BUILDING 1970

R EDGRAVE HALL WAS SITUATED IN THE NORTHERN PART OF SUFFOLK
NEAR THE NORFOLK BORDER, seven miles west of Diss. The first
house on its site is thought to have been built early in the thirteenth
century by the Abbot of Bury St Edmunds to whom the manor belonged.
Following the Dissolution of the Monasteries Redgrave was granted by
King Henry VIII to Sir Nicholas Bacon, who became Lord Keeper of the
Great Seal under Elizabeth I and was the father of Sir Francis Bacon.

Redgrave remained in the Bacon family until 1702 when it was bought
by Sir John Holt, Lord Chief Justice of the King's Bench. On his death
without children in 1709 the estate passed to his brother Rowland
(1652–1719) and subsequently to his son Rowland II (1698–1739) and

53 Redgrave Hall:
Sir Nicholas Bacon's
house, showing the
wings added to the
original structure to
enlarge the house in
the 1560s.

his grandson Rowland III (1723–86), whose mother was a cousin of George Washington, first President of the United States of America. On his death, unmarried, in 1786 the estate passed to his brother, Thomas, who bequeathed it to his sister Lucinda's son, Admiral George Wilson, in whose family (later Holt-Wilson) it remained until the house was demolished.

THE HOUSE that Bacon acquired was described in 1542 as 'sore decayed', but some part of it was incorporated in Sir Nicholas's new house.[1] Parts of Bacon's building survived the rebuilding of the house in the eighteenth century, and the last part of Redgrave to remain standing was the cross-wing of the house he built.

Lord Keeper Bacon's house was one of the earliest examples of the U-plan houses built in this part of England and was more sophisticated than both Hengrave and Little Saxham, further south in the county, which 'were both firmly in the English late mediaeval tradition'.[2] It was begun in 1545 and completed in its original form nine years later. It was a rigidly symmetrical house with crow-stepped gables and a central octagon turret. Its symmetry reflected the influence of Renaissance architectural ideas and extended not only to the front but also to the inner faces of the side wings. The hall of the house was to the left of the central block off a screens passage with private accommodation in the wing. The kitchens and service rooms were to the right of the passage, and in its planning therefore the house continued the medieval tradition. The house had a running water system, with the water drawn from a spring three-quarters of a mile from the house.[3] This facility, a plan of which survives, was retained in the eighteenth-century remodelling of the house.

Bacon, who had a considerable interest in architecture himself, appears to have played a major part in its design, but he was advised by John Gybbon, a mason from Southwark, who was a craftsman of some distinction, having been employed by King Henry VIII on works at Westminster Hall in the 1530s.[4] It was Gybbon who prepared the initial ground plan for the house. Bacon also altered the river flowing in front of the house and had a bridge built over it with raised causeways to provide a direct approach to the house. Edward Withipoll, who had been responsible for the building of Christchurch Manor in Ipswich between 1548 and 1550, was involved in the building of the bridge, and it has been suggested on account of the similarities between the two houses that his craftsmen may also have been involved in the building of Redgrave Hall.[5]

Queen Elizabeth is said to have told Bacon that Redgrave was not a sufficiently grand house for a man in his position, to which Bacon replied that it was she who had made him too great for his house. Whether there is any truth in this story and whether it related to Redgrave or to Bacon's principal seat at Gorhambury is not clear. However, what is known is that he enlarged Redgrave in the early 1560s, when two flanking wings were added on each side, thus increasing the size of the house without destroying its symmetry.

There is no record of any major changes being made to the house over the two centuries after Sir Nicholas Bacon's additions in the 1560s, and the house he built seems to have survived intact until the 1760s, more than twenty years after Rowland Holt III inherited the estate. Initially Holt commissioned Lancelot ('Capability') Brown to redesign the parkland, and this work began about 1763 with the construction of a lake which submerged Bacon's bridge and causeway. Stables, an orangery and a boathouse were built together with an octagonal building, the Round

54 Redgrave Hall: the entrance and west fronts of the house rebuilt for Rowland Holt in the 1760s; the surviving parts of Sir Nicholas Bacon's house stood behind the new building.

HALL REDGRAVE.

House (a cottage), as a landscape feature. Plans for rebuilding the house followed later in the decade.

Capability Brown's plans involved the building of new facades and principal rooms with an enclosed central courtyard. The front and sides of the house were clad in Suffolk white brick with stone dressings. The house was of nine bays on both the front and side elevations. The central three bays of the south (entrance) front had a portico with four Ionic columns supporting a pediment in which the Holt family's arms were placed. The west front had a pediment over the three central bays, and this feature was presumably mirrored on the east front. The great hall and service rooms of Bacon's house were converted into domestic offices, forming the rear of the enclosed courtyard, and the octagonal turret above the former main entrance was retained. Architectural drawings and floor plans of the house made in the 1930s show how these elements of the Tudor house were incorporated into Rowland Holt's somewhat austere new house.[6]

These plans show that the house had a saloon (which also served as the entrance hall), staircase hall, drawing room, dining room, two libraries, morning room and billiard room. These rooms occupied the whole of the south and west sides of the building and with the exception of the billiard room were all intercommunicating. The north and east sides contained the kitchen and scullery, a housekeeper's room, servants' hall, butler's bedroom and, adjoining the dining room, the butler's pantry. There was also a muniment room. The first floor was approached by the principal staircase and by a secondary staircase situated in the north-west of the courtyard. There were eight principal bedrooms and three dressing rooms in two intercommunicating sets. Two of these bedrooms appear to have been created out of larger rooms windows in which had been blocked up. At the north-east corner of the house over the servants' hall and other service quarters there were three floors: the 'mezzanine' floor (consisting of three bedrooms), the floor above it and an attic room being served by a separate staircase. The creation of an additional floor in this part of the house appears to have been achieved by some of the service rooms being at a lower level than the principal rooms on the ground floor and the height of the rooms also being lower.[7]

In the autumn of 1771 the Hon. William Hervey recorded in his journal that 'the water is very fine ... the house well situated, nine windows in front and nine in flank, a hall and a good room on each side'

– clearly the work was substantially completed by that time. By 1773 Capability Brown, who used his associate Henry Holland senior, a London builder, to oversee the brick and masonry work and John Hobcraft to supervise the carpentry and joinery, had been paid £10,000 of which £9,440 had been paid over to Holland and Hobcraft. Brown proposed to Rowland Holt the building of flanking wings, but these were not executed.[8]

THE ESTATE remained in the ownership of the Holt-Wilson family until 1971. In the middle years of the nineteenth century the family responded to financially straitened circumstances by vacating the house, and it was occupied by tenants. However, in the 1860s the house was refurbished and the family moved back. The agricultural depression of the last quarter of the century resulted in the estate slipping further into debt, and in 1895 the family finally moved out of the house and it became tenanted once again.

During the Great War, the house was occupied by troops. Between 1919 and 1921 the bulk of the estate muniments were sold to the University of Chicago, and in 1936 the contents of the house were also sold.[9] The house was occupied as a country club in the 1930s and by troops again during World War II, when a large temporary hospital was built on the estate.[10] By 1946 the house was in a dilapidated state, and in June that year much of the building was sold for demolition, which took place the next year. At this stage the surviving part of the Tudor house was retained with a view to it being refurbished with two new Tudor-style wings.[11] These were never built, and in 1970 the remains of the house were demolished.

Redgrave was a house of considerable historical and architectural interest, which suffered from its owner's financially straitened circumstances in the early nineteenth century and the effects of the agricultural depression at the end of that century. As in the case of many other houses, its occupation by the armed forces in the twentieth century resulted in damage and dilapidation. These influences sealed its fate in the period before historic buildings became protected by legislation. The Orangery was demolished in the 1960s, and all that survive of Capability Brown's buildings are the Round House and the kennels.

RENDLESHAM HALL

DEMOLISHED 1949

R ENDLESHAM HALL, FROM 1796 UNTIL AFTER THE GREAT WAR THE
SUFFOLK SEAT OF ONE BRANCH OF THE THELLUSON FAMILY, was
situated five miles north-west of Woodbridge. The house, which was
demolished in 1949, replaced in the 1870s an earlier and 'far more
important' house burnt down forty years previously.[1]

In 1552 the manor of Rendlesham and various properties in that and
neighbouring parishes were purchased from John Harman by James
Spencer of Bexwell in Norfolk.[2] The family also owned other manors in
the parish notably that of Naunton Hall held by the Harman family
since the late fifteenth century, which appears to have been one of the
most important, having annexed to it a house of that name which became
part of the Rendlesham estate. The property passed through succeeding
generations of the Spencer family until it was inherited by Anne Spencer,
co-heiress of Edward Spencer, who died in 1727. In 1737 Anne Spencer
married as his third wife the fifth Duke of Hamilton, bringing
Rendlesham into the hands of the Hamilton family.[3] The sixth Duke
sold it to Sir George Wombwell from whom it was acquired by the
Thelluson family.

Peter Thelluson, a London banker with West Indian commercial
interests, was the son of Isaac de Thelluson, Swiss ambassador to the
Court of Louis XV of France. He settled in England in the 1760s,
amassed a large fortune from his financial and commercial ventures, and
in about 1790 acquired the manor of Brodsworth in Yorkshire.[4] In 1796,
the year before he died, the Rendlesham estate was bought in the name of

his son, Peter Isaac Thelluson, although on Peter Thelluson's death it
appears to have been part of his estate.[5] By his extraordinary will Peter
Thelluson left £100,000 to his widow and children and the remainder of
his fortune, some £600,000, to accumulate until the death of his last
surviving grandson, when it was to be divided between the eldest male
descendants then living of his three sons. The will was contested but
upheld by the courts, although concern that property could be left to
accumulate in the hands of trustees for a long period led to the
Accumulations Act 1800 (the 'Thelluson Act'), which imposed
restrictions on the length of accumulation periods in trusts.[6]

Peter Thelluson's last surviving grandson, Charles Thelluson, died in
1856 and the accumulation period came to an end. One of Peter

Thelluson's three sons had been killed in the Peninsular War and had no descendants and, following a further court judgment, the estate fell to be divided into two lots. In 1856 the Court of Chancery appointed Commissioners to report on the property and make the division. They reported in 1857.[7] The Yorkshire estate at Brodsworth and all other property in the north of England, together with part of the Hertfordshire estate, were allocated to the late Charles Thelluson's son, also Charles (of Brodsworth), and the Suffolk estate and the remainder of the Hertfordshire estate to the 'eldest male descendant' of Peter Thelluson's eldest son, Peter Isaac Thelluson, who had been created Baron Rendlesham in 1806. Further litigation then ensued to determine who was, in law, Peter Thelluson's 'eldest male descendant', the oldest in years or the senior by primogeniture, who was the fifth Lord Rendlesham. The House of Lords eventually upheld Lord Rendlesham's claim, and in 1859 both the Rendlesham estate and extensive property in Hertfordshire were transferred to him.

THE HOUSE at Rendlesham which Anne Spencer brought to the Hamilton family was an early seventeenth-century house. About 1780, during the sixth Duke's time, alterations were made for which it is thought Henry Holland was responsible, but what that work involved is not known.[8] The early years of the Thelluson family's ownership saw substantial alterations to the seventeenth-century house. The architect John Buonarotti Papworth provided designs for the addition of a glazed loggia with a new entrance porch and large wings, all in the Gothic style and battlemented.[9] H. Davy's drawing of 1825 (illustration 55) shows these additions together with a tower, which appears to date from the same period; behind them is the older building. Papworth did not himself execute his design, this work being undertaken by another architect, Henry Hakewill.[10] At the same time as the house was enlarged the park in which it stood was laid out by Humphrey Repton.[11]

On 2 February 1830 Rendlesham Hall was destroyed by fire, and it was to be forty years before its replacement was built. The family's residence on the site in the intervening years was described shortly before its demolition as 'but an apology for the homestead of the Rendlesham's waiting only for the Thelluson riches to be replaced by a mansion worthy of the name'.[12] Following the transfer of Rendlesham to the fifth baron in 1859 the East Anglian architect Richard Makilwaine Phipson produced plans for a large country house.[13] This was to have 'ten sleeping rooms with dressing rooms attached, twelve bachelors' bedrooms and male and female servants' rooms over the offices'.[14] This design in the Gothic style was never executed and, later in the decade, William Burn, a prolific country house architect who was nearing the end of both his career and his life, produced what has been described as a large, uninspired design in the Jacobean style with a plentiful supply of curvilinear gables, a porte-cochère and a large conservatory.[15] This design, executed between 1868 and 1871, was finished after Burn's death. The new house was located near to the site of the old hall, that site being occupied by the stables, estate office and gardener's cottage. The new house was of red brick with stone dressings irregular in design with, on the garden front, a main block of five bays on two storeys with attics. To this were appended on one side a large conservatory and on the other a substantial wing with a tower surmounted by a cupola.

In May 1898 fire struck again and burnt for nearly two days. To quote a contemporary newspaper reporter, 'the interior was completely burned out, although the well-built walls, the innumerable chimneys and gables, and the stone framework of the windows, are all left standing'.[16] The furniture was saved and the house itself was subsequently restored.

Rendlesham Hall was a house built for entertaining on a grand scale: it had eight reception rooms including a ballroom, a conservatory, twenty-five principal bedrooms with dressing rooms, nine secondary and thirteen servants' bedrooms, five bathrooms, eleven lavatories and the extensive domestic offices needed to service a house of this size. Outside there were twenty-five acres of pleasure grounds with tennis and croquet lawns and a four-acre walled kitchen garden in a park which extended to 250 acres.[17]

DURING the fifth Lord Rendlesham's long tenure, the estate played a major part in the social life of Suffolk, but his death in 1911 heralded the impending break-up of the estate and the sale of the house. The selling of outlying parts of estates was, in many cases, the first step in their decline occasioned by the need to raise funds to meet family obligations or taxation liabilities. 1914 saw the sale of the outlying portion of the Rendlesham estate when nearly 6,000 acres of mainly tenanted farms and other properties went under the hammer. This sale, which took place three weeks before the commencement of the Great War, raised nearly £48,000, but owing to the war completion of many of the sales did not take place until 1920.[18]

In May of that year the Home Portion of the estate including Rendlesham Hall was placed on the market in 123 lots. There were no bids for the house and only forty-two lots were sold, raising a total of some £37,000.[19] Three months later fourteen properties were offered for sale, with three remaining unsold.[20] In 1921 agreement was reached for the sale of the house to a London medical practitioner, but this sale did not proceed to completion, and in July 1922 the property was on the market again.[21] It was withdrawn when bidding reached £25,000; a farm in the same sale was withdrawn at £13,000 and only lots worth some £10,000 were sold. The history of these attempts to dispose of the house and of agricultural land exemplifies the lack of interest in such properties in the early years after the Great War. The final sale of estate property took place in 1925.

In 1923 the house itself was sold and became a nursing home run by Norwood Sanatorium Limited, which it remained until World War II. During the war it was occupied by the Army and by the Womens' Land Army. After the war it was never occupied again, and in 1949 it was demolished. A newspaper report referred to an advertisement, announcing 'Building materials (secondhand) for sale: Rendlesham Hall' and continued:

> the hall is now being demolished – once the scene of glittering functions at which royalty were entertained. ... Now the windows are blank, footsteps of workmen echo dully in the spacious rooms and water drips desolately through the lofty ceilings. ... Where panelling has gone old hand printed wallpaper is seen. Upstairs a soldier's number or rank still shows on peeling wallpaper.[22]

Another house which in Victorian times had been the centre of a large estate and important in the social life of Suffolk had disappeared. The walled garden and two lodges to the house survived. The lodges dated from the end of the eighteenth century, and have been described as 'two of the most memorable follies of Suffolk' – one a single-storeyed building has flying buttresses supporting the chimney and the other is a sham ruin in the Norman style.[23]

ROUGHAM HALL

RUINED BY BOMBING IN 1940

ROUGHAM HALL, THE RUINS OF WHICH STAND NORTH OF THE ROAD FROM BURY ST EDMUNDS TO STOWMARKET, was the only country house in Suffolk whose demise is attributable to enemy action in World War II. The house that was bombed was the successor to an earlier Rougham Hall, which stood further south in the parish.

The manor of Rougham Hall was one of the many manors possessed by the Abbey of Bury St Edmunds until the Dissolution of the Monasteries, when it was granted to Thomas Howard, third Duke of Norfolk.[1] It was then acquired by John Drury, remaining in his family for a century. After two generations of Burwell ownership it passed by marriage to the father of Sir Robert Walpole and was then sold to Sir Robert Davers, who had made his fortune in Barbados. Davers' son married the eldest daughter of Thomas, second Baron Jermyn of St. Edmundsbury. In the first decade of the eighteenth century, he sold Rougham to his son-in-law Clement Corrance. Nearly a century of Corrance ownership ended with its sale in 1792 to the Reverend Roger Kedington from whom it descended to Philip Bennet of Widcombe in Somerset who also had an estate at Tollesbury in Essex. His son, also Philip, built the new house in the 1820s: the old one was burnt down shortly afterwards. Philip Bennet II was succeeded by his son, another Philip.

57 Rougham Hall:
the garden front.

THE NEW HOUSE was a brick-built edifice whose design reflected the style espoused by Regency period architects such as James Wyatt, Sir Jeffry Wyatville, Thomas Hopper and Robert Smirke for many of the mansions they designed. The architect of what was described as a large picturesque mansion in the Gothic and Tudor styles is not known.

On the west (entrance) front a three-storey single bay block at the north end was linked by a two-storey range with a large porte-cochère to a larger two-storeyed tower-like block which had an oriel window on the upper floor. On the south (garden) front this block had a two-storey projecting bay surmounted by pinnacles in Jacobean style. This block was connected by a lower five-bay two-storey range to an octagonal tower of three storeys at the eastern end of the house to which was attached a conservatory. Behind the central ranges of the entrance and garden fronts there was another octagonal tower, taller than the one on the garden front and further buildings. To the rear of the house there was a stable courtyard.

The house was extended later in the nineteenth century by the addition of a substantial wing joining the rear of the house to the stable block. This work appears to have been undertaken in the last twenty years of the century.[2]

AFTER THE DEATH of Philip Bennet III in 1875 it appears that the house was acquired by Edwin James Johnstone, but whether he bought the whole estate is not clear. Philip Bennet IV seems to have retained both the lordship of the manor and the advowson of the parish through into the 1880s. It may be assumed that Johnstone was responsible for the enlargement of the house, although it was occupied by Spencer Brunton for part of his period of ownership.[3]

In 1905 the estate was acquired by Sir George Agnew, and it has remained in his family's ownership since that date. The house was occupied by the Armed Forces when it was bombed in September 1940 during a series of Luftwaffe raids on the area where an ammunition dump was being established.

During the war restoration was not possible, and following deterioration of the building no attempt was made to do so after 1945. In 1975 concerns over the dangerous condition of the west tower led to it being demolished.[4] Ten years later the owner, Major Keith Agnew, predicted that eventually the building would have to be demolished, but the remains of this once substantial mansion still stand in a derelict state.[5] Its stable block and other service buildings survive.

RUSHBROOKE HALL

DESTROYED BY FIRE DURING DEMOLITION 1961

Rushbrooke Hall, which stood some three miles south-east of Bury St Edmunds, belonged to the Abbey of Bury St Edmunds in medieval times but is said to have been occupied from late in the twelfth century by ancestors of the Rushbrooke family to whom the property passed again in 1808. The memorial in Rushbrooke Church to Robert Rushbrooke, who died in 1829, records that he 'after it had been successively possessed during a period of six centuries by the families of Jermyn and Davers became the proprietor of this seat of his ancestor'. The house, which survived until 1961, is believed to have been built by Edmund Jermyn about 1550 or some twenty-five years later by Sir Robert Jermyn.[1]

The Jermyn family was prominent in Suffolk and Norfolk, various members of it serving as Sheriffs of those counties.[2] Queen Elizabeth I was entertained at Rushbrooke during her East Anglian progress in 1577. Members of the family were notable in the next century for their support of the Royalist cause. Henry Jermyn, who was created Baron Jermyn of

58 Rushbrooke Hall: the house in the nineteenth century.

St Edmundsbury in 1643, Earl of St Albans in 1660 and a Knight of the Garter in 1672, served in the Court of Queen Henrietta Maria and lived in exile as head of her household after the execution of King Charles I. He is reputed to have been clandestinely married to the Queen, and one unproven account alleges that he fathered King Charles II.[3] There are accounts of him as a gamester, bully and coward, 'an adventurer of a base type' and 'a coarse and brutish libertine'.[4] His nephew, another Henry, is said to have married Mary, Princess of Orange, daughter of King Charles I and Queen Henrietta Maria, but there does not appear to be any evidence to support this suggestion. A portrait of William, Prince of Orange (later King William III) as a boy holding an arquebus was included in the 1919 sale of the contents of Rushbrooke and can be seen in the photograph of the staircase (illustration 60). This Henry was a Roman Catholic and, being a supporter of King James II, went into exile with his monarch.

The Jermyn male line came to an end in 1708 with the death of Henry, third Lord Jermyn. He had succeeded his brother Thomas whose son (also Thomas) had been killed aged 16 by the falling of a ship's mast in 1692. The eldest of Thomas, Lord Jermyn's daughters had married Sir Robert Davers and he bought out the Rushbrooke interests of his four sisters-in-law. The Davers family came from nearby Rougham where they had acquired property with a fortune made in Barbados where, in the early part of the seventeenth century, they had an estate reputedly worth £30,000.[5] Sir Robert's father had been made a baronet for services to Kings Charles I and II. His second son, Sir Jermyn, the fourth baronet, greatly enhanced Rushbrooke in the mid-eighteenth century. Sir Robert, the fifth baronet, was murdered at Lake Huron in Canada in 1763. His brother, Sir Charles, who succeeded him, also seems to have been an adventurer in North America where, although officially unmarried, he has been attributed with having married a miller's daughter or someone named Coutts. However, 'no Lady Davers ever came to England'.[6]

Sir Charles died in 1806, leaving eight illegitimate children, five sons and three daughters, all by Frances Treice. Rushbrooke passed to his heir at law, Frederick William, fifth Earl and later first Marquess of Bristol, whose father (the Earl Bishop who built Ickworth) had married Sir Jermyn Davers' daughter Elizabeth. The Earl of Bristol retained the estate for only two years, exchanging it in 1808 for the estate at Little Saxham of Colonel Robert Rushbrooke who had married Frances, one of the daughters of the last Davers baronet. Thus the Rushbrooke family returned to what had reputedly been the home of their ancestors, and it was to remain the family's seat until shortly after the Great War during which one of Colonel Rushbrooke's great-grandsons, Bartle Davers Rushbrooke, was killed in action in the first Battle of Ypres.[7]

THE HOUSE built by the Jermyns was one of the most important sixteenth-century houses in Suffolk. Built of red brick as a rectangular 'U'-shaped house, it had nine bays on the south-facing cross-wing and seven on the projecting wings facing into the courtyard. There were two pedimented dormer windows on each of the wings and three on the cross-wing. A brick-built bridge spanned the moat directly opposite the stone entrance porch, which had Tuscan columns at the corners and an upper storey with a coat of arms above the doorway flanked by pilasters surmounted by heraldic supporters. Below its small pediment was a clock. The external corners of the house had polygonal turrets with ogee roofs of the type commonly seen in East Anglian houses of the period. These had small windows and there was a sundial high on the south-east turret. The house had thirteen bays on the west front, with a pedimented section of three bays occupying the fifth, sixth and seventh bays from the southern end. This facade was not, therefore, symmetrical. The north front of eleven bays had a three-bay pedimented section in the centre. The east side of the house, approached by a wooden bridge over the moat, had one large wing and an assortment of other extensions evidently added at various stages during the building's existence. Part of an earlier house, on whose moated site the Tudor house was built, is thought to have been incorporated in the building.

The house was altered and embellished in the time of Sir Jermyn Davers, who inherited the house in 1729 and died in 1743. The north front was refenestrated with sash windows and surmounted by a three-bay pediment with a circular window. The new frontage was built with the Tudor polygonal turrets retained at the east and west ends. The south front and the wings were also refenestrated, although this work did not extend to the dormer windows and the windows on the south ends of the wings, which remained either mullioned or mullioned and transomed with leaded panes. The eighteenth-century alterations included the introduction of rococo stuccowork and handsome doorcases in the two-storeyed hall where the pedimented marble fireplace had two caryatids and a garland of fruit from which the face of a young person emerged at the centre. Above the fireplace was an ornate overmantel with a broken pediment flanked by garlands suspended from shells in which grotesque masks were fixed. The dining room also had rococo stuccowork. The decorations are said to have included carvings by Grinling Gibbons.

Unlike so many houses built in earlier centuries Rushbrooke, although updated, did not suffer the addition of a substantial service wing and additional accommodation to cater for the large house parties that were a feature of late Victorian country house living. The basic integrity of its rectangular 'U'-shape remained. To the south it looked out over parkland from which it was separated by its moat and a wrought iron fence with piers surmounted by urns.

THE RUSHBROOKE family's ownership of the estate came to an end when Captain Robert Basil Wyndham Rushbrooke put the estate up for sale in 1919. Why the family decided to sell is not clear, but the lack of any additions to the building in the nineteenth century suggests that this was not a wealthy family, and the agricultural depression in the last quarter of that century may have taken its toll of the resources needed to maintain the property.

The estate of 358 acres was sold in a number of lots in October 1919, the house with 195 acres being bought privately before auction by Captain Philip Ashworth of West Dean Park, Chichester.[8] Following the sale of the estate the contents of the house were sold.[9] They included two pictures (in addition to that of William, Prince of Orange), which can be seen above the staircase in illustration 60. These were of Mary (Moll) Davis (the actress and mistress of Charles II) by Sir Peter Lely and of Lady Dover, wife of Sir Henry Jermyn, Earl of St Albans, whose portrait in his Garter Robes was sold for 500 guineas. Brussels tapestries were reported to have sold for up to 1,200 guineas and a portrait of Queen Henrietta Maria fetched £490.[10] The Marchioness of Bristol bought a number of Jermyn and Davers portraits for the Ickworth collection.[11] A local newspaper reported the forthcoming sale, noting that after the death of Sir Charles Davers in 1806 there had been a sale of furniture at Rushbrooke but that the main seventeenth-century furniture had remained in the house.[12]

Captain Ashworth's period of ownership was short. In June 1922 a letter to *Country Life* from the Secretary of the Society for the Protection

TOP RIGHT:
59 Rushbrooke Hall: the west front.

RIGHT:
60 Rushbrooke Hall: the staircase with the portrait of William, Prince of Orange holding an arquebus at the top of the first flight of stairs.

of Ancient Buildings raised concerns that the house might be demolished.[13] However, this was followed within a month by a report that the property had been sold to Lord Islington.[14] Sir John Dickson-Poynder, Lord Islington, was a distinguished public servant who had inherited the Hartham estate in Wiltshire, which he sold on purchasing Rushbrooke.[15] He had been Governor of New Zealand before the Great War and had served in the wartime governments of Asquith and Lloyd George. He died in 1936 and two years later Rushbrooke was sold to Lord Rothschild.

Lord Rothschild's purchase was followed by extensive refurbishment of and alterations to the house, involving substantial work to the east wing to provide a new corridor where bedrooms had previously been intercommunicating.[16] The house was provided with mains water and electricity, heating and domestic hot water systems, security systems, steel stairways in two of the turrets as fire escapes, pumping equipment to supply fire hydrants, fireproof bookcases in the library and strongrooms. Garages and accommodation for chauffeurs and gardeners were built and the driveway to the house altered to increase privacy with a ha-ha to provide views from the house unobstructed by fences. New greenhouses were built with potting sheds and propagating frames. New farm buildings were constructed on the estate, the size of which had been increased by acquisition of farms sold off separately in 1919. All this heralded a renaissance for Rushbrooke, but as the work was being finished war broke out, and in 1941 the house became a convalescent home for servicemen run by the Red Cross. The Rothschild family never returned to live in the house, although they have retained the estate and occupy a house there.[17]

In 1947 the house was handed over to West Suffolk County Council for twenty-one years for use as a hostel for a farming institute, but this project did not come to fruition because of the lack of suitable agricultural land in the vicinity, and in 1949 the lease was surrendered.[18] In 1950 a *Country Life* article on the Gower Report referred to the possible dereliction of 'this famous and beautiful old house'.[19] Over the next decade other uses for the house were sought, with it being offered to, among other bodies, Thingoe Rural District Council, the British Limbless Ex-Servicemen's Association and the War Office. In 1955 it was reported that the Historic Buildings Council was unable to provide grant assistance as the interiors were 'insufficiently important'. The lack of heating (the house needed five tons of coal a day to heat) and the spread of dry rot led to its deterioration. Estimates of the cost of restoration varied, with figures as diverse as £50,000 and £100,000 being quoted.[20]

In 1961 it was decided that the house should be demolished. Before demolition the front porch was dismantled for use elsewhere and oak panelling was taken out and given to the local Council for their Council Chamber. The chimneypiece from the hall and an Adam-style doorcase were installed in St Edmund's Roman Catholic Church in Bury St Edmunds.[21] During demolition fire broke out and the house was severely damaged. What else might have been salvaged but for the fire is a matter of speculation. Subsequently the moat was cleared of the rubble tipped in during demolition and incorporated in the garden of the house created by the Rothschild family from the Garden Cottage.

'Rushbrooke Hall may lay claim to very high distinction even in a county which possesses such splendid houses as Melford, Hengrave and Helmingham,' wrote the *Country Life* reporter at the time of the sale of the house to Lord Islington in 1922. It was a house whose charm reflected its Tudor origins and whose stylishness derived from the alterations of the 1730s and, undoubtedly, its destruction was among the greatest losses in the history of Suffolk houses.

STOKE PARK

DEMOLISHED c. 1930

TOKE PARK STOOD SOUTH OF THE ROAD FROM IPSWICH TO BELSTEAD
in the parish of Stoke St Mary, which was within the Liberties of
Ipswich. It was described in 1918 as lying 'upon an easy acclivity rising
from the Western bank of the River Orwell, and commands exceedingly
beautiful prospects of the scenery along the River Banks'.[1]

The manor of Stoke was held before the Reformation by the Abbey
of Ely, and on the Dissolution of the Monasteries passed to the Dean
and Chapter of Ely Cathedral. By the early seventeenth century an
interest in Stoke Park was held by William Acton, who left it to his
cousin, the William Acton who acquired property in Bramford from
1595 onwards.[2] The 1829 edition of *The Suffolk Traveller* refers to 'the
manor of Stoke-hall, by which word we do not mean the modern house
by the church but what is now called Stoke-park', stating that it was held
by Nathaniel Acton of the Dean and Chapter of Ely.[3] A map dating
from 1787 shows an unnamed building located near the site of Stoke
Park, and one dating from 1801 shows Stoke Hall on the north side of
the Belstead road near the church of St Mary near the Orwell.[4] These
are presumably the two different buildings to which reference is made in
The Suffolk Traveller.

*61 Stoke Park: the
garden front.*

In 1840 Stoke Park was acquired by the Honourable Merrick Lindsey Peter Burrell, a member of a family whose seat since the late seventeenth century had been at Langley Park, Beckenham in Kent.[5] It seems likely that the estate came on the market following the death of Nathaniel Lee Acton in 1836.

Burrell was the younger son of the first Lord Gwydyr who married the eldest daughter of the third Duke of Ancaster (also Lord Willoughby de Eresby), joint hereditary Lord Great Chamberlain, a position which she inherited. Burrell died in 1848, to be succeeded at Stoke by his eldest surviving son, Peter Robert Burrell, who became the fourth Lord Gwydyr, succeeding a cousin in that barony but not inheriting the office of Lord Great Chamberlain, which passed in the female line. He died at the age of 99 in 1909, and on the death of his only son six years later the barony became extinct and the Stoke Park estate was inherited by his grand-daughter, the wife of Sir John Henniker Heaton.

STOKE PARK is stated to have been 'built on the site of an old house of the same name according to plans approved by the late Peter Lord Gwydyr'.[6] Little appears to be known about the house that it replaced, except that the Tithe Map of 1840 shows a large building consisting of two blocks, the south side of one overlapping contiguously the north side of the other.[7]

The new house may have been designed by Richard Makilwaine Phipson, the East Anglian architect, but this is by no means certain.[8] It had eight bays on the south (garden) front and five on the flank, the windows on the upper floors being sashed. It was a three-storeyed building with a wing projecting to the rear on the west side and a two-storeyed wing to the north-east containing the domestic offices. It was built of white Suffolk bricks with a hipped roof and string courses. The entrance was at the southern end of the west front with an Ionic-pillared porte-cochère leading into a single-storey entrance hall. On the garden front there was single-storeyed open colonnade of nine pillars on to which French doors gave access. On the east front there was a single-storey extension matching the entrance hall and leading to a conservatory.

The house had five 'noble entertaining' rooms – saloon, two drawing rooms, library and dining room – together with a billiard room and study. The main rooms had decorated ceilings and marble chimneypieces, the principal drawing room being decorated in the Adam style with a marble and scagliola chimneypiece inlaid to represent fluted columns with Ionic capitals. The oak staircase from the saloon led to thirteen bedrooms in the south wing, those on the first floor being arranged in two suites of three rooms each. The west wing contained four bedrooms on each floor. In all there were three bathrooms.[9]

The domestic quarters in the north-east wing provided all the offices normally required in a house of this size – butler's pantry, strongroom, housekeeper's room, servants' hall, kitchen, scullery, larder, laundry rooms, game larder, brush room, lamp room, knife room, shoe room, wood house, oil room, coal houses and two cellars. On the upper floor of this wing there were nine servants' bedrooms, a housemaid's room, two pantries, drying room and box room.

The coach yard provided stabling for ten horses with a coach house, harness room and other offices together with a coachman's house. The kitchen and fruit gardens had a range of glass houses (comprising vineries and peach, cucumber, tomato and propagating houses), potting and tool sheds and the head gardener's cottage. There were extensive pleasure grounds and gardens including tennis and croquet lawns.

In July 1918 the whole of the Stoke Park estate was put up for sale by auction by Lady Henniker Heaton. It extended to 1,050 acres of which 300 were parkland, with parts of the estate being described as having 'fine prospects for future development'. The house together with its contents and other parts of the estate (including tenanted farms producing an income of over £1,000 a year) were offered for sale initially as a single lot. If no such sale was achieved the house (either with or without its contents) was to be sold separately, with the rest of the estate being offered in twenty lots of which five (totalling nearly 130 acres) were described as suitable for housing.

The auction does not appear to have resulted in a sale, but subsequently in March 1919 the estate was sold (according to a press report) 'to a London gentleman', presumably referring to Mr Long of Cox Long & Co. Limited, the company that paid £50,000 for it.[10] The purchase appears to have been a speculative one by a property developer. Evidently the 'writing was on the wall' as far as the future of the estate as an entity was concerned, but to what extent Cox Long & Co. itself developed any of the estate is not clear.

Another auction of the house and estate was fixed for May 1919, but with what outcome is not known. In October of that year the contents of the house were sold. In September 1921 the house with sixty-two acres, the Home Farm of eighty-two acres, fourteen residential sites and other land was put up for sale by auction, the sale particulars giving details of a proposed new road through the estate.[11] The next owner of a major part of the estate was Percy Barker, but his initial purchase did not include the Home farm of 179 acres, although this was transferred to him in January 1922.[12] In 1927 Barker sold seventy-six acres of land to Alderman W. F. Paul, who presented it to Ipswich Borough Council for a public park.[13] In the following year the house, with only twenty-two acres, was again on the market.[14] Over a period of ten years the estate had been broken up.

Exactly when the Burrell's house was demolished is unclear, but in 1933 or 1934 what remained of the estate (some eighty acres) was bought by Sir John Ganzoni, the Member of Parliament for Ipswich and later the first Lord Belstead. By 1935 a new house had been built to the designs of H. R. Hooper, a local architect, whose work here was in the style of C. F. A. Voysey.[15] This house was itself demolished in 1968 and the estate was acquired for housing development.[16] Over a period of fifty years the whole of the Stoke Park estate other than the park provided by Alderman Paul had become a suburb of Ipswich.

SUDBOURNE HALL

DEMOLISHED 1951

SUDBOURNE HALL, ONE MILE FROM ORFORD, IS NOTABLE FOR ITS ASSOCIATION WITH SIR RICHARD WALLACE whose considerable wealth and artistic taste were engaged in building up what became the Wallace Collection, bequeathed to the nation by his widow.

The manor of Sudbourne belonged at various times in the Middle Ages both to the Bishop of Norwich and to the priory and convent of Ely from which it passed to the Crown at the Dissolution and was granted again to the Bishop of Norwich. In the time of Queen Elizabeth I it reverted to the Crown, and in 1600 was bought by Sir Michael Stanhope, who was a courtier to both Queen Elizabeth I and King James I. Following his death in 1621 it passed to his daughter and co-heir Jane who that year married Sir William Withipole. Their daughter and heir married Leicester Devereux, sixth Viscount Hereford, and the property descended to the tenth Viscount, who died in 1748.[1] In 1753/4 Sudbourne was sold to Francis Seymour Conway, first Marquess of Hertford. It remained in his family until the last quarter of the nineteenth century.

The fourth Marquess of Hertford died in 1870 when the title and the family's estates at Ragley in Warwickshire and at Sudbourne entailed to the marquessate passed to a cousin. His residuary estate was left to Richard Wallace, who is believed to have been his illegitimate son (his name was originally Richard Jackson) and who was brought up in Paris by the third marquess's widow with whom he enjoyed a close relationship. Wallace's parentage has never been unequivocally determined, the fourth marquess never publicly acknowledging that he was Wallace's father, and he was thought at one time to have been his illegitimate half-brother.

For many years Wallace acted as secretary to his putative father who was a connoisseur of the arts and amassed a large collection of paintings and other works of art. In addition to buying on behalf of his employer Wallace also collected on his own account until 1857, but thereafter devoted himself to buying only for the Marquess. Living in Paris, Wallace enjoyed an opulent lifestyle, being paid £1,000 a year for his services and from time to time having his debts paid off by his employer. He lived with Julie Castenau, the daughter of a French army officer, whom he married in 1871 after the death of the fourth Marquess. They had a son, Edmond Richard, who was born in 1847 and who predeceased his father. During the Franco-Prussian War Wallace contributed very large sums of money

TOP RIGHT:
62 *Sudbourne Hall: house designed for the first Marquess of Hertford by James Wyatt as it looked about 1800.*

RIGHT:
63 *Sudbourne Hall: the garden front in 1901 after the alterations made for Sir Richard Wallace.*

to relieve poverty in Paris when it was besieged. For this philanthropic work he was made a baronet in 1871.[2]

On the fourth Marquess's death his will leaving his residuary estate to Richard Wallace was disputed, and a long-running lawsuit ensued in the Irish courts. This was eventually settled by the Hertford family's Irish estate at Lisburn being transferred to Wallace on payment of £400,000 to the fourth Marquess's brothers, who had claimed that the codicil incorporating the bequest of the residuary estate to Wallace was invalid.[3] Shorn of the residuary estate, the fifth Marquess was unable to support both of the entailed estates, and in 1871 Wallace bought the Sudbourne estate for £298,000.

Wallace's tenure of Sudbourne lasted twelve years. During this period he was a generous benefactor in the locality, and it was his hope that his son would succeed him and adopt the life of an English country gentleman.[4] However, that hope was not fulfilled and Edmond returned to live in Paris with his mistress and four children, where he died in 1887. Lady Wallace also preferred living in Paris, and eventually Sir Richard, a disillusioned man, gave up his seat in Parliament and returned to Paris, where he died in 1890. The magnificent collection of art treasures that he had inherited from the fourth Marquess had been transferred to London in the 1870s, and on her death in 1897 Lady Wallace bequeathed it to the nation.

In 1884 Sir Richard had sold Sudbourne to Arthur Heywood, who further extended the estate before it was sold in 1897 to Arthur Herbert Edward Wood, whose ownership lasted only seven years. The house was then bought by Kenneth Mackenzie Clark of Paisley, whose family had made a large fortune in the cotton trade. Clark's son, also Kenneth Mackenzie Clark, was Director of the National Gallery from 1934 to 1945, became a leading adviser on and exponent of the arts, was created a life peer in 1970 and was made a member of the Order of Merit. He was brought up at Sudbourne.

SIR MICHAEL STANHOPE is said to have replaced an earlier house known as 'Chapmans or Sudburn Howse' by a house with two single-storey wings.[5] This house, built in the early years of the seventeenth century, survived until the last quarter of the eighteenth century but, writing in August 1755, Horace Walpole said that he 'went to see Orford castle and Lord Hertford's house at Sudbourne. The one is a ruin and the other ought to be so.' Clearly, Walpole was not impressed by what he saw, but it was another thirty years before Stanhope's house was replaced by a new house (illustration 62) designed by James Wyatt.[6] An early nineteenth-century account of the house built for the first Marquess of Hertford describes it as a 'plain quadrangular building … covered with a white composition, and the staircase is executed with his [*Wyatt's*] usual skill and taste, the whole conveying an idea of simplicity rather than elegance'.[7] The house had nine bays on the garden front and four on the flank and was of three storeys with a plain parapet and hipped roofs.

Wallace's acquisition of Sudbourne was followed by considerable alterations to the house.[8] These included the building of a service wing to the right of the entrance front, the removal of the 'white composition' and the refacing of the house in red brick with stone quoins. On the garden front a single-storeyed semi-circular bay with pairs of pilasters between the windows was added to the central three bays, conservatories were built to the left of this front and new gardens were laid out.[9] The plain parapet of Wyatt's house was replaced by a balustrade.

64 Sudbourne Hall: the entrance front about 1905 after the alterations made for Kenneth Mackenzie Clark

BOURN HALL.

In addition to enlarging the house Sir Richard Wallace increased the size of the estate, and new estate cottages were built some of which were 'cottages ornées' with thatched roofs.[10]

The purchase of Sudbourne by the Clark family was followed by further alterations to the building, including the erection of a tower over the entrance front and the building of a garden room or palmhouse to replace the Victorian conservatory. There was a major refitting of the interior in an elaborate Jacobean style to the designs of Fryers & Penman.[11]

The house after the Victorian and Edwardian additions was a substantial residence. On the ground floor it had outer and central halls, the latter containing the staircase with galleries at first and second floor levels. There were a drawing room with Ionic columns and pilasters and an Adam-style marble mantelpiece, a dining room, library, boudoir, billiard room, business and secretary's rooms, a 'shooter's room' and the palmhouse. On the first floor there were six bedrooms, two dressing rooms and three bathrooms, some of these rooms being arranged in suites. There were also day and night nurseries with their own bathroom. On the second floor there were twelve bed and dressing rooms and two bathrooms.[12]

The domestic offices in a separate wing were extensive, as befitted a house of this size: a servants' hall with its own pantry, housekeeper's and butler's rooms, a still room and a number of pantries, the kitchen with three larders and a scullery and, outside, the servants' lavatory, the cook's sitting room and the bakehouse. The first floor of this wing had nine bedrooms and a bathroom for women servants. The men's rooms were 'shut off from the [women's rooms] by a door, and, when this is closed, these rooms consisting of three bedrooms, bathroom … and W.C. are reached by a winding Staircase leading from the Offices'.[13]

Outside there were the laundry premises with accommodation for four servants, the stable yard with stabling for eleven horses, coach house, a four-car garage, kennels, an engineer's house, a groom's house, the head chauffeur's house and other premises. On the first floor of the stable buildings there were bedrooms for eleven men, 'odd man's quarters, consisting of large sitting room, two bedrooms, Loft and W.C.' and hay and straw lofts. There was also an octagonal game larder.[14]

The park extended to 300 acres and included a fourteen-hole golf course and large formal gardens. There were walled vegetable and fruit gardens and a large range of glass houses. The garden buildings included a head gardener's house with four bedrooms, packing and storage rooms and a bothy with living accommodation including six bedrooms.[15]

IN 1918 THE ESTATE of over 11,000 acres was put up for sale by Walter Boynton, who had previously contracted to purchase it from Clark but had not completed his purchase.[16] Boynton's interest appears to have been speculative and made with a view to acquiring the timber on the estate. The result of Boynton not completing the purchase appears to have been that Clark remained at Sudbourne for two more years, although some of the farms, houses and cottages were sold in 1918. The next owner was Joseph Watson, created Lord Manton in January 1922, two months before he died while hunting. Following his death, although his family retained part of the estate, Sudbourne Hall and the rest of the estate were sold. The purchaser was Jeremiah Malcolm Lyon, but financial difficulties led to him selling off part of the estate in the 1920s and 1930s. During this period Sir Bernard Greenwell bought up parts of the estate as they became available, and after Lyon's bankruptcy bought Sudbourne Hall in 1935. The Forestry Commission also bought part of the estate from Lyon.

In 1942 Sudbourne was taken over by the War Department and 9,500 acres became a battle training area. The village was evacuated and did not return to civilian occupation until 1948.[17] The house itself suffered considerable damage during military occupation, and the Ministry of Works undertook works to repair it before it was released from requisitioning in 1950. When inspected for the Historic Buildings List it was reported that this Wyatt house 'is in very bad repair' and 'had undergone so many alterations that the earlier work is now so subordinate to the later additions, and the condition is so deteriorated as to make grading as II on architectural and historical grounds not defensible'.[18]

The house did not long survive de-requisitioning. In August 1951 the local press reported that 'the prohibitive cost of repairing the Hall, said to be many times the payable compensation', had brought about its demolition. It described the house as 'a casualty of the war' and published a photograph of demolition work in progress.[19] 'Such was the fate of the former Suffolk seat of the Marquesses of Hertford.'[20] The two service wings, the stable block and a number of other subsidiary buildings were retained, and these have been converted to houses. The octagonal game larder also survived.

TENDRING HALL

DEMOLISHED 1954

TENDRING HALL AT STOKE-BY-NAYLAND, EIGHT MILES NORTH OF COLCHESTER, stood on high ground overlooking the River Stour. William Tendring's house of the late thirteenth century had passed by the end of the fifteenth century to the Howards, Dukes of Norfolk.[1] The medieval house of the Howards was rebuilt after the estate was acquired by Sir Thomas Rivett in 1563. A tower from this Tudor house survived when the rest was taken down in the eighteenth century. After the Rivetts Tendring was owned by the Windsor family for three generations.[2]

In the first half of the eighteenth century Tendring was owned by Sir John Williams, an alderman of the City of London, a merchant 'at the head of the Turkey trade' and 'one of the greatest exporters of cloth in England'.[3] In 1748 he settled the estate on his son, Richard Williams, a 'dealer and chapman'.[4] Richard became bankrupt shortly thereafter and his financial affairs were the subject of an Act of Parliament. While the assets his wife had brought to their marriage were reserved for her and their children the estates which he enjoyed under his father's settlement were allocated to his creditors. Tendring was sold in March 1750 to Admiral Sir William Rowley, the first of a line of distinguished naval officers.[5] In the years that followed the land holdings of the Rowleys were increased by the purchase of a number of neighbouring estates, including in 1785 the nearby Shardelowes estate from the trustees of Sir John Williams.

On his death in 1768 Sir William was succeeded by his son, Joshua, Rear Admiral of the White, who was created a baronet in 1786. Sir Joshua's wife, Sarah, was the daughter and heiress of Bartholomew Burton, Governor of the Bank of England, a painting of whom by George Dance which hung at Tendring was sold to the Bank in 1933.[6] Sir Joshua was responsible for the rebuilding of Tendring Hall, his new house dating from 1784–6 being designed by Sir John Soane.[7]

TENDRING, one of Soane's earliest country houses, was built of white brick with a portico and dressings in Portland stone.[8] The rectagular house of three storeys including the basement had five bays, with the two central bays on the south (garden) front having a three-window semi-circular bow, thus providing seven windows on each floor with uninterrupted views over the valley below.[9] The entrance portico to the north had four Ionic columns. As designed by Soane it was also semi-

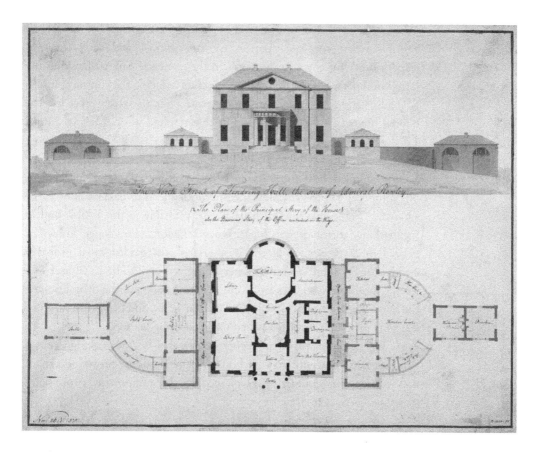

circular, reciprocating the bow on the opposite front of the house.
However, the portico was either never built as designed or was rebuilt in
rectangular form in Victorian times.

Internally the house had a circular staircase with a delicate iron
balustrade, the accommodation on the principal (ground) storey
consisting of a withdrawing room of which the south front bow formed
part, a library, billiard room, eating room and a chamber. The bedchamber
storey had five bedrooms and Lady Rowley's room overlooking the park.
The basement storey with its kitchen court to the west provided the
domestic offices. Garret rooms were provided for the servants.

The original contract for the building, for which Soane was not only
architect but also acted as contractor, provided for the erection of the
house itself, the kitchen court and offices, stable buildings, the kitchen
garden including a hot house, two lodges, park paling and farm buildings.
The total cost was to be £12,050. Soane's clients were the trustees of Sir

65 Tendring Hall: drawing by Sir John Soane of the entrance front, showing the semi-circular portico, which was either not built or subsequently replaced by a rectangular portico

William Rowley's will (authorised by Act of Parliament), but Sir Joshua and his eldest son were parties to the contract and took financial responsibility for any cost overruns. In the event the park palings and the farm buildings were not built by Soane, thus reducing the contract sum to £10,520 (£544 of which was never paid), but the costs exceeded the quoted figure by £1,282. The dispute that resulted was not resolved until 1792 when arbitrators awarded Soane a final sum of £992. The total cost to the Rowley family was £10,968.[10]

The completion of the house in 1788 was followed by the employment of Humphrey Repton to landscape the parkland.[11] His Red Book of 1790 survives.[12] Sir Joshua's father had already, probably in the 1750s, built a fishing lodge to the designs of Sir Robert Taylor.[13] This lodge, known as 'The Temple', was sited at the west end of the garden canal probably created for Sir John Williams earlier in the century.[14] The canal and The Temple both survived later landscaping of the park and the demolition of the house itself. However, Sir Joshua died in 1790, and implementation of Repton's proposals must have been undertaken by his son.

As was the case with many other houses that had been designed as a compact late eighteenth-century house, Soane's building proved too small in Victorian times, and it was enlarged by the addition of two single-storey wings each of three bays.

OCCUPATION by the Rowley family did not continue for many years into the twentieth century: the family had another estate at Holbecks, some four miles away, near Hadleigh, and this became their principal residence. Tendring Hall became a tenanted property, let in 1913 to the Hon. Henry Coventry and subsequently in 1931 to David Davies (later Lord Davies, of Llandinam).[15] The house was let furnished with the heirlooms forming part of the settled estate included, although in the 1920s the silver and plate was taken out of the settlement.[16] Lord Davies took the house with sixteen acres and the sporting rights over 3,000 acres and the obligation to maintain the gardens. However, within a year these terms had been varied to permit the kitchen garden to be grassed over except for one acre, which was to include the asparagus beds. This alteration to the lease probably reflected the difficulties of maintaining, in the changed circumstances of the years of the economic depression, the large gardens with their glass houses and other outbuildings that had been an essential part of a country estate in late Victorian times.

The late 1930s and 1940s saw substantial reductions in the size of the estate, there being no fewer than ten private treaty sales of land and two auction sales between 1937 and 1950.[17] World War II saw the requisitioning of the house by the War Department. Occupation by military personnel resulted in considerable damage to the fabric, and the family never reoccupied the house.

About 1950 a scheme to reduce the house was proposed, the architect being Raymond Erith.[18] By June 1953 this scheme, which involved pulling down the wings and reducing the height of the central block, had progressed to the stage of an application being made for the conversion work to be done. The estimated cost was £20,300. However, dry rot had taken hold of the building, and in February 1954 the scheme was abandoned. Later in the year the building was sold to Sam Walton, a demolition contractor from Melton near Woodbridge, with the entablature and two brick buildings at the entrance to the stable courtyard being reserved out of the sale. Demolition commenced in October 1954, to be followed in December by an auction of materials from the house. The entrance portico survived and remains standing in the park.

Ptolemy Dean writes that the demolition of Tendring Hall was one of the greatest Soane losses.[19] Like many other houses that were demolished after World War II, it had ceased to be its owning family's main house, had suffered considerable damage during the war years and deteriorated to such an extent that its rehabilitation ceased to be viable.

66 Tendring Hall: the garden front showing the wings added to Sir John Soane's building.

THORINGTON HALL

DEMOLISHED 1949

THORINGTON HALL, SOME FOUR MILES SOUTH-EAST OF HALESWORTH, was the home of the Bence family from the end of the seventeenth century until its demise in the late 1940s. It replaced an earlier house on a different site, which was demolished in the first quarter of the nineteenth century.

Early in the seventeenth century Thorington was acquired by Sir Edward Coke, who was Chief Justice of the King's Bench and from whom the Earls of Leicester are descended. In 1691 the Coke family, having inherited Holkham in Norfolk from a cousin, sold the estate to the Bence family.[1] The Bences were originally merchants in Aldeburgh but in the seventeenth century built up considerable manorial and landed interests in Suffolk. In addition to Thorington these included the manors of Carlton, Ringsfield and Benhall and the Heveningham estate, which was sold in 1752 to Sir Joshua Vanneck.

In 1735 Thorington was owned by Alexander Bence, and on his death was inherited by his daughter Ann.[2] In 1762 she married George Golding of Poslingford in the west of the county, when the estate formed part of their marriage settlement.[3] Ann Golding had no children, and on her husband's death in 1803 the property passed to the Reverend Bence Sparrow. Sparrow was descended from Alexander Bence's brother Robert whose daughter Anne had married Robert Sparrow of Worlingham. In 1804 he changed his name to Bence in compliance with Ann Golding's testamentary wishes, and five years later conveyed the estate to his son, Lt Col. Henry Bence Bence.

In 1815 Henry Bence Bence married Elizabeth Starkie, the co-heiress of Nicholas Starkie of Huntroyde near Preston in Lancashire and East Riddlesden Hall near Keighley in Yorkshire. She brought substantial wealth to the Bence family, wealth that may have made possible the building of a new mansion at Thorington. Henry and Elizabeth Bence's second son Edward was to inherit £130,000 from a member of his mother's family, enabling the Kentwell Hall estate at Long Melford to be bought for him in 1838.[4]

WRITING IN 1819, in his *Excursions through the county of Suffolk*, Cromwell reported that 'the old hall is now demolished and a new one erecting, about half a mile from the site, by Henry Bence, esq'.[5] Henry Bence

Bence's architect for the new house built between 1817 and 1820 was probably Thomas Hopper.[6] The house is said to have cost £16,000.[7] Described when it was put on the market after World War II as a 'Bold Georgian Mansion', Bence's brick-built house was of two storeys with five bays on the entrance front and seven on the flanking garden front. The entrance front facing south had a massive portico with four Ionic pillars. On the garden (west) front the three central bays were framed by pilasters, and each side of the middle bay there were semi-circular pilasters matching the pillars that supported the entrance portico. On its north side to the rear of the house there was a service wing of lower height than the main block.

The house had a stone paved entrance hall, salon, drawing room, dining room, library and smoking room and substantial domestic offices. The salon had a panelled plaster-domed ceiling with a circular roof light,

67 Thorington Hall: the garden front.

iNGTON HALL. (2).

and the other rooms had 'highly enriched plaster ceilings and cornices'. The staircase rose in two flights from a staircase hall to the galleried landing on the first floor, which was on two levels, the higher one providing access to five principal bedrooms. The lower level gave access to the north wing, which had six secondary bedrooms on the first floor and five staff bedrooms on the second.[8]

There were substantial stabling and garage premises, kitchen garden with cool frames, a heated sunken forcing house, glass house comprising vinery, nectarine and forcing divisions, orchard and a circular dovecot built of brick with a thatched roof. The gardens consisted of a balustraded terrace, lawns with yew hedges, herbaceous borders, shrubberies, Irish yew walk, rose garden and lily pond.[9]

Henry Bence Bence enjoyed his new house for forty years. On his death in 1861 Thorington was inherited by his eldest son, Henry Starkie Bence, one of whose daughters, Millicent, who married Guy Lambert (changing his name to Bence-Lambert), remained at Thorington until the house was requisitioned by the War Department in 1940.

This brought to an end the Bence family's occupation of Thorington, and in 1945 the whole estate of 876 acres was put on the market. The house was still subject to requisition, and contemporary photographs show the gardens to be in a derelict state.

No record of the outcome of the 1945 sale appears to have survived, but it seems unlikely that the house was lived in again and in 1949 it was pulled down.

THORNHAM HALL

THORNHAM HALL, PREVIOUSLY CALLED MAJOR HOUSE, STOOD IN THE VILLAGE OF THORNHAM MAGNA, three miles south-west of Eye. Before being acquired by John Major, a Yorkshireman by descent who was created a baronet in 1765 and who also owned Worlingworth and other properties in Suffolk, Thornham had been the property of the Briseworth, Wiseman and Bokenham families before passing by marriage to the Killigrew family in 1681.[1] On Sir John Major's death in 1781 his baronetcy passed to John Henniker, the husband of his elder daughter Anne. Thornham was inherited by his younger daughter, who married the second Duke of Chandos, and on her death without children it was inherited by the Henniker family. Sir John Henniker, the son of a Russia merchant, was created a baron in the peerage of Ireland in 1800.

THE HOUSE that Sir John Major bought was a Tudor rectagular U-shaped moated house typical of its period with pedimented windows on the ground floor, a central projecting double-storey entrance porch

68 Thornham Hall: the entrance front.

surmounted by a steeple or cupola in the centre of the cross-wing and polygonal turrets at the angles. It was recased in the seventeenth century, the porch and polygonal turrets being removed, a clock and bell tower built at the centre of the ridge of the cross-wing roof and the original fenestration replaced by sashed windows. A plan of the house before its nineteenth-century transformation shows what must have been the great hall divided by a partition into a dining room and library, with a screens passage and the left-hand wing devoted to domestic offices.[2] The other wing contained an ante room and the drawing room. Substantial additions, including a staircase hall, had been built to the rear of the cross-wing. The house of the second Lord Henniker and his nephew who succeeded him remained basically a Tudor house altered to accommodate new styles of living in the late seventeenth and eighteenth centuries.

On inheriting the house on the death of his father in 1832, the fourth Lord Henniker commissioned J. P. Deering to produce plans to extend and modernise it.[3] Deering's proposals involved rebuilding parts of the house in the Regency style espoused by his contemporary, Sir Jeffry

69 Thornham Hall; the garden front.

Wyatville, but this scheme was not adopted.[4] Whether this was because it was not to his client's taste or because Deering was gradually giving up his architectural practice is not known. What is clear is that within four years Lord Henniker had substantially greater funds available. In January 1837 he married Anna Kerrison, the daughter of Sir Edward Kerrison of nearby Oakley and Brome, her marriage portion being £20,000 (the equivalent of some £850,000).[5]

Lord Henniker then employed Sydney Smirke, his father-in-law's architect, to undertake substantial alterations and extensions to the house.[6] Smirke had remodelled Kerrison's eighteenth-century house at Oakley in a neo-classical style, but at Thornham he adopted a style which has been described as 'resembling a French chateau' with Jacobean features.[7] Much of the existing house was retained and reorganized, with a new drawing room added on the east side. New stables and outbuildings were erected. From March 1837 through to at least February 1839 Smirke produced plans, drawings and specifications, and until the work was completed wrote frequently to Lord Henniker making additional proposals and discussing the fitting out of the building.[8] Work started while the building scheme was still being developed. In June 1838 this resulted in delay as the design for the staircase was not completed because Smirke was heavily engaged in work at Westminster Abbey in preparation for the Queen's Coronation. Later that year Smirke was recommending finishes for the dining room panelling and proposed the purchase of a chimneypiece which had been removed from a house in Hammersmith built by Lord Chancellor Hatton in the reign of Queen Elizabeth I. Nor did the work progress without difficulties. In June 1838 after the drawing room had been built a wall collapsed during the creation of a new wine cellar underneath the room – the cellar was a late addition to the plans. Smirke attributed the collapse to the 'soft boggy situation' and surmised that this was because the cellar was located on the bed of 'some old moat'.

The building contractor was Samuel Grimes of Colchester. The total of Grimes's account for the major works done from 1837 to the end of 1839 amounted to £8,689.[9] In addition he charged £1,304 for further day works and £844 for 'sundry alterations' between June 1837 and February 1838.[10] These figures did not include the cost of bricks, which were provided from the estate, nor the cost of plasterwork in the drawing room, the dining room chimneypiece, and other finishes such as wallpaper and the tower pinnacles.[11] Grimes was still engaged at Thornham in 1840, sorting out leaking windows, chimney problems and painting which had been not been done to specification. The work had taken three and a half years.

On his succession in 1870 the fifth Lord Henniker planned to extend the house, and in 1872 the architect James Colling produced proposals to build over part of the domestic offices to provide three bedrooms adjoining the main part of the house, day and night nurseries and seven servants' rooms.[12]

IN THE 1890s the financial position of Lord Henniker, who had been a Lord in Waiting to Queen Victoria and who was appointed Governor of the Isle of Man in 1895, was such that the family ceased to occupy the house. His brother, Col. Arthur Henniker, acquired the contents and in 1896 the agent, F. J. Cheney of Ipswich, was planning to find a tenant. From 1903 until 1936 the house was let furnished to Lt.-Col. Michael Hughes, although after the Great War he only used it in the summer months, which is not, perhaps, surprising as this thirty-five bedroom house was old-fashioned, having neither electricity nor central heating and only two bathrooms.[13]

The ending of the Hughes tenancy was followed by consultations with John D. Wood & Co. about the future of the house.[14] They offered two alternatives, letting or demolition and replacement with a new house of between ten and fourteen bedrooms (not to cost more than £3,000 plus the break-up value of the old house), stating that it should not be so large as to deter possible tenants but should be what the family might want in the future. At the same time the Bristol architect G. D. Gordon Hake produced proposals for reducing the size of the house.[15] Hake pointed out that Smirke's additions were structurally independent of the earlier house and could be removed without difficulty. His proposed reduction left the house with an entrance hall, dining and drawing rooms, library and kitchen quarters, with twelve bedrooms and four bathrooms. The attic would provide a further five or six bedrooms and one or two bathrooms.

Contemporaneously somewhat perfunctory negotiations were being conducted with a group of people who were planning to set up a 'Country House Home' for 'the children of "unemployed" middle class men, children of little business owner or farmer [sic], children of underpaid clerks, railway officers or Civil Servants who are in financial difficulties owing to unforeseen or unfortunate circumstances'. The group claimed that they had the patronage of the Bishop of Liverpool, but his response to Lord Henniker's application for a reference was distinctly guarded. In the event these negotiations, which started in March 1936, lapsed four months later. No tenant was found, the interest of one enquirer failing to survive the information that the house had only two bathrooms.

In May 1937 John D. Wood & Co. held a five-day auction sale of furniture, pictures and books which fetched £10,780.[16] The next month Perry & Phillips, a firm from Bridgnorth in Shropshire who specialised in demolition sales, sold the fixtures and fittings of the house in 393 lots for nearly £1,800, which included £720 for that part of the fabric that was not to be retained.[17] The sale catalogue stated that 'The portion of the Mansion that is being retained is the part forming the original front; and this will be found to be clearly marked and can easily be left intact.' A contract for converting the retained portion of the house was signed the following year.[18]

After the reduction of the house the sixth Lord Henniker moved back, but lived there for only a short time as during World War II the house was taken over by the War Department and used as divisional headquarters. After the war the house became a small preparatory school for boys. In November 1954 the building was destroyed by fire, which was reported as spreading 'along the wooden panelling fanned by wind coming through the first floor windows which had been broken by [the] heat'. Only the shell of a major part of the house remained standing.[19]

Thornham Hall was, in terms for its demise, a hybrid – lost in part by the demolition in the 1930s of most of the exuberant additions of its Victorian heyday as a major country house and sixteen years later the original structure destroyed by fire. A new house was built on its site, and this incorporates a tower that survives from Smirke's work. The outbuildings also survive. The walled garden and part of the estate have been made over for countryside pursuits with a field centre and waymarked walks.

UFFORD PLACE

DEMOLISHED 1956

U FFORD PLACE, SITUATED THREE MILES NORTH OF WOODBRIDGE, stood in parkland, which, since the demolition of the house, has become the site of a housing development, a hotel and a golf course. Unlike many country houses, it was never the seat of the lord of the manor, there having been another hall elsewhere in the parish.

The house is said to have been the property of the Hammond family in the late 1620s and to have been rebuilt by William Hammond, who is recorded as having a house with six hearths in 1674.[1] By the fourth decade of the eighteenth century it was owned by Samuel Thompson, who married Anne, a daughter of Sir Charles Blois, first baronet.[2] It descended to their daughter, also Anne, who married Reginald Brooke.[3] Ufford was to remain in the ownership of the Brooke and Blois families until the middle of the twentieth century, although its descent in those families was somewhat complex. Reginald and Anne Brooke's son, Francis Capper Brooke, who died in 1886 and his son (by his second marriage), Edward, owned the estate for over eighty years, and it was during their tenure that Ufford Place was considerably enlarged. Francis Capper Brooke was clearly concerned that his estate should eventually pass to male members of his family, and he provided that, although the estate passed on Edward's death to his sister Constance, it was thereafter (if he had no male descendants) to be inherited by the heir male of Sir Thomas Brook, who had died in 1418, failing whom to the second and succeeding sons of Sir John Blois, eighth baronet of Cockfield. This last provision took effect, and the estate passed in 1930 to Eustace Steuart Blois, who took the name of Brooke on inheriting Ufford.

THE DEVELOPMENT of the house is largely undocumented, but it is said to have been originally a timber-framed building with gables and mullioned and transomed windows. On an 1823 map of the Reverend Capper Brooke's lands it is shown as a rectangular U-shaped building with a substantial rectangular building abutting the left-hand wing.[4] The rear of the building faced north, and on this side the cross-wing had a substantial canted bay in the centre. An 1828 map shows a similar configuration, but the projecting wings on the south side had been connected by a further cross-wing to create an internal courtyard.[5]

A photograph of about 1880 (illustration 70) shows a sash-windowed

TOP RIGHT:
70 *Ufford Place: the house about 1880.*

RIGHT:
71 *Ufford Place: the north front after the alterations and encasement of the late nineteenth century.*

three-storeyed house, the full-height centre canted bay on the north front now flanked by single-storey square bays on each side. This front was of seven bays. The porticoed entrance, presumably created when the open courtyard was enclosed in the 1820s, was on the west front, occupying the two right-hand bays of this four-bay side of the house. To the right of the entrance portico there was a two-storeyed wing. This was, it seems, the service wing, as an incomplete plan of the house in 1866 shows the principal rooms on the ground floor of the three-storeyed main block but no service quarters.[6]

At the time that plan was drawn up the rooms on the ground floor consisted of a front hall, inner (staircase) hall, an 'old dining room', a dining room and a library, all with windows on the north front (the library also having windows to the east), and a 'long room' and 'new library' on the east front. The fact that two of these rooms have the designations 'old' and 'new' suggests that changes to the internal layout of the house had been made relatively recently.

At some date after 1880, no doubt during Edward Brooke's tenure, the house was altered and encased in brick, the single-storey bays on the north front being replaced by chimneys and an orangery being built on the northern end of the east front, forming an extension to the north front. An arched entrance way led from the drive on to a balustraded terrace overlooking the garden on the north side of the house. The west front was also altered, the entrance being moved to the two-storey side wing and replaced by a chimney. A large extension was added at the north end of this front. The east front of seven bays also had a balustraded terrace overlooking a lawned garden.

The recasing and alterations created a massive mansion, heavy in appearance with large chimneys running up the external walls, a substantial string course in ornamental brickwork between the first and second floors, pilasters, parapets concealing the roofs, bay windows, and the house refenestrated with mullioned and transomed windows. What had started life as a seventeenth-century U-shaped house, altered into a plain late Georgian building, had metamorphosed into a very substantial late Victorian or Edwardian mansion.

A complete account of the house's accommodation does not appear to exist, but the 1930 sale catalogue lists a large number of rooms.[7] On the ground floor these included entrance, inner and staircase halls, a dining room, library, the 'long room' and domestic offices, and on the first floor a music room and a china room, eight bedrooms, three dressing rooms and a nursery. On the second floor there were five further bedrooms. Additionally the house had five maids' bedrooms and three men's bedrooms. There must also have been other rooms from which furniture and effects were not included in this sale.

THE NINETEENTH century had seen the expansion of the Ufford Place estate with the purchase of further land, particularly in the 1860s.[8] As with other Suffolk estates the first quarter of the twentieth century saw a substantial reduction in its size when, in 1921, following the death of Edward Brooke, 800 acres in Ufford and neighbouring parishes were put on the market.[9] His sister Constance Brooke's death in 1930 was followed by the sale in over 1,500 lots of the Brooke family's furniture and effects: presumably Eustace Brooke (Blois) imported his own.[10]

During World War II the house was occupied by the Army, and is said to have been left in such a dreadful state that after the war the family was unable to restore it. Eustace Brooke died in December 1955, and six months later the contents of the house were put up for sale in 700 lots.[11] A contemporaneous report of the sale stated that the library, 'reputed to have been one of the most valuable collections in the country', had already been sold to London dealers: in 1908 Edward Brooke's library had been said to contain over 36,000 volumes.[12] Photographs taken in the early 1950s show a house that looks uncared for and with its gardens unkempt, and the statement in the sale report that it was to be demolished proved correct. In late 1956 it was pulled down.[13]

The orangery survived and was converted into a house designed for R. G. Staddon by John Penn.[14] The coach house also survives as a residence. The wrought iron gates to the grounds of the old house remain as the entrance to an estate of houses and bungalows that have been built within the grounds.

APPENDIX

IN THE 1974 BOOK *The Destruction of the Country House* the list of Suffolk houses lost in the century commencing in 1875 contained thirty-seven names. Eric Sandon also listed thirty-seven houses in his book *Suffolk Houses*, published in 1977. In G. Worsley, *England's Lost Houses* the list for Suffolk contains the names of forty-three houses either demolished or destroyed by fire in the twentieth century. The present book gives an account of forty houses. Some readers may wish to know why some houses listed in earlier works have been omitted from this book and others not previously listed are included here.

The 1974 list omitted Barking Hall, Holton Hall and Downham Hall of whose former existence the authors of *The Destruction of the Country House* were presumably unaware. Included in that list was Hurts Hall, a house built by Samuel Wyatt at the beginning of the nineteenth century and destroyed by fire ninety years later, when it was replaced by a new house which still survives. Also included were Nettlestead High Hall, which N. Pevsner in *The Buildings of England: Suffolk* (London 1961) described as 'clearly only a fragment', although Sandon states that he could find no evidence for this assertion. Theberton Manor is included in the 1974 list, apparently erroneously, as the Old Manor House in Theberton is still standing: its inclusion seems to have arisen from confusion with Theberton Hall, part of which had been demolished. Thistleton Hall, which is also listed, was demolished in 1955 but falls outside the scope of this work as this once-large timbered house had long ceased to be anything other than a farmhouse prior to being closed up during World War II, when it was within the boundary of Debach airfield. Kenton Hall (a remnant of a very large timbered house on a moated site) and Wamil Hall, both of which suffered damage by fire in the twentieth century, were both rehabilitated.

Sandon's list covered a period of two hundred years and included houses demolished before 1900 or only partly demolished (one of which, Tostock Place, had only lost one wing, the rest of the house having survived and been converted into a number of residential units) and Wamil Hall. It omitted Acton Place, Barking, Carlton, Chediston, Henham, Holton and Hunston Halls, Drinkstone Park, Easton Park and Stoke Park.

Worsley's list in 2001 gives the names of forty-three lost Suffolk houses. It omitted Barking, Downham and Hunston Halls and included Kenton Hall, Nettlestead High Hall, Theberton Manor, Thistleton Hall, Tostock Place and Wamil Hall.

There were other houses, some of considerable antiquity, which were demolished in the twentieth century and which had, in former centuries, been important houses but whose status had declined by the time of their destruction. These included Badingham Hall, Brundish Hall and Letheringham Abbey. There were also other houses such as Gippeswyk Hall (part of the Stoke Park estate outside Ipswich) and Holy Wells Park (the home of the Cobbold brewing family, also outside Ipswich), demolished in the twentieth century but which, not being the 'big houses' in their locality, fall outside the scope of this book.

NOTES TO THE TEXT

Abbreviations

Burke's Peerage and Baronetage – Burke's Peerage
Burke's Genealogical and Heraldic History of the Landed Gentry – Burke's
　　Landed Gentry
Suffolk Record Office, Bury St Edmunds – SRO(B)
Suffolk Record Office, Ipswich – SRO(I)
Suffolk Record Office, Lowestoft – SRO(L)

Note: The titles of particulars of sale of property and sale catalogues of chattels (however entitled as printed) are stated as *Particulars of Sale* and *Sale Catalogue* respectively, followed by the date(s) of sale.

INTRODUCTION, pages 1–11

1　R. Strong, M. Binney and J. Harris, *The Destruction of the Country House* (London 1974) offered a contemporary perspective on the fate of country houses.

2　Books that provide detailed commentaries on the economic, social and political factors affecting landed estates in the nineteenth and twentieth centuries include:
F. M. L. Thompson, *The Landed Estate in the Nineteenth Century* (London 1963);
D. Cannadine, *The Decline and Fall of the British Aristocracy* (New Haven and London 1990);
P. Mandler, *The Fall and Rise of the Stately Home* (New Haven and London 1997).

3　Books on the demolition of country houses include: J. Cornforth, *Country Houses in Britain: Can they Survive?* (London 1974); M. Binney and E. Milne (eds), *Vanishing Houses of England* (London 1982); J. Harris, *No Voice in the Hall* (London 1998); G. A. Worsley, *England's Lost Houses* (London 2002); J. Harris, *Moving Rooms – The Trade in Architectural Salvages* (New Haven 2007). Books on 'lost' houses in a number of individual English counties have also been published.

4　The financing of the building of country houses in the seventeenth, eighteenth and nineteenth centuries is examined in R. Wilson and A. Mackley, *Creating Paradise – The Building of the English Country House 1660–1880* (London 2000).

5　Worsley, *England's Lost Houses.*

6　Lists of houses in Suffolk demolished or destroyed by fire have been included in previously published works. The composition of those lists and the differences between them are discussed in the Appendix.

ACTON PLACE, pages 12–15

1   W. A. Copinger, *The History of the Manors of Suffolk*, I (London 1905), pp. 5–13. Copinger's account of the Daniel family's ownership of manors in the parish of Acton contains discrepancies, but it appears that the family was seated there from at least the third decade of the sixteenth century.

2   *The Annual Register* 1798 reported Jennens's death on 19 June that year. He also had a residence in Grosvenor Place, London.

3   *Suffolk Chronicle & Mercury*, 17 October 1930 gives this figure without stating its source, but W. Harrison and G. Willis, *The Great Jennens Case* (Sheffield 1879), p. 108 quote a figure of £1,091,000.

4   H. Colvin, *Biographical Dictionary of British Architects, 1680–1840* (3rd edn) (New Haven and London 1995). p. 402. James Gibbs (1682–1754), elected a Fellow of the Royal Society in 1729, was noted for his designs for public buildings and large mansions. These included the Senate House at Cambridge, the Radcliffe Library at Oxford, the building named after him at King's College, Cambridge, St Martin-in-the-Fields, Ragley Hall, Wimpole Hall, Burlington House, Kelmarsh Hall and Houghton Hall.

5   Quoted in D. E. Johnson, *Some Notes on the History of the Church and Parish of Acton, Suffolk* (5th edn) (Acton 2003).

6   Harrison and Willis, *The Great Jennens Case*, pp. 98–9, quoting Davy's Suffolk Collections.

7   The reference to Lynders is probably intended to be a reference to Frans Snyders (1579–1657), a Flemish artist renowned for his still life and animal paintings.

8   Harrison and Willis, *The Great Jennens Case*, p. 100, quoting T. Cromwell, *Excursions in the county of Suffolk*, I (London 1818), p. 55.

9   Cromwell, *Excursions*.

10   The sales were advertised in the *Ipswich Journal*, the auctioneer being Mr Thyne. The advertisements were quoted by Harrison and Willis, *The Great Jennens Case*, pp. 113–14, as preserved in Davy's Suffolk Collections, fo. 22.

11   Colvin, *Biographical Dictionary of British Architects*.

12   The Tithe Map for Acton 1839 (SRO(B) T92/2) shows the driveway leading from the road from Long Melford to Acton dividing towards each of the buildings, which are shown as rectangular 'U's with a void between them but with avenues and paths beyond the site of the former central block leading south towards Long Melford. The related Apportionment shows that the house stood in thirty-four acres and that Earl Howe owned nearly 2,000 acres of land in the parish.

13   White, *Directory of Suffolk 1844*.

14   White, *Directory of Suffolk 1874*.

15   These improvements involving the enlargement of bedrooms and general repairs as well as the new buildings were a condition of the lease of the house in 1891 to Mrs Mary Braithwaite and were paid for by the owner, Earl Howe (SRO(B) 993/5/1).

16   H. R. Barker, *West Suffolk Illustrated* (Bury St Edmunds 1907), p. 3.

17   Minutes of Melford Rural District Council, Plans and Building Licences Committee, 28 July 1958 (SRO(B) EF501/1/27).

18   *East Anglian Daily Times*, 5 August 1960.

ASSINGTON HALL, pages 16–18

1   W. A. Copinger, *The History of the Manors of Suffolk*, I (London 1905), pp. 16–19. For the descent of the Gurdon family, see *Burke's Peerage* (1970 edn): under Cranworth.

2   D. E. Smith, *Assington through the Ages* (1974) (SRO(B) 942.64 ASS). In a letter to the *East Anglian Daily Times*, 28 December 1974, Smith pointed out that Assington was a typical East Anglian building with brick infilling to the timber frame.

3   R. Gibson, *Annals of Ashdon* (Chelmsford 1988), pp. 15–32.

4   The enclosure map of 1817 shows the house with its projecting wings (SRO(B) 993/8/1).

5   R. C. Knight & Sons, *Particulars of Sale 15 July 1938* (SRO(I) SC014/4).

6   Ibid.

7   *The Times*, 29 August 1957; *Essex County Standard*, 30 August 1957; *Suffolk Chronicle & Mercury*, 30 August 1957.

BARKING HALL, pages 19–21

1   W. A. Copinger, *The History of the Manors of Suffolk*, 2 (Manchester 1908), p. 246.

2   Ashburnham Archive (Suffolk Estates) (SRO(I) HA1): documents in this collection (including details of his will dated 10 February 1763) provide evidence that Crowley was a shipowner and had interests in businesses in London, Blackwall, Greenwich, Stourbridge, Walsall, Ware and Wolverhampton and in Co. Durham.

3   Elizabeth Crowley is said to have had a fortune of £200,000.

4   G. E. Cockayne (ed. The Hon. V. Gibbs), *Complete Peerage*, I (London 1910), p. 273 and the East Sussex Record Office's Catalogue of the Ashburnham Archive (Administrative History).

5   Reverend H. A. Harris's papers (SRO(I) HD 78/2671) include two photographs of the 'old wing', which appears to be detached from the main house (see note 8).

6   J. Kenworthy-Browne et al., *Burke's & Savills Guide to Country Houses, III – East Anglia* (London 1981), p. 214.

7   Plan of Barking Hall by E. and G. N. Driver, Whitehall 1832 (SRO(I) HA1/HB5/1/3). The off-centre position of the entrance also gives rise to the possibility that it was placed in the same position as the entrance to the predecessor building, i.e. opening into a great hall with a screens passage, and that the projecting bays stood where the wings of a rectangular 'U'-shaped building had once been.

8   It is not clear whether the rear extension joined the main building to the 'old wings'. The 1904 25-inch Ordnance Survey shows an outline of the house as a complete unit, but photographs suggest that the two buildings remained separate, and that this was the case is supported by the fact that when the fabric was sold for demolition the main block and the wing containing the servants' quarters were sold as individual lots.

9   Newspaper report (unattributed), 15 April 1926 (SRO(I) HD78/2671).

10   Newspaper report (unattributed and undated) (SRO(I) HD78/2671).

11   Woodward & Woodward, *Sale Particulars 11 December 1917* (SRO(I) HE402/2/1917/6).

12 Newspaper report (unattributed), December 1917 (SRO(I) HD78/2671).

13 Newspaper report (unattributed), 15 April 1926 (SRO(I) HD78/2671).

BARTON HALL, pages 22–26

1 Bunbury Papers, catalogue note (SRO(B) E18/3).

2 Folkes/Hanmer Marriage Settlement (SRO(B) E18/310/1–2).

3 Bunbury Papers, Introduction (SRO(B) E18) and catalogue of documents relating to Barton (SRO(B) E18/152/1).

4 *Bury Free Press*, 15 September 1978: article on Great Barton.

5 *Bury Free Press*, 17 January 1914.

6 J. Kirby, *The Suffolk Traveller* (Ipswich 1735), p. 155.

7 Sir William Chambers RA (1723–96) trained in Paris and Rome, journeyed to India and China, was tutor in architecture to George, Prince of Wales 1757 and architect of the King's Works (with Robert Adam), laid out Kew Gardens and designed buildings including the Chinese Pagoda and Orangery, and was the architect of Somerset House.

8 J. Kenworthy-Browne et al., *Burke's and Savills Guide to Country Houses, III – East Anglia* (London 1981), p. 215. A design (dated 1767) for a doorcase in the library is in the Drawings Collection at Sir John Soane's Museum (Drawer 43 Set 6).

9 T. Cromwell, *Excursions in the county of Suffolk*, I (London 1818), post p. 96 (T. Higham, engraved by W. Wallis 1818).

10 Kelly, *Directory of Suffolk 1896*.

11 'Peeps into the Past', article by W. S. Spanton (SRO(B) HD526/113).

12 A history of the house and a comprehensive account of the fire appeared in the *Bury Free Press*, 17 January 1914.

13 Ibid.

14 Norbury-Smith & Co., *Sale Particulars 15 and 16 July 1915* (SRO(B) HC539/B/1).

15 Norbury-Smith & Co., *Sale Particulars 13 October 1915* (SRO(B) HD1346/11). The sale was reported in the *East Anglian Daily Times*, 15 October 1915.

16 Advertisement, 1916 (unattributed and undated) (SRO(B) HD526/11/41).

17 Manuscript note about sale on 28 June 1916 by Lacy Scott & Sons. The buyer was T. W. Rodwell of Hacheston, Wickham Market (SRO(B) HD526/11/38).

BOULGE HALL, pages 27–29

1 White (Boulge) Manuscripts: Report of the Historical Manuscripts Commission and Supplements (SRO(I) HA244). The Introduction and the note to document no. 1 give brief details of the Purcell/FitzGerald and White families. For the descent of the White family, see *Burke's Peerage* (1970 edn): under White of Boulge Hall.

2 Suffolk County Council, Sites and Monuments Record BOU008 (SF10257), referring to D. E. Davy (British Museum Add. MS 19113, Wilford Hundred, Boulge). When inspected under the listing provisions of the Town and Country Planning Act 1944, the core of the house and the stables (timber-framed and

plastered with pedimented centre break and a bell turret) were attributed to the late eighteenth century and the interior was reported to have retained 'original' panelling, which photographs also indicate to have been of eighteenth-century date.

3   C. Brown, B. Haward and R. Kindred, *Dictionary of Architects of Suffolk Buildings 1800–1914* (Ipswich 1991).

4   White (Boulge) Manuscripts (SRO(I) HA244, documents 66 (Property Purchases 1891–1910), 74 and 75 (Correspondence 1887–1901 and 1891–1905)).

5   Bidwells, *Sale Particulars 29 May 1945* (SRO(I) HA244, supplement 3, document 1483).

6   Lady White's correspondence from Bidwells (SRO(I) HA244, supplement 2, documents 754 and 755).

7   *East Anglian Daily Times*, 20 July 1955.

8   *East Anglian Daily Times*, 7 September 1955.

BRAMFORD HALL, pages 30–32

1. R. Wilson and A. Mackley, *Creating Paradise – The Building of the English Country House 1660–1880* (London 2000), p. 405 n. 112, pointing out that over two centuries the estates of the Lee, Acton, Fowle and Middleton families descended to the Barons de Saumarez. The final descent of Bramford was to a sister of the wife of the 4th Baron de Saumarez.

2   The 2007 deposit of part of the de Saumarez archive contains Sir William Fowle Fowle Middleton's notebook 1813–1824 in which he records that William Acton (died 1616) was the son of George Acton of Chattisham Place (which William sold) and that, in addition to purchasing Bramford, he inherited Stoke Park from his cousin William Acton (SRO(I) SA/1/2/21).

3   The Loraine Family Archive (SRO(I) HA61) contains numerous deeds relating to the purchase of the manors by William Acton and purchases of land by John Acton between 1622 and 1656.

4   Matthias Candler, *Collections etc.* (British Library Add. MS 15520) stated that 'John Acton Esq … hath built an house in Bramford'. However, in the *The Book of Bramford: A Suffolk Parish and Its People* (Bramford 2003), which gives a brief résumé of the history and fate of Bramford Hall, the building of the house is attributed to William Acton's grandson.

5   Documents in the Loraine Family Archive relating to works at Bramford show work done to meet requirements of incoming tenants including alterations paid for by tenants (SRO(I) HA61 436/881).

6   Three albums of photographs from the years 1895–1902 by Vick, an Ipswich photographer (SRO(I) K475/2–4).

7   The papers of the Hon. John Henniker as agent for Sir Percy Loraine are in the Henniker Archive (SRO(I) HA116 Acc 4676/36 and 37). This collection contains correspondence and other papers regarding the management of the estate and the works to the house in the 1930s.

8   The Loraine Family Archives include a specification for the 1857 works, the cost of which was £637 (SRO(I) HA61/881).

9   Richard Makilwaine Phipson (1827–84) started work in London but moved to Ipswich in 1849 and practised principally in Suffolk and Norfolk, being appointed

Surveyor for the latter county in 1859. He was responsible for the rebuilding of the church of St Mary le Tower in Ipswich and the restoration of St Peter Mancroft in Norwich, and was one of the Norwich Diocesan Surveyors under the Ecclesiastical Dilapidations Act 1871. His obituary was published in *The Ipswich Journal*, 3 January 1885 and in *The Builder*, 10 January 1885.

10 The Henniker Archive (SRO(I) HA 116 Acc 4676/36 and 37) contains a summary of the 'Bramford Improvement Fund' to 1 January 1938. The builders were Sparrows of Needham Market.

11 Phillips Son & Neale, *Sale Catalogue 18/19 March 1953* (SRO(I) SC 063/2).

12 *East Anglian Daily Times*, 29 March 1956 reports the sale and has a photograph of timbers from the house piled up by the entrance drive. A photograph in the 20 April 1956 issue of the paper shows the house in an advanced stage of demolition.

13 *East Anglian Daily Times*, 29 December 1972.

14 *Evening Star*, 15 December 1974.

BRANCHES PARK, pages 33–38

1   W. A. Copinger, *The History of the Manors of Suffolk*, 5 (Manchester 1909), pp. 203ff. gives the history of the manors of Cowling(e) and Shardeloes in Cowlinge.

2   R. Tricker, *St Margaret of Antioch, Cowlinge: Brief History and Guide* (1993). The memorial to Francis Dickins was the work of Peter Gaspar Scheemakers (1691–1781), who was born in Antwerp, the son of a sculptor. He came to London in 1720 and in the course of a fifty-year career in England was responsible for the memorial to William Shakespeare in Westminster Abbey, a bust of William Harvey for the Royal College of Physicians, the massive Shelburne memorial in High Wycombe church and many other monuments.

3   The purchases of farms and other land (Hardhouse Farm in 1705, Grove's estate in 1714, Church House Farm in 1720, Swans and Newtons between 1715 and 1728, Cocks in 1734, Hildershaws in 1732 and Brick Kiln Meadow in 1734) are documented in SRO(B) 744/2/20 (papers deposited by E. Longhurst & Sons Limited).

4   T. Williamson, *Suffolk's Gardens & Parks* (Macclesfield 2000), pp. 60–2.

5   Hoggart & Phillips, *Sale Particulars 25 July 1817* by order of the assignees (SRO(B) E3/10/5/2). This contains detailed descriptions of the 'Noble Brick-Built Mansion' and of the estate, which was stated to produce £1,818 p.a. plus fines and a further £800 derived from the rectory property leased from Trinity Hall (see note 6).

6   Francis Dickins took a twenty-one-year lease of the Rectory in 1791, which passed to Kemp in 1807 (but assigned to John Goodeve Sparrow of Gosfield to secure Kemp's borrowings) and to Henry Usborne in 1820, when he paid £2,427 plus annual grain payments for a new lease, which was renewed for twenty-one years in 1825 (SRO(B) E3/10/5.1).

7   Henry Usborne married Phoebe Ann Birch. Their marriage settlement, dated 15 August 1816, was one of a number of documents deposited with Hoare, Bennett & Hoare (bankers), which also included title deeds and a mortgage deed dated 12 and 13 May 1820, securing £22,380 to Jos. Birch, T. N. Birch, John Usborne and Thos. Usborne. Henry Usborne also assigned the Rectory of Cowlinge as additional security (SRO(B) E3/10/5.4).

8 The valuation shows the gross annual value of the estate at £2,446 (net £2,212), the capital values being the Mansion House £4,000, cottages £1,500, copyhold lands £3,456, the Manor £1,000 and the remainder of the estate £53,760, with adjustments for repairs and leaseholds (SRO(B) E3/10/5.4).

9 Copinger, *History of the Manors of Suffolk*, 5, p. 208.

10 Lease by Mrs Phoebe Ann Usborne to the Reverend Martin John Lloyd, dated 23 August 1844 (SRO(B) 744/2/10).

11 Copinger, *History of the Manors of Suffolk*, 5, p. 208, quoting from the *Ipswich Journal*, 16 August 1845.

12 James Simpson (the elder)'s testamentary dispositions are recited in a disentailing assurance of June 1880 (SRO(B) 744/2/15).

13 The transmission of Branches through the Simpson family is documented in a number of deeds (SRO(B) 744/2/10). These include a deed of enfranchisement of the 'capital messuage and lands' called Branches' copyhold of the Honor of Clare. When sold in 1817 the estate was described as freehold, although it appears that this may not have been the strict legal position as regards the whole of the property. The estate that Cockburn purchased was smaller than the one Simpson had bought in 1845, at least one farm, Rosalia, having been sold off to Sir Robert Pigot Bt (SRO(B) 744/2/28).

14 Late nineteenth-century photographs in the Spanton Jarman collection (SRO(B) K505/2526 and K505/2527) show the house apparently unchanged from that shown in the drawings by G. E. Madeley lithographed by Ingres & Madeley of Strand, London when the house was for sale by auction by G. Robins, possibly in the 1820s (SRO(B) E3/10/5.5).

15 Hoggart & Phillips, *Sale Particulars 25 July 1817*.

16 C. Brown, B. Haward and R. Kindred, *Dictionary of Architects of Suffolk Buildings 1800–1914* (Ipswich 1991): under Hornblower & Tonge.

17 Ibid. Whether Tonge was acting as an amateur architect in conjunction with Hornblower or his interest in Hornblower's practice was financial is not known. He is not recorded in the British Architectural Library as having been in partnership with Tonge.

18 Tonge's insurance policy for 1904/5 refers to 'new wings now or lately in course of erection, all brick or stone built and tiled or slated' and to the increase in the sum insured from £13,400 to £32,600 from Michaelmas 1904 (SRO(B) 744/3/3.

19 John D. Wood and Dilley, Theakston & Read, *Sale Particulars 3 July 1929* (SRO(B) HD/1750/28).

20 Brown, Haward and Kindred, *Dictionary of Architects*.

21 *Suffolk County Handbook* (Ipswich 1939) lists Mrs Tonge as resident at Cheveley. The Clare Rural District Council Valuation List for the early 1940s shows Mrs Fitzgerald as the owner of Branches Park, and for many of the farms on the estate her name is recorded in place of that of the Executors of G. A. Tonge (SRO(B) EF509/2/35). There is an annotation on the list stating that from March 1946 part of the house was being used for storage.

22 *Newmarket Journal*, 5 July 1956.

23 *Newmarket Journal*, 15 November 1956.

24 Winkworth & Co., *Sale Particulars 12 December 1956* (SRO(B) HE/502/3/1).

25 *Suffolk Chronicle & Mercury*, 22 March 1957: the article about Branches refers also to the demolition of Cavenham, Ousden and Fornham and the impending loss of Rushbrooke.

26 R. C. Knight & Sons in conjunction with John D. Wood & Co., *Sale Particulars 10 April 1957* (SRO(B) HE502/4/1).

BREDFIELD HOUSE, pages 39–41

1 Provisional List of Buildings of Architectural or Historic Interest 1947: Deben Rural District Council (citing Ryce, *Suffolk Manors & Halls*, p. 149) and J. Kenworthy-Browne et al., *Burke's and Savills Guide to Country Houses, III – East Anglia* (London 1981).

2 Robert Marryott had a son of the same name whose daughter, Dorothy, married Edmund Jenney of Campsea Ashe.

3 Lachlan White Papers (SRO(I) HD 1409): title on the sale of Bredfield House in 1859 stemmed from this marriage settlement of which Nathaniel Acton of Bramford and John Affleck of Dalham were the trustees.

4 The house is described in detail in the Historic Buildings List (see note 1). The inspection appears to have taken place after demolition had started when floorboards taken up were found to have inscriptions recording the dates of eighteenth-century work – 'Daniel Pensing Junr. laid this floor in the years 1735–6' and 'James Tollet and William Theldrake re-laid this floor May 4th in the year 1756'. There is also a description of the house and copies of 1946 plans of the building in *Proceedings of the Suffolk Institute of Archaeology and History*, 38 (Ipswich 1996), pp. 495–8.

5 Suffolk County Council, Sites and Monuments Record BFD 028 (SF13622).

6 E. Martin, 'Garden Canals in Suffolk', in *East Anglia's History: Studies in Honour of Norman Scarfe* (ed. C. Harper-Bill, C. Rawcliffe and R. G. Wilson) (Woodbridge 2002), p. 213, stating that the canal was probably built for Arthur Jenney who died in 1729 and noting that 'interestingly there is a reference to "a summer house and ponds" in this area in 1663'. Other features of the eighteenth-century garden have survived, including a bank on which the summer house once stood, a walkway and ha-ha (Suffolk County Council, Sites and Monuments Record BFD 029 (SF13623)).

7 The inventory was taken on 29 August 1852 when the house was let by William Jenney to Robert Knipe Cobbold. In 1860 Joseph White insured the house for £1,000, the stables and coach house for £300 and the contents of the house for £700 (SRO(I) HD1409).

8 Historic Buildings List (see note 1).

9 In 1900 Captain Lachlan White purchased the Home Farm and various cottages as they came on the market. In 1917 he purchased the Manor of Bredfield with Windervilles for £130 (SRO(I) HD1409).

10 Hampton & Sons in conjunction with Robert Bond & Sons, *Sale Particulars 9 July 1946* (SRO(I) SC477/63).

11 *East Anglian Daily Times*, 1 February 1950.

12 *East Anglian Daily Times*, 12 October 1948: letter from Charles Ganz, Hon. Member of the Omar Khayyam Club.

BROME HALL, pages 42–46

1   Sir Thomas Cornwallis acquired the manor of Brome, which had passed through a number of families in the medieval period (Davillers, Bacon, Calthorpe, and Hyde), in about 1550. For an account of the history of the manors in the parish of Brome, see W. A. Copinger, *The History of the Manors of Suffolk*, 3 (Manchester 1909), pp. 235–43.

2   D. Dymond and P. Northeast, *A History of Suffolk* (Chichester 1985), p. 73.

3   Culford was inherited by Frederick Cornwallis from his stepfather, Sir Nathaniel Bacon (grandson of Lord Keeper Bacon, the builder of Redgrave), who, in 1614, married Jane, widow of Sir William Cornwallis of Brome.

4   C. Brown, B. Haward and R. Kindred, *Dictionary of Architects of Suffolk Buildings 1800–1914* (Ipswich 1991).

5   T. Cromwell, *Excursions through the county of Suffolk*, 2 (London 1819), p. 20.

6   George Wyatt (1782–1856), a pupil of James Wyatt (his father's cousin), designed buildings in both neo-classical and Gothic styles.

7   Millar, Son & Co., *Particulars of Sale 29 September 1924* (SRO(I) HB112:12540/2).

8   Lewis William Wyatt (1777–1853), a pupil of his uncles Samuel and James Wyatt, was Clerk of Works at the Tower of London from 1818 and at Hampton Court during 1829–32. His best work was in the neo-classical style but he also designed in Tudor and Jacobean styles. His commissions included additions and alterations to many country houses (including Hackwood in Hampshire, Sherborne in Gloucestershire, Lyme Park and Tatton Park, both in Cheshire) and church building (the most notable example being Stockport Parish Church).

9   Letter dated 21 June 1815 from George Wyatt to Lewis Wyatt, explaining that he had made two journeys to Brome, furnished working drawings and also made designs for the old Hall; the cost of the works had been £2,000 excluding materials, and he was seeking advice on the fee he should charge. Lewis Wyatt's advice was 5% plus journey costs (Fitch Collection: Hartismere Volume A–O (SRO(I) qs 9).

10 Letter dated 14 June 1815 from George Wyatt to an unknown addressee (Fitch Collection: Hartismere Volume A–O (SRO(I) qs 9).

11 Millar, Son & Co., *Particulars of Sale 29 September 1924.*

12 Rowland Frederic William Hodge (1859–1950), created a baronet in 1921, was a prominent Tyneside shipbuilder, founder and managing director of Northumberland Shipbuilding Co. Ltd and a director of Canning Town Glass Works Ltd. He is said to have made a substantial fortune building ships during the Great War but was discredited when convicted of hoarding food, which was an offence at that time.

13 Millar, Son & Co., *Particulars of Sale 29 September 1924*: the copy at SRO(I) is marked 'Miss Tacon Contract' and gives the amounts she paid for various lots.

14 *Eastern Daily Press*, 24 June 1953.

15 Thos. Wm. Gaze & Son, *Particulars of Sale 19 October 1953.* The sale was described as 'In the Estates of Sir Thomas Henry Tacon, Deceased and Miss Maude Tacon, Deceased', and included cottages and commercial properties (a warehouse, a granary with a railway siding, and coal and timber yards) in Eye and residential properties in Denham.

16 *East Anglian Daily Times*, 20 October 1953. A manuscript note in SRO(I) Pre-1977 Cuttings file: Brome written by Mr Eric King of Bungay (whose father had

been Head Gardener at Brome) states that the clock from the hall was removed to the Science Museum but was subsequently, in May 1982, sold at Sotheby's.

17 *Eastern Daily Press*, 1 May 1958.

CAMPSEA ASHE HIGH HOUSE, pages 47–49

1   Some sources refer to William Glover as a servant of Thomas, Earl of Norfolk not Thomas, Earl of Suffolk. However, as the earldom of Norfolk was not created until 1644, three years after Glover's death in 1641, it appears likely that the more common attribution of service under the Earl of Suffolk is correct. The killing of William Glover is noted in 'Campsea Ash 1790', a bound album incorporating Collections towards the History and Antiquities of Elmeswell and Campsey Ash; Bibliotheca Topographica Britannica No. 52, dated 1790 and manuscript notes and press cuttings relating to Campsea Ashe (Lowther Archive SRO (I) HA47/C5/1).

2   The house in the early nineteenth century is illustrated in T. Cromwell, *Excursions in the county of Suffolk*, 2 (London 1819), p. 64.

3   Campsea Ash 1790 (see note 1) contains a handwritten note that records J. G. Sheppard's jury service in the Tichborne trial and its effect on his health is noted.

4   *East Anglian Daily Times*, 11 July 1883 (reproduced in 1933). The sale of the Campsea Ashe and Bawdsey estates took place in London when the Bawdsey estate was sold to W. C. Quilter of London and Broke Hall, Nacton for £22,600.

5   Provisional List of Buildings of Architectural or Historic Interest 1947: Deben Rural District Council (SRO (I) 720.942646). Extracts from the 1883 Particulars of Sale in the handwritten note in 'Campsea Ash 1790' (see note 3) include references to the two ceilings retained by Salvin.

6   W. C. Mitchell & Sons and Hampton & Sons, Limited, *Sale Particulars 9 November 1949* (SRO(I) SC88/5).

7   Detailed descriptions of the gardens can be found in *Country Life*, xviii (15 July 1905), p. 54, in an article by Viscount Ullswater; in *The Royal Horticultural Society Journal*, January 1928; and in Kathryn Bradley-Hole, *Lost Gardens of England* (London 2004), p. 114. An article by P. F. Springett, '"Westbury-in-Suffolk?" or the Lost Garden of Ashe High House', *Garden History Journal* (c. 1973) contains an analysis of the layout of the garden and surrounding parkland (SRO(I) Pre-1977 Cuttings File: Campsea Ashe).

8   Springett, '"Westbury-in-Suffolk?"

9   'Campsea Ashe 1790' (see note 1).

10 G. A. Worsley, *England's Lost Houses* (London 2002), p. 118, refers to the purchase of Campsea Ashe by the Desborough Settlement Trustees as part of 'careful provision' in advance of Lady Desborough's death. The acquisition of agricultural land was frequently used as a device in Estate Duty mitigation schemes. Lady Desborough, whose three sons had died before her (two, including the poet Julian Grenfell, were killed in the Great War), died in 1952. Her own house, Panshanger in Hertfordshire, was demolished after her death. The Suffolk Record Office copy of the sale particulars (SRO(I) SC88/5) is annotated to show the lots bought by the Public Trustee.

11 *East Anglian Daily Times*, 10 November 1949.

12 English Heritage, *Register of Parks and Gardens of Special Historic Interest in England: Part 39 Suffolk*: the remains of the gardens are Grade II*-listed.

CARLTON HALL, pages 50–52

1   Archaeological investigation of the site of Carlton Hall provided no evidence of buildings earlier than the eighteenth century (Suffolk Sites and Monuments Record KCC 022 (SF14899)).

2   Matthias Candler, *Collections etc.* (British Library Add. MS 15520).

3   Evidences of Title to the estates of the Reverend Bence Bence (formerly Sparrow) 1809, including extracts from the will of Alexander Bence (SRO(I) HB441/A/24).

4   Deeds relating to repurchase, 25/26 June 1753 (SRO(I) HB441/A/1).

5   Administrative history of documents relating to Carlton Hall forming part of the Turner, Martin and Symes (solicitors) collection (SRO(I) HB441/A). These documents include mortgage and security deeds relating to land included in the marriage settlements of Osborne Fuller and Harriott, daughter of the Reverend James Carter of Kelsale 1781, and of Edward Fuller and Harriott Mary, daughter of William Tatnell of Kelsale 1810 (SRO(I) HB441/A/25).

6   Marriage settlement of Henry Frederick Bonham and Augusta, daughter of the Reverend Sir Christopher Musgrave Bt 1850 (SRO(I) HB441/A/44). The evidences of title to the estate settled in 1875 (see note 7) include the admission of Edward Walter Bonham to copyholds in 1856 and the deed enfranchising copyhold lands of the manor of Carlton in 1860 (SRO(I) HB441/A/45).

7   Marriage settlement of Henry Walter Musgrave Bonham and Georgiana Mary Sheriffe 1875 (SRO(I) HB441/A/45).

8   R. A. Whitehead, *Garretts of Leiston* (London 1974) and V. B. Redstone, *The Suffolk Garretts* (published privately 1916) provide histories of the business and family.

9   Kelly, *Directory of Suffolk 1885* (and later years to 1904).

10 Evidences of title 1907 include Sir Ronald Lane's notice to exercise the option for £20,000 (SRO(I) HB441/A/55).

11 Frank Newman & Son and Knight, Frank & Rutley, *Sale Particulars 28 September 1937* (National Monuments Record SB00234).

12 The attribution of the house to the eighteenth century was confirmed during monitoring of the site during residential development in 2002 when walls and the cellar of that period were exposed for inspection (Suffolk Sites and Monuments Record (see note 1)).

13 J. Kenworthy-Browne et al., *Burke's & Savills Guide to Country Houses, III – East Anglia* (London 1986), p. 221.

14 Frank Newman & Son and Knight, Frank & Rutley, *Sale Particulars 28 September 1937.*

15 Newell & Bailey and Flick & Son, *Sale Particulars 1 December 1948* (National Monuments Record SB00334).

CAVENHAM HALL, pages 53–55

1   W. A. Copinger, *The History of the Manors of Suffolk*, 4 (Manchester 1909), pp. 142–5.

2   Waddington family documents (SRO(B) 853).

3   The Waddington family came from Ely and were of substantial means. Henry Spencer Waddington (senior) and his brother each inherited over £14,000 from their father. The Cavenham estate formed part of the 1810 settlement of H. S.

Waddington (the elder) when he married Mary Anne Milnes of Fryston, Yorkshire, a settlement that provided £25,000 for the younger children of the marriage and a jointure of £1,000 p.a. for his widow (SRO(B) 853).

4   C. R. Paine, *The Culford Estate 1780–1935* (Ingham 1993), p. 2.

5   The location of the old house near the road and its rectangular 'U' footprint are shown on the Cavenham Enclosure map of 1802 (SRO(B) Q/R1 10).

6   *The Builder*, 18 May 1901, p. 491.

7   Andrew Noble Prentice (1866–1941) undertook a considerable amount of domestic (country house) work. He also designed the Joint Examination Halls for the Physicians and Surgeons and the interiors of ships for the Orient Line.

8   C. Brown, B. Haward and R. Kindred, *Dictionary of Architects of Suffolk Buildings 1800–1914* (Ipswich 1991).

9   *The Builder*, 17 June 1899, p. 496; 18 May 1901, p. 491; and 1 June 1901, p. 536. The narrow bricks were supplied by Allan & Co of Sudbury and the tiles by Brosely Tilery Company. Clement Jeakes & Co. were the heating and hot water supply engineers and Tewson & Streatfield the electrical engineers. The drawing room ceiling was executed by Jackson & Sons and the modelled figures and other ornaments to the mantlepiece were by Taylerson. The drawings for the house were exhibited at the Royal Academy in 1899.

10   H. Muthesius, *Das Englische Haus* (Berlin 1904/5; English translation, London 1979). Muthesius wrote: 'An artist who has moved steadily closer to this classicising trend is A. N. Prentice, who first made his name with his fine drawings of Spain. One must regret this change of heart all the more since in his first projects Prentice raised great hopes of a more independent attitude and at the beginning was in every way one of the most promising talents. His taut, forceful style of drawing, of which he was an undisputed master, has had great influence on the youngest generations. His ground plans are always extremely lucid and precise.'

11   *The Builder* articles (see note 9).

12   Knight, Frank & Rutley, *Sale Particulars 26 September 1918* (SRO(B) HD1325/63).

13   Bidwells, *Sale Particulars 20 June 1946* (SRO(B) HD1180/18).

14   Harrods, *Sale Catalogue 30 September 1946* (SRO(B) 1325/75).

15   *East Anglian Daily Times*, 26 August 1949 article, 'Another Suffolk House To Go'.

CHEDISTON HALL, pages 56–57

1   Chediston Estate Map 1845 (SRO(I) HB26: 10975/6).

2   Suffolk County Council, Sites and Monuments Record CHD057 (SF13603).

3   J. Kirby, *The Suffolk Traveller* (Ipswich 1735), p. 122.

4   T. Cromwell, *Excursions through the county of Suffolk*, 2 (London 1819), p. 107.

5   The Reverend A. Suckling, *The History and Antiquities of Suffolk*, 2 (London 1848), p. 95. Suckling's account is supported by the fact that when the outlying farms on the estate were sold in 1917 the sale particulars stated that title was to commence with a Royal Warrant of 1846 under the Royal Sign Manual of Her Late Majesty Queen Victoria (SRO(I) HD78:2671).

6   Edward Blore (1787–1879), architect and antiquary, completed work at Buckingham Palace started by John Nash and later in his career designed the palace's

facade facing the Mall. He worked at Lambeth Palace, St James's Palace and Windsor Castle, and produced designs for many other buildings in England and Scotland. C. Brown, B. Haward and R. Kindred, *Dictionary of Architects of Suffolk Buildings 1800–1914* (Ipswich 1991) note that the work undertaken did not accord with Blore's plans.

7   Suckling, *History and Antiquities of Suffolk*, 2, p. 195.

8   Provisional List of Buildings of Architectural or Historic Interest 1947: Blyth Rural District Council gives a description of the house under the name Chediston Grange, a house on the south side of the Chediston-to-Halesworth road. The listing description, however, accords with photographs of Chediston Hall.

9   SRO(I) HB26: 10975/6.

10 Suffolk County Council, Sites and Monuments Record attributes the canal to the eighteenth century (see note 2), although J. Kenworthy-Browne et al., in *Burke's and Savills Guide to Country Houses, III – East Anglia* (London 1981) suggest that it was part of a former moat. However, no other evidence of medieval origins of the house has been found.

11 Lease of 'Cheston-hall and other farms' by William Plumer of Gilston Hall, Hertfordshire to Mr John Beales jnr (SRO(L) 1019/3/2).

DOWNHAM HALL, pages 58–60

1   A detailed account of the 'sand-flood' is contained in J. Kirby, *The Suffolk Traveller* (London 1829), pp. 438–43, quoting a letter written by Thomas Wright (see note 2).

2   An Abstract of Title to the Downham Hall Estate recites an indenture of 1664 by which Thomas Wright leased the Impropriate Rectory and Parsonage of Downham 'late parcel of the then late dissolved priory of Ixworth with messuages, houses, buildings and tithes' to other members of the family for a term of 900 years at a rent of £40 p.a. (SRO(B) HA536/CD24).

3   The Earl and his son, the Hon. Henry Cadogan, who was killed at Vittoria, are commemorated by wall tablets in Santon Downham Church.

4   The Abstract of Title (see note 2) recites the will of the Duke of Cleveland.

5   *Burke's Landed Gentry* (1883 edn): under Mackenzie of Fawley Court.

6   The Abstract of Title (see note 2) gives details of the acreage of the various parts of the estate.

7   Suffolk County Council, Sites and Monuments Record STN017 (SF7598) suggests that the late eighteenth-century work at Downham constituted a remodelling of the earlier house.

8   Lewis Vulliamy (1791–1871) was a pupil of Sir Robert Smirke and designed buildings in a variety of styles (Classical, Elizabethan, Italianate, Romanesque and Gothic) as suited the taste of his clients. He designed many churches and made alterations to a large number of country houses as well as designing public buildings and town houses. His largest new country house was Westonbirt, Gloucestershire for R. S. Holford, built in the Elizabethan style. (H. Colvin, *Biographical Dictionary of British Architects 1680–1840* (3rd edn) (New Haven & London 1995). He is also recorded as working at Newton House, Yorkshire for the Duchess of Cleveland in 1846 (E. Waterson and P. Meadows, *Lost Houses of York and the North Riding* (York 1990), p. 38).

9   J. Kenworthy-Browne et al., *Burke's & Savills Guide to Country Houses, III – East Anglia* (London 1981), p. 228.

10 Kelly, *Directory of Suffolk 1892*.

11 Col. E. P. Mackenzie (1842–1929) is commemorated by a wall tablet in the church.

12 The Abstract of Title (see note 2) recites a number of property transactions involving F. W. Wateridge, British Farm Lands Limited, partners in Smith Vane & Co., Downham Syndicate Limited, Land Cultivations Limited and other parties and their mortgagees in the period following the purchase by Wateridge in 1917. These relate to the dismemberment of the estate prior to most of the land passing to the Forestry Commission.

13 The Reverend J. A. Fitch [Rector 1960–70], *The Church in the Forest – St Mary the Virgin, Santon Downham* (1996 edn).

DRINKSTONE PARK, pages 61–63

1 Suffolk County Council, Sites and Monuments Record DRK010 (SF14657) and S. Wright, *Drinkstone Revisited – More Stories from a Suffolk Village* (2007).

2 R. Workman, 'The Joshua Grigbys: Some Materials for a History of the Joshua Grigbys of Bury St Edmunds 1659–1829', pp. 75–83. This is an unpublished manuscript in book form (with illustrations), which contains a history of the family and a brief account of the building of the mansion at Drinkstone (SRO(I) HD1339).

3 Workman, ibid., contains an appraisal of Grigby's wealth and suggests the lower figure.

4 Wright, *Drinkstone Revisited*.

5 J. Kirby, *The Suffolk Traveller* (London 1764), p. 223. The statement in that book that Drinkstone was the 'seat of Joshua Grigby Esq.' provides no evidence as to whether it was Joshua Grigby II or Joshua Grigby III who was responsible for the building of the house. Workman attributes it to the former and Wright to the latter.

6 As described in letting particulars in 1936, quoted in Wright, *Drinkstone Revisited*.

7 Workman, 'The Joshua Grigbys'.

8 *East Anglian Daily Times*, 24 January 1951, under the heading 'Another Suffolk Mansion Goes', reported the sale by Thomas W. Gaze & Son of Diss in conjunction with Mr R. T. Innes of Crowborough.

EASTON PARK, pages 64–67

1 W. A. Copinger, *The History of the Manors of Suffolk*, 4 (Manchester 1909), pp. 253ff. and T. Cromwell, *Excursions through the county of Suffolk*, 2 (London 1819), p. 109.

2 *Burke's Peerage* (105th edn): under Hamilton & Brandon.

3 The Duke's interests extended to keeping a motor vessel, the 'Thistle', at Ipswich.

4 Architect's drawings (undated) of designs for the north and south fronts of 'The Rt. Honble. the Earl of Rochford's House at Easton' show a three-storey house and are therefore not of the house as executed (National Monuments Record (AA72/1910).

5 Quoted in Copinger, *History of the Manors of Suffolk*, 4.

6 Suffolk County Council, Sites and Monuments Record ETN 005 (SF8293).

7   Woodward & Woodward, *Sale Particulars 29 April 1919* (SRO(I) fSC142/1) provides a detailed description of the property.

8   £80,000 of the Duke's mortgages was consolidated in 1892 (The Easton Park (Fforde) Collection, SRO(I) HA222): papers regarding mortgages at HA222:1335/9/8). The earliest mortgage loan extant in 1892 amounting to £10,000, dated from 1791, with further Rochford loans totalling £20,000 and the balance having arisen in the twelfth Duke's time.

9   The Hamilton Estates Act 1918 (SRO(I) HA222: 1335/1/1).

10 Woodward & Woodward, *Sale Particulars 29 April 1919*.

11 The conveyances of Capon's sales to underbuyers (including the sale of the White Hart Inn in Easton to Tollemaches Ipswich Brewery Ltd) were direct from the Marchioness of Graham (SRO(I) HA 222:1335/1/3).

12 Moore Garrard & Son, *Sale Particulars 29 June 1922* (SRO(I) HA222:1335/1/3).

13 SRO(I) HA222:1335/1/3. A report in the *Evening Star*, 9 August 1982 (SRO(I) pre-1977 Press Cuttings file) stated that the house was bought by Mr Percy Vestey of Aldeburgh who hoped to live in it but whose architect was unable to come up with a proposal to make it much smaller, and it was therefore demolished. This report appears to have been inaccurate.

EDWARDSTONE HALL, pages 68–70

1   The name Edwardstone Hall now (2009) attaches to another house (formerly called Lodge Farm), which stands opposite the gateway to the old house.

2   W. A. Copinger, *The History of the Manors of Suffolk*, I (London 1905), pp. 99–103.

3   Edwardstone Hall passed to the Lowry-Corry family (Earls Belmore) through the marriage of the third Earl to a daughter of William Shepherd of Brabourne, Kent, whose mother was a daughter of Thomas Dawson (*Burke's Peerage*, 1902 edn).

4   Deeds relating to the purchase in 1897 (SRO(B) 391/4).

5   Suffolk County Council, Sites and Monuments Record EDN014 (SF14595) suggests that the site of the house near Edwardstone Church indicates its early origin and notes that it appears on Hodskinson's Map, The County of Suffolk Surveyed 1783. Sir John Brand was High Sheriff of Suffolk in 1691.

6   W. Goult, *A Survey of Suffolk Parish History*, I (Ipswich 1990).

7   Historic Buildings List 1980: Cosford Rural District Council.

8   John D. Wood & Co., with Strutt & Parker, *Sale Particulars 27 January 1951* (The Georgian Group library).

FLIXTON HALL, pages 71–75

1   N. Evans, 'The Tasburghs of South Elmham: The Rise and Fall of a Suffolk Gentry Family', *Suffolk Institute of Archaeology and History*, 34, part 4 (1980), pp. 269–80. This article contains a history of the family and its connections with Flixton.

2   For the descent of the Adair family, see *Burke's Peerage* (105th edn). Sir Robert Shafto Adair for whom Salvin rebuilt Flixton was created a baronet in 1838, and his eldest son, Sir Robert Alexander Shafto Adair, was created Lord Waveney in 1873, the barony becoming extinct on his death in 1886.

3   T. Cromwell, *Excursions in the county of Suffolk*, 2 (London 1819), p. 101.

4   Watercolour by Thomas Sandby, subsequently engraved for W. Angus, *Seats of the nobility and gentry, in Great Britain and Wales* (Islington 1787).

5   *East Anglian Daily Times*, 29 November 1950 refers to a fire in 1832 but no corroboration of this has been found.

6   C. Brown, B. Haward and R. Kindred, *Dictionary of Architects of Suffolk Buildings 1800–1914* (Ipswich 1991). Anthony Salvin (1799–1881), born in Co. Durham, after spending some time in John Nash's office in London commenced practice at an early age, certainly before 1826. He remained in practice for the rest of his life, with some two hundred commissions to his name. His practice extended to castle and cathedral restoration, work on the royal palaces, the building or remodelling of country houses and churches, the building of many rectories and smaller houses and work on colleges in the universities.

7   Unidentified source: reprinted article of December 1846 (SRO(I) Pre-1977 Cuttings File: Flixton).

8   Photographs by the Diss (Norfolk) photographer Cleer S. Alger, reproduced in E. Goldstein, *18th Century Weapons of the Royal Welch Fuziliers from Flixton Hall* (Gettysburg 2002). This book gives a history of the house, its Adair owners and the weapons collection previously housed there.

9   J. Allibone, *Anthony Salvin: Pioneer of Gothic Revival Architecture 1799–1881* (Columbia 1987), pp. 74–5.

10 Provisional List of Buildings of Special Architectural & Historic Interest 1947: Wainford Rural District Council and Allibone, *Anthony Salvin*, p. 193 (catalogue raisonné).

11 A watercolour drawing from Salvin's office reproduced in Allibone, *Anthony Salvin* shows what appear to be sixteenth- or seventeenth-century buildings behind a curtain wall linking two other buildings.

12 William Harroway's list of works and their cost, quoted in ibid., p. 172.

13 Sir George Gilbert Scott (1811–78), a leading architect of the Victorian Gothic revival, was President of the Royal Institute of British Architects in 1873. His early practice was as a designer of workhouses but his later work was principally in church architecture (including St John's College Chapel, Cambridge, the Cathedral Church of St Mary the Virgin, Glasgow and the restoration of a number of cathedrals) and in the design of public buildings (including St Pancras Station and the Foreign and Commonwealth Office).

14 Fairfax Bloomfield Wade (1852–1919) was a pupil of A. W. Blomfield. His work included church and house restorations and extensions, including Londonderry House, Ballymena Castle and Castle Ashby, including the Great Hall and the building of a new church at Handbridge, Cheshire for the Duke of Westminster (described by Blomfield as 'a very fine work and carefully studied in every detail') (Royal Institute of British Architects, Fellowship Nomination Papers 1888).

15 *East Anglian Daily Times*, 29 November 1950.

16 *East Anglian Daily Times*, 21 February 1951.

17 *East Anglian Daily Times*, 7 March 1951 and 20 April 1951.

18 *East Anglian Daily Times*, 9 June 1952.

FORNHAM HALL, pages 76–79

1   W. A. Copinger, *The History of the Manors of Suffolk*, 6 (Manchester 1910), pp. 268–71.

2   H. R. Barker, *West Suffolk Illustrated* (Bury St Edmunds 1907), pp. 143–6.

3   White, *Directory of Suffolk 1874*, p. 544, referring to the purchase of two-thirds of the Fornham All Saints estate.

4   D. Stroud, *Capability Brown* (London 1975), pp. 197–8: it is interesting to note that prior to his first visit Brown had stayed at nearby Ickworth and met Sir Gerard Vanneck (of Heveningham), Sir John Rous (of Henham) and Charles Kent but that only one of them, Vanneck, utilised the services of Capability Brown on his estate.

5   James Wyatt (1746–1813) studied in Italy 1762–8 and established his reputation with the building of the Pantheon in Oxford Street, London, in 1772. He was appointed Surveyor of Westminster Abbey in 1776, Architect to the Board of Ordnance in 1782, Surveyor and Comptroller of the Office of Works in 1796. Elected a Royal Academician in 1785, Wyatt was involved in designs for public buildings, cathedrals, colleges and country houses. His country house work covered more than one hundred properties and included five in Suffolk (Broke Hall, Fornham Hall, Henham Hall, Heveningham Hall (interior) and Sudbourne Hall.

6   H. Davy, *Views of the Seats of the Noblemen and Gentleman of Suffolk* (Southwold 1827).

7   Robert Abraham (1774–1850) commenced work as a surveyor, measuring building works at the time when 'measure and value' was the normal method of billing for building works, a method of valuation for large works largely superseded by 'contract' during his lifetime. Abraham's knowledge of both methods of valuation led to his professional practice as an arbitrator and referee. After the Napoleonic Wars he was introduced to some of the leading Roman Catholic families and 'much valuable private connection'. His work included conservatories and garden buildings for the Earl of Shrewsbury at Alton Towers and works at Arundel, Worksop, Fornham and Norfolk House for the Duke of Norfolk. His obituary was published in *The Builder*, 21 December 1850.

8   The Georgian Group – Pardoe Collection: notes to engraving of Thomas Wright's picture of Fornham.

9   Thomas Wright's picture, engraved by W. B. Cooke.

10   Arthur Rutter, Sons & Co., *Sale Particulars 25 October 1950* (SRO(I) SC166/2).

11   Arthur Rutter, Sons & Co., *Sale Catalogue 30 and 31 March & 1 April 1950* (SRO(I) 728.8).

12   Arthur Rutter, Sons & Co., *Sale Particulars 25 October 1950*.

13   Newspaper report (unattributed), 20 October 1950 – the reference to the eleventh Duke of Norfolk was erroneous, Bernard Edward Howard being the twelfth Duke.

14   *East Anglian Daily Times*, 14 June 1951. The similar report in the *Bury Free Press*, 16 June 1951 states that the house had not been privately occupied for thirty years and that the internal decorations included some magnificent examples of Adam work.

15   *Bury Free Press*, 17 August 1951.

16   *Evening Star*, 16 September 1951.

17   *The Georgian*, Autumn/Winter 2004, p. 49 reports the listing of what remains of Wyatt's work at Fornham and the Group's intervention to influence the appropriate conversion of the remaining buildings.

HARDWICK HOUSE, pp. 80–85

1   The Reverend E. Farrer, *Hardwick Manor House* (c. 1928) gives a history of Hardwick. The title of this book derives from the new Elizabethan-style house built in the grounds of Hardwick after the demolition of Hardwick House.

2   Salter, Simpson & Sons, *Sale Particulars 11 December 1924* (SRO(B) HH1924(2)).

3   Matthew Habershon (1789–1852) was an architect of Yorkshire origin who came to London in 1806 and trained at the Royal Academy Schools. In 1836 he published *The Ancient Half-Timbered Houses of England.*

4   Salter, Simpson & Sons, *Sale Particulars 11 December 1924.*

5   A. L. Hagger and L. F. Miller, *Suffolk Clocks and Clockmakers* (London 1974).

6   *Burke's Landed Gentry* (1906 edn): under Milner-Gibson-Cullum.

7   G. G. Milner-Gibson-Cullum ceased farming the Home Farm in 1916 when there was a sale of live and dead stock prior to the farm being let (SRO(B) HH1916).

8   Salter, Simpson & Sons, *Sale Catalogue 24–27 June 1924* (SRO(B) HH1924).

9   *Bury Free Press*, 28 June and 5 July 1924 reports the sale, stating that the Painted Panelling (originally from Hawstead) was sold to an Ipswich dealer for 160 guineas.

10 Salter, Simpson & Sons, *Sale Particulars 11 December 1924.*

11 *Bury Free Press*, 14 December 1924.

12 Ibid.

13 Arthur Rutter & Sons, *Sale Particulars 14 May 1925* (SRO(B) HH1925).

14 *Bury Free Press*, 16 May 1925: report of sale (a photograph of G. C. Gooday was also printed).

15 Perry and Phillips in conjunction with Woodward & Woodward, *Sale Catalogue 16–18 November 1926* (SRO(B) HH1926).

16 *Bury Free Press*, 20 November 1926, reporting the sale with prices and purchasers for the principal items and also containing a report of an action in the Sudbury County Court in which G. C. Gooday and other were the defendants in a property dispute.

17 Farrer, *Hardwick Manor House.*

HENHAM HALL, pages 86–89

1   The Blythburgh Society, *The History Notes: Henham Hall – A Lost House* (www.blythweb.co.uk).

2   James Byres (1734–1817), a Scotsman who trained as an artist in France and Italy but who was unsuccessful as an architect, very few of his designs being executed.

3   James Wyatt (1746–1813): for biographical details see Fornham Hall, note 5.

4   *The Builder*, 16 March 1867.

5   For a detailed account of the building of Henham, see A. Mackley, 'The Construction of Henham Hall', *The Georgian Group Journal*, VI (1996), pp. 85–96.

6   Edward. M. Barry (1830–80), son of Sir Charles Barry, the architect of the Palace of Westminster.

7   C. Brown, B. Haward and R. Kindred, *Dictionary of Architects of Suffolk Buildings 1800–1914* (Ipswich 1991).

8   *The Builder*, 16 March 1867.

9   *Evening Star*, 23 April 1953.

10 Newspaper report (unattributed and undated) (SRO(L) cuttings file: Henham).

11 Thos. Wm. Gaze & Son, *Sale Particulars 21 & 22 April 1953* (SRO(L) AR274/38).

12 *Evening Star* and *The Times*, 23 April 1953.

13 *East Anglian Daily Times* and *The Times*, 23 April 1953.

HOBLAND HALL, pages 90–92

1   Dr Robin Darwall-Smith, archivist of Magdalen College, in letters to the author 2007. Tenants in the period 1724 to 1816 included Schutz 1724 and 1731; Pitcarne 1738 and 1747; Trotter 1753; Urquhart 1759, 1766, 1773, 1780 and 1787; Fowler, 1794 and 1801; Thirkill 1808 and 1816 (Magdalen College Register of Entry Fines).

2   Thirkill's name is also stated as Thirtell and Thurtell.

3   Provisional List of Buildings of Architectural or Historic Interest 1949: Lothingland Rural District. The listing included the walled garden's wrought iron gate, which was contemporaneous with the house.

4   John Thirkill paid entry fines in 1808 and 1816 but went bankrupt in 1823 after which his property, comprising a manor and mansion with 362 acres, the equity of redemption of estates at Bradwell, Hopton, Belton and elsewhere, together with the sites of the manors of Hobland and Hopton, were sold by auction (*Ipswich Journal*, 26 July 1823).

5   R. C. Knight & Sons, *Sale Particulars 13 June 1953* (Norwich Record Office BR184/41).

6   Kelly, *Directory of Suffolk 1883*, when Mrs Barber (a widow) was resident and T. Q. Barber lived at nearby Hobland House.

7   *East Anglian Daily Times*, 26 January 1961: report of the fire and brief details of the history of the house in the twentieth century.

8   Biographical details of John Thurtell and a brief history of Hobland Hall can be found at www.zentus.com/kraushaar/johnthurtell.htm.

HOLTON HALL, pages 93–95

1   Holton: Waveney District Council Conservation Area – Character Appraisal 2006.

2   The marriage settlement of Wilkinson and Jane Teresa Fitzgerald, dated 15 May 1832. The property settled included the Mansion and two cottages and the estate of 281 acres to secure half of the widow's jointure by way of a rent charge of £200. The sum of £5,175 was provided to secure a further £200 p.a. (SRO(L) 878/B1/1).

3   Tithe Map of 1839 and Apportionment of 1841 (SRO(I) FDA135/A1/1a and 1b).

4   White, *Directory of Suffolk 1844.*

5   SRO(L) 878/B1/2.

6   White, *Directories of Suffolk 1865, 1868 and 1869*. These show Major General H. B. Turner as the tenant.

7   White, *Directory of Suffolk 1874*.

8   E. Walford, *County Families of the United Kingdom* (London 1886).

9   The mortgage dated from 1867, the mortgagor was the late Andrew Johnson and the original mortgagee was Thomas Fowell Buxton. Neither the circumstances in which the mortgage was held in 1886 by Johnson's trustee nor the nature of Easton's interest in the property before 1887 are clear.

10 Charles Smith (1832–1912) practised in Reading for fifty years. Most of his work was the design of public buildings – halls, hospitals, workhouses and children's homes. These were mainly in Berkshire and Oxfordshire, and how he came to be the architect for the rebuilding of Holton Hall is not known. His obituary in *The Builder*, 16 February 1912 makes no reference to the design of domestic buildings.

11 C. Brown, B. Haward and R. Kindred, *Dictionary of Architects of Suffolk Buildings 1800–1914* (Ipswich 1991).

12 Flick & Son and Lenny, Smith & Stanford, *Sale Particulars 26 July 1886* (SRO(L) 1229/4/1).

13 Farebrother, Ellis & Co., *Sale Particulars 14 July 1937* (SRO(I) HE402/2/1937/28).

14 War Memorial tablet in Holton Parish Church.

15 Farebrother, Ellis & Co., *Sale Particulars 14 July 1937*.

16 Garrod Turner & Sons, *Sale Catalogue 10 January 1947* (SRO(I) HE402/1/1947/1).

17 The history of Holton Hall has also been the subject of research by Martin Bates, the results of which are available on his website at www.batesuk.cwc.net/Holton/Holton_hall.htm.

HUNSTON HALL, pages 96–97

1   W.A. Copinger, *The History of the Manors of Suffolk*, I (London 1905), pp. 325–7.

2   Suffolk County Council, Sites and Monuments Record HUN001 (MSF6914).

3   Copinger, *History of the Manors of Suffolk*, I.

4   White, *Directories of Suffolk 1844, 1855, 1858, 1888, 1900, 1904 and 1922*.

5   *East Anglian Daily Times*, 1 August 1917.

6   George Symonds, *Sale Particulars 30 July 1919* (SRO(B) E2/41/6).

LIVERMERE HALL, pages 98–103

1   1702 Abstract of Title (Saumarez Family Archive: SRO(I) HA93/2/794).

2   Deed dated 7 October 1603 (SRO(I) HA93/2/775).

3   William Cooke's son, Richard, bought Peggs Farm in Great Livermere for £850 (SRO(I) HA93/2/778).

4   The 'Final Accord', dated 11 October 1709, describes the property bought by Lee as the manors of Murrells and Broomhall, 15 messuages, 2 dovehouses, 6 gardens, 6 orchards, 650 acres of land, 100 acres of meadow, 250 acres of pasture,

1,200 acres of heath … and the Advowson of Little Livermere Church (SRO(I) HA93/2/806).

5   This picture (photographed at Shrubland, then the Suffolk seat of the de Saumarez family) was reproduced in *Country Life*, 3 December 1953 with a letter from Christopher Hussey who stated that he suspected that the artist was Peter Tillemans (c. 1684–1734). He referred to the house being acquired in 1722 from the third Duke of Grafton and stated that it 'appears to have been a red-brick Charles II house, to which large wings were added'. Hussey's reference to the third Duke, who was born in 1735 and did not succeed to the dukedom until 1757, must be erroneous. The extensive archive of the de Saumarez family (SRO(I)) does not seem to contain any documents indicating that any part of the title to the Livermere estate derived from the second Duke of Grafton (1683–1757), whose father was an illegitimate son of King Charles II by Barbara Villiers. The Grafton archive (SRO(B)) contain only a few papers relating to the second Duke, and none of these appear to have any relevant references to Livermere. The property sold by Arundell Coke to Thomas Lee in 1709, described in his receipt dated 6 May 1709 (SRO(I) SA/16/1/4/13), included 'All and singular the Mannors, Messuages … whatsoever of me the said Ar. Coke … late the estate of Richard Coke my late Father deceased'. The 'Final Accord' (see note 4 above) refers to the manor of Murrells (the Little Livermere manor) and to fifteen messuages, but whether Livermere Hall was embraced in the term 'messuages' is not known. It should, however, be noted that J. Kirby, writing in *The Suffolk Traveller* (Woodbridge 1735), p. 123, states that Livermere is 'now the Lordship and Demesne of Baptist Lee esq; who has lately erected a neat Mansion there, and made it his seat'.

6   R. Wilson and A. Mackley, *Creating Paradise – The Building of the English Country House 1660–1880* (London 2000), p. 405 n. 112.

7   Knight, Frank & Rutley, *Sale Particulars 28 October 1919* (SRO(B) HD1750/114).

8   J. Kenworthy-Browne et al., *Burke's and Savills Guide to Country Houses, III – East Anglia* (London 1981), p. 250. The attribution of this work to Samuel Wyatt (1737–1807) has been made on stylistic grounds. Wyatt had an extensive country house practice: other houses with which he was associated were Culford Hall and Hurts Hall, Saxmundham, in Suffolk, and Gunton Park and Holkham Hall in Norfolk.

9   Kenworthy-Browne et al., *Burke's and Savills Guide.*

10 De Carle's Wages Book 1790–1811 (SRO(B) Ref 2285): references to Livermere cease in 1797.

11 Evidence of the decline in the population of Little Livermere in Baptist Lee's time is provided by the decline in the number of baptisms (24 per decade 1700–40, 3 per decade 1750s and 1760s) and the number of burials in the churchyard of people who had died in other places (9% of all burials between 1700 and 1750, 50% or more in the 1750s and 1760s) (from Bishop's Transcripts, cited in *Proceedings of the Suffolk Institute of Archaeology and History*, 37, part 1 (1988), p. 85).

12 Knight Frank & Rutley, *Sale Particulars 28 October 1919.*

13 Humphrey Repton (1752–1818) established himself after 1788 as the leading landscape gardener of his time, filling the 'vacancy' left by the death in 1783 of Lancelot 'Capability' Brown. In all Repton undertook more than two hundred commissions, often working with the architect John Nash and also with his son, John Adey Repton, who acted as his 'architectural adjutant' (T. Williamson, *Suffolk's Gardens*

and Parks (Macclesfield 2000), pp. 95–8). In Suffolk (the county of his birth) Humphrey Repton worked at a number of other country seats, including (in addition to Livermere) Culford, Henham, Little Glemham, Rendlesham, Shrubland and Tendring. Many of his more than seventy Red Books, with their 'as it is now' and 'as it could be' watercolour drawings of the landscapes on which he worked, have survived, including that for Livermere (SRO(I) HA93:14688/1). Repton's work on the landscape at Livermere is referred to in E. Hyams, *Capability Brown and Humphrey Repton* (London 1971).

14 Williamson, *Suffolk's Gardens and Parks*, pp. 106–8.

15 Some details of N. L. Acton's expenditure in the last years before his death can be found in a small collection of estate and domestic accounts and correspondence, which include his Wages Book for the years 1818–35 (SRO(B) 1338/1 and 1338/3/1–25). Acton's estates at Bramford, Bailham and Claydon produced rents of over £5,000 a year in the three years before his death in 1836. His gardener, John Lines, was paid £20 wages a quarter both in 1819 and 1829, and was paid £42 for fruit trees and garden plants in 1831. Acton's Assessed Taxes composition statement for the five years from 5 April 1835 covered ten servants, four four-wheeled carriages, ten horses for riding, fourteen dogs and armorial bearings, the total payable being £94.14.2.

16 Wilson and Mackley, *Creating Paradise*, p. 350.

17 Knight, Frank & Rutley, *Sale Particulars 28 October 1919*.

18 *Bury Free Press*, 1 November 1919.

19 The sale of Livermere contributed £43,300 towards the total of £165,000 realised from the trustees' sale of the estates of Sir William Fowle Middleton between 1912 and 1931 (SRO(I) SA/4/1/2/18).

20 B. Dyson, *A Parish with Ghosts* (2001), p. 28.

21 Kenworthy-Browne et al., *Burke's and Savills Guide*.

THE MANOR HOUSE, MILDENHALL, pages 104–106

1   A. Sampson (comp.), *A History of Mildenhall* (Mildenhall 1893).

2   Survey of Mildenhall, July 1st 1608 (SRO(B) ET/15).

3   Lord Keeper Bacon was granted a thirty-year lease of Mildenhall in 1570 but died in 1578–9, and it seems likely that thereafter Henry North acquired the lease. The grant by the Crown to Sir Henry North in 1614 is in Patent Roll, Chancery, 12 James I, p. 3, no. 5.

4   Sir C. J. F. Bunbury (ed.), *Memoir and Literary Remains of Sir Henry Edmund Bunbury (bart)* (London 1868), p. 242. The chapter on Mildenhall written by Sir H. E. Bunbury states that 'The Mansion-house was probably built by the first Sir Henry North, who died in 1620.'

5   J. Kirby, *The Suffolk Traveller* (Woodbridge 1819).

6   F. Schoberl, *A Topographical and Historical Description of the County of Suffolk* (London 1818).

7   J. Carter Jonas & Sons, *Sale Particulars 28 July 1933* (SRO(B) HD1750/64).

8   White, *Directory of Suffolk 1844*.

9   Post Office, *Directory of Suffolk 1865* and White, *Directory of Suffolk 1874*.

10 K. Burrows, *Mildenhall in Edwardian Times* (Mildenhall 1978).

11 C. M. Dring, *Mildenhall in Old Postcards* (Zaltbommel 1993).

12 Kelly, *Directory of Suffolk 1904*.

13 Wamil Hall, two miles west of Mildenhall, was a late sixteenth-century house that was partly destroyed by fire in 1898 when it was owned by the Bunbury family. It was partially restored and sold in 1911 in the first estate sale. It was again seriously damaged by fire in 1955. It was restored again after the second fire.

14 Burrows, *Mildenhall in Edwardian Times*.

15 H. C. Wolton, *Sale Catalogue 18/19 March 1932* (SRO(B) HD1124/18).

16 J. Carter Jonas & Sons, *Sale Particulars 28 July 1933*.

17 The SRO(B) copy of the 1933 sale particulars (see note 7) has annotations giving prices offered with, where applicable, the letter 'W', which is assumed to denote that the lot was withdrawn.

18 *Bury Free Press*, 9 June 1934 and the Reverend G. Benton, 'Wall-paintings Discovered at the Manor House Mildenhall', *Proceedings of the Suffolk Institute of Archaeology and Natural History*, 22, part 1 (1934), p. 108 in which Benton describes the painting as a typical piece of Renaissance ornament, consisting of scroll work, with a sphinx-like figure on the right and a lion rampant on the left, the hind leg of which appears to be being bitten by a cockatrice. Benton also states that further wall paintings were totally destroyed.

MOULTON PADDOCKS, pages 107–109

1 Moulton Enclosure Award and Map 1841 (SRO(B) Q/R1.31).

2 Moulton Tithe Map and Apportionment (SRO(B) T136/1 and 2).

3 A mortgage dated 1850 in favour of Sir Robert Pigot Bt describes him as of Moulton Paddocks (Staffordshire & Stoke-on-Trent Archive Centre D4544/C/1), and in White, *Directory of Suffolk 1855* the property is described as 'his occasional seat'.

4 In White, *Directory of Suffolk 1868* the property is named Fidget Hall, but in the 1875 edition as Moulton Paddocks.

5 The Mountbatten Papers (Hartley Library, University of Southampton) contain photographs of the Mountbattens at Moulton Paddocks.

6 White, *Directory of Suffolk 1885*.

7 Newman & Newman, *Sale Particulars 14 June 1895* (SRO(B) EF506/10/17).

8 Knight, Frank & Rutley, *Sale Particulars 25 April 1922* (SRO(B) HD1750/70).

9 J. Kenworthy-Browne et al., *Burke's & Savills Guide to Country Houses, III – East Anglia* (London 1981).

10 Newman & Newman, *Sale Particulars 14 June 1895*.

11 Knight, Frank & Rutley, *Sale Particulars 25 April 1922*.

12 George Trollope & Sons and Lacy Scott & Sons, *Sale Particulars 9 October 1941* (SRO(B) HD1325/73).

13 *East Anglian Daily Times*, 10 June 1950.

OAKLEY PARK, pages 110–115

1   S. J. Govier, 'The Story of Hoxne Hall' (lecture at Hoxne, 23 September 2004).

2   W. A. Copinger, *The History of the Manors of Suffolk*, 4 (Manchester 1909), pp. 50–4.

3   Map of Hoxne New Park 1619 (SRO(I) HD40/422).

4   Matthias Candler, *Collections etc.* (British Library Add. MS 15520) stated that 'Robert Style hath built an house anno 1654 or 1655'. An article in *Country Life*, 4 January 1908 stated that the house was rebuilt by Style in 1654. While a brand-new house may have been built in the 1650s, it seems unlikely (but not impossible) that it had fallen into disrepair by 1700, when the house is depicted as having only two bays and a central entrance. Govier, 'Story of Hoxne Hall' stated that three bays were still standing in 1700. It may, of course, be the case that the depiction of the building on the 1700 map is not accurate, but it seems likely that Style's work was less a complete rebuild than the improvement of the existing house. The building history of Hoxne Hall in the sixteenth and seventeenth centuries remains unclear and merits further investigation (Map of 1700, SRO(I) HB21/280/1).

5   *Country Life*, 4 January 1908.

6   C. Brown, B. Haward and R. Kindred, *Dictionary of Architects of Suffolk Buildings 1800–1914* (Ipswich 1991). Sydney Smirke (1798–1877) was the younger brother and pupil of Sir Robert Smirke, a leading architect of the Greek Revival. Sydney Smirke's best-known works included the Circular Reading Room at the British Museum, the Imperial War Museum, The Carlton Club and Brookwood Cemetery.

7   J. Mordaunt Crook, 'Sydney Smirke: the architecture of compromise', in *Seven Victorian Architects* (ed. J. Fawcett) (London 1976), pp. 58ff.

8   Ibid.

9   Ibid.

10   Full descriptions of the house are given in Castiglioni & Scott, *Sale Particulars 18 May 1920* (National Monuments Record SC 1002) and John D. Wood & Co., *Sale Particulars 4 October 1921* (SRO(I) SC 230/4).

11   Rowland Frederic William Hodge (1859–1950) (see Brome Hall, note 12).

12   Abstract of title reciting an indenture of November 1919 from which Hodge's title to the estate derived (SRO(B) HD1708/2/1).

13   Castiglioni & Scott, *Sale Particulars 18 May 1920*.

14   Details of Bateman-Hanbury's purchase contained in the indenture of conveyance of 7 December 1920 are recited in a 1923 abstract of title (SRO(I) FC82/A5/2).

15   John D. Wood & Co., *Sale Particulars 4 October 1921*.

16   The conveyance of 31 July 1923 by the National Bank shows Lord Terrington as purchaser for £22,590 and Lister as sub-purchaser for an additional £3,910 (SRO(I) FC82/A5/2).

17   Harry H. Arnold, *Sale Particulars 30 June 1923* (Norfolk Record Office MC14/198).

OUSDEN HALL, pages 116–120

1   I. Lymn, *What's In a Name? (A History of Ousden)* (Ousden 2001), pp. 95ff. provides an account of the history of the estate and house.

2   Mackworth-Praed family papers: correspondence, draft advertisements, valuations and other papers regarding the sale of the property 1908–1912 (SRO(I) HA543/2/2/4/3/1–4).

3   Correspondence with Biddell & Blenclowe, land agents of Bury St Edmunds, regarding the shooting and with Lawrence Chalmers of Bickley, Kent and of Brown Shipley (the City acceptance house) who rented the house and sporting rights from 1905 until the estate was bought by Algernon Mackworth-Praed in 1913 (SRO(I) HA543/2/2/4/3/1).

4   Valuation by Drivers Jonas (SRO(I) HA543/2/2/4/3/3).

5   Correspondence, statements of account and other papers 1912–14. Of the £41,965 that Algernon Mackworth-Praed paid £26,500 was left outstanding on mortgage. £800 of this was paid off out of the proceeds of sale of Cator's Farm at Cowlinge to Gilbert Tonge of Branches Park (SRO(I) HA543/2/2/4/3/5–6).

6   E. Martin's essay 'Garden Canals in Suffolk', in *East Anglia's History: Studies in Honour of Norman Scarfe* (ed. C. Harper-Bill, C. Rawcliffe and R. G. Wilson) (Woodbridge 2002) refers to the canal at Ousden being the eastern arm of the former rectangular moat around the hall. Suffolk County Council, Sites and Monuments Record OUS003 (SF11617) suggests that, considering the various configurations of the house on old maps and the relationship of the moats on the site to the building, the Tudor house may have been a remodelling of an earlier house. The house before the addition of the Georgian wings is depicted in a drawing reproduced in Lymn, *What's in a Name?*

7   The sketch of the house (illustration 49) was made from drawings of the house in 1804 and 1807 and shows the new wings together with the original seven-bay Tudor or Jacobean house.

8   William Emes (1729–1803), landscape gardener, whose work (without mention of Ousden) is outlined in the *Oxford Dictionary of National Biography* and in *Country Life*, 15 October 1987, p. 152.

9   Thomas Rickman (1776–1841) practised as an architect in Birmingham and London, and worked on churches and public buildings, including New Court, St John's College, Cambridge. His domestic work included the main entrance gate at Audley End House, Essex for the third Lord Braybrooke and alterations and additions at Rose Castle for Hugh Percy, Bishop of Carlisle. The entertainment of King William IV at Ousden is referred to in *East Anglian Daily Times*, 25 October 1955.

10 Messrs Beadel, *Sale Particulars 18 June 1864* (SRO(B) HD526/106/4).

11 The Blomfield family had a long-standing connection with the village of Ousden, Isaac Blo(o)mfield (1683–1770) being churchwarden c. 1738–65.

12 Correspondence and accounts for alterations and additions (SRO(I) HA543/2/2/4/1/17).

13 H. C. Wolton & Son, *Sale Catalogue 17 and 18 July 1952* (SRO(B) 728.8): 8). A sale of silver and books was held on 5 September 1952 (*East Anglian Daily Times*, 6 September 1952).

14 Lymn, *What's in a Name?*: the sale of the estate of 2,593 acres (including seven farms, the village inn and school, cottages and market gardens and 'much Veneer Quality Standing Oak Timber') was scheduled for 23 June 1954, but the property was sold before auction.

15 Hampton & Sons in conjunction with H. C. Wolton & Son, *Sale Particulars 23 June 1954*.

16 *East Anglian Daily Times*, 25 October 1955.

17 R. Meyrick, *The Ousden Clock* (Bury St Edmunds 1981).

18 See J. McCann, *Dovecotes of Suffolk* (Ipswich 1998), p. 92 for a full description of the Ousden dovecote.

19 *Country Life*, 6 June 1908: the advertisement of the estate for sale by Biddell & Blencowe contains a description of the stable block.

THE RED HOUSE, IPSWICH, pages 121–124

1 *Burke's Landed Gentry* (1914 edn): under Edgar of Red House Park.

2 Feoffment dated 1 December 1641 vesting property in Lionel Edgar, son of Lionel Edgar and the latter's grandchildren William and Mary (SRO(I) HA247/1/8).

3 The Reverend Mileson Gery Edgar's 1840 Marriage Settlement records land holdings in Tuddenham, Witnesham, Swilland, Hemingstone, Coddenham, Gosbeck, Westerfield and Whitton (SRO(I) HB54/E20/28).

4 One of the roads in the housing development on land formerly part of the Red House estate is named 'Borrowdale Avenue', possibly to perpetuate the past connection of the area with the Edgar family.

5 *Burke's Landed Gentry* (1914 edn).

6 Elizabeth was the daughter of William Arkell of London and was Mileson Gery Edgar's second wife. They were married in 1840. He had no children by either of his marriages.

7 J. Kenworthy-Browne et al., *Burke's and Savills Guide to Country Houses, III – East Anglia* (London 1981), p. 257 attributes the house to the early eighteenth century, with the wings being built later in that century. Although the Suffolk County Council, Sites and Monuments Record IPS459 (SF21889) survey did not indicate any pre-eighteenth- century activity on the site of the house, the attribution of the house to the early eighteenth century appears to be erroneous.

8 Garrod Turner & Sons, *Sale Particulars 28 April 1937* (SRO(I) SC242/85).

9 Twentieth-century photographs of the entrance front of the house show it unchanged from Henry Davy's etching of 1840 (illustration 52).

10 Garrod Turner & Sons, *Sale Particulars 28 April 1937*.

11 Agreement to lease by the trustees of Elizabeth Edgar's Estate (Mileson Edgar, Arthur Thomas Schreiber and Herman Biddell) to Edward Arthur Maund. This agreement, dated 10 December 1895, provided that the lessee was to spend not less than £300 fitting out bathrooms and heating as approved by the trustees and install a new kitchen range, half the cost being returnable on termination of the lease, which was for ten years, terminable after seven by either party (SRO(I) HB54/E20/28).

12 Christie Manson & Woods, *Sale Catalogue 29/30 March 1900* (SRO(I)
HD1/9/18). The copy at SRO(I) bears no indication that the 'property of a
Gentleman' to be sold in 241 lots was from the Red House, and this attribution
arises from the SRO(I) accession correspondence. The items sold included porcelain,
objets de vertu (including souvenirs of Napoleon) and furniture.

13 Kelly, *Directories of Suffolk 1908, 1912* and *1922* each give the names of occupiers
in those years.

14 Agreement for Sale: Mrs Elizabeth Edgar to the Ipswich Burial Board 1855
(SRO(I) HB54/E20/28).

15 Garrod Turner & Sons, *Sale Particulars 1 July 1936* (SRO(I) SC242/84).

16 Garrod Turner & Sons, *Sale Particulars 28 April 1937*.

17 *East Anglian Daily Times*, 29 April 1937. The sale included cottages, smallholdings
and other properties forming part of the estate in outlying villages, and fetched
about £2,500.

REDGRAVE HALL, pages 125–129

1 A plan of the ground floor of the house (one of a set of plans and elevations
made in 1937 by Basil Oliver FRIBA) is annotated to show where a small section of
thirteenth-century stonework was incorporated in Bacon's rebuilding of Redgrave.
Oliver's drawings are included in T. Holt-Wilson's website of the history of Redgrave
and its owning families (myweb.tiscali.co.uk/redgravehistory).

2 M. Airs, 'The Designing of Five East Anglian Houses', *Architectural History*, 21
(1978), pp. 58/9. Various aspects of the building of Redgrave are also referred to in
M. Airs, *The Tudor and Jacobean Country House: A Building History* (Stroud 1995).

3 E. R. Sandeen, 'The Building of Redgrave Hall 1545–1554', *Proceedings of the
Suffolk Institute of Archaeology*, 29, part 1 (1961), pp. 1–33.

4 Ibid.

5 Ibid.

6 Plans and elevations by Basil Oliver (see note 1).

7 Oliver's plan of the ground floor shows the corridor serving the servants' hall and
the butler's pantry as being a ramp downwards to the rear of the building, although
his sectional drawing of the house looking to the rear shows the floor of the servant's
hall at the same level as the principal rooms of the house. The bedrooms above the
servants' hall (which had a lower ceiling height than the principal rooms of the
house) appear to have had short windows at floor level, these being the upper
portions of the windows serving the rooms beneath. This arrangement avoided
disturbing the regular fenestration of the house when viewed externally.

8 D. Stroud, *Capability Brown* (London 1975), p. 112 gives a description of the
house and its rebuilding, and quotes the Hon. William Hervey's journal for 25
October 1771.

9 J. Sheehan, *Redgrave Reflections* (Redgrave 1993).

10 Holt-Wilson website (see note 1).

11 *East Anglian Daily Times*, 14 June 1946.

RENDLESHAM HALL, pages 130–134

1   J. Kenworthy-Browne et al., *Burke's & Savills Guide to Country Houses, III – East Anglia* (London 1981), p. 258.

2   Conveyance by bargain and sale, dated 4 November 1552, of the manor together with property in Rendlesham, Loudham, Iken, Bredfield and North Glemham, which Hugh of Naunton had received from John Holbroke and his wife Pernell in 1327 (SRO(I) HB416/b1/57/1).

3   The fifth Duke died in March 1742/3, and nine years later his widow married the Hon. Richard Nassau of Easton Park. Although Rendlesham was sold by the sixth Duke, Easton passed to the Hamiltons on the expiry of the Nassau (Earls of Rochford) line.

4   The Georgian house, Brodsworth Hall, bought by Peter Thelluson was pulled down in the 1850s. Charles Sabine Augustus Thelluson, Peter's great-grandson, built a new house which, after passing to the Grant-Dalton family, was given to English Heritage in 1990 (English Heritage, *Brodsworth Hall and Gardens* (London 2000)).

5   Evidences of Title to the property conveyed on 6 and 7 June 1796 to Peter Isaac Thelluson of Philpot Lane, London (SRO(I) HB416/A2).

6   *Thelluson* v *Woodford* (1799): the courts upheld the validity of the will in this notable legal action.

7   Thomas Fisher Salter of Attleborough and John Peirson of Thornton Fields, Gisboro': Report and Division of the Thelluson Estates – 5 June 1857 (SRO(I) HB416/A2/14). The Thelluson Estates comprised 29,945 acres in Yorkshire, Co. Durham, Hertfordshire, Warwickshire, Northamptonshire and Suffolk. 11,705 acres passed to the Brodsworth branch of the family and 18,327 acres to the Rendlesham branch. The Report of the Commissioners details all the property in the estates with names of tenants and acreages.

8   D. Stroud, *Henry Holland – His Life and Architecture* (London 1966), pp. 58/9 refers to papers in Sir John Soane's Correspondence, which suggest that Holland may have been connected with alterations at two Suffolk houses at this time, i.e. about 1780 (the other was Redgrave). Subsequently Soane was asked by Holland to go to Rendlesham to correct excessive charges made by Richard Norris, the surveyor.

9   John Buonarotti Papworth (1775–1847) was the son of a stuccoist employed by the Office of Works under Sir William Chambers. At the age of 18, on behalf of his principal, Philip Norris, he designed Ray Lodge, Woodford, Essex, for Sir James Wright and by the age of 25, having worked for a builder and for a decorator as well as having attended the Royal Academy Schools, he was well established. The author of various books on architecture, he developed an extensive practice, especially building and altering country houses.

10   Henry Hakewill (1771–1830), who studied at the Royal Academy Schools, undertook a wide range of work designing and altering both public buildings – the Middle Temple, the Radcliffe Camera and Infirmary in Oxford and Rugby School being examples – and country houses including Lamport Hall (in the Gothic style) and Packington Hall.

11   Humphrey Repton (1752–1818): for biographical details, see Livermere Hall, note 13.

12   Report from an unidentified newspaper of unknown date around 1868 (SRO(I) Pre-1977 Cuttings File).

13 Richard Makilwaine Phipson: for biographical details, see Bramford Hall, note 9.

14 C. Brown, B. Haward and R. Kindred, *Dictionary of Architects of Suffolk Buildings 1800–1914* (Ipswich 1991).

15 William Burn (1789–1870), the son of an Edinburgh builder and architect, was a pupil in Sir Robert Smirke's office. He practised in Edinburgh in the early years of his career, building up an extensive practice in country house work in a variety of styles (Grecian, Elizabethan, Jacobean, Italian Renaissance and Scottish vernacular). From 1844 onwards he practised in London, and his work in East Anglia included designs for Orwell Park, Holkham Hall, Cheveley Park and Blickling Hall.

16 *East Anglian Daily Times*, 11 May 1898.

17 Knight, Frank & Rutley, *Sale Particulars 27 May 1920* (SRO(I) fSC335/2).

18 *East Anglian Daily Times*, 15 July 1914. Various sale agreements changed the completion date from 6 January 1915 to 11 October 1920 (SRO(I) HB416/B1/94 and others).

19 *East Anglian Daily Times*, 28 May 1920. Among the purchasers was Lord Alastair Graham, brother of the Marquis of Graham (later sixth Duke of Montrose), who married Lady Mary Hamilton of Easton Park, whose forebear had married Anne Spencer of Rendlesham.

20 *East Anglian Daily Times*, 28 July 1920.

21 Agreement between Lord Rendlesham and Sir Henry Lunn MD for the sale of the house for £35,000, part of which was to remain outstanding on mortgage for ten years (SRO(I) HB416/B1/100).

22 *East Anglian Daily Times*, 26 October 1949.

23 N. Pevsner, *The Buildings of England: Suffolk* (2nd edn) (London 1974).

ROUGHAM HALL, pages 135–136

1 W. A. Copinger, *The History of the Manors of Suffolk*, 6 (Manchester 1910), pp. 322–8.

2 The extension is not shown on the 1884 edition of the 25-inch Ordnance Survey but appears on the 1904 edition.

3 A Note on the Monuments and Memorials of St Mary's Church, Rougham states that Johnstone acquired the manor of Rougham from the Bennet family in 1875, following the death of Philip Bennet III (SRO(B) HD116/51). Kelly's *Directory of Suffolk 1885* and the 1888 and 1892 editions state that Spencer Brunton was then the occupier of Rougham Hall. The 1896 and 1900 editions state that Rougham was Johnstone's 'property and residence'.

4 *Bury Free Press*, 25 April 1975.

5 *Bury Free Press*, 6 December 1985.

RUSHBROOKE HALL, pages 137–143

1 *Country Life*, 10 October 1903 contains an illustrated article on Rushbrooke, and there is a chapter on the house in G. A. Worsley, *England's Lost Houses* (London, 2002), pp. 246–7.

2 See G. E. Cokayne, *The Complete Peerage*, 7 (ed. H.A. Doubleday and Lord Howard de Walden) (London 1929): under Jermyn of St Edmundsbury for the descent and a brief history of the Jermyn family.

3   A. Adolph, ' "... and in My Lady's Chamber" Jermyns and Stuarts: Illicit Liaisons', *Genealogists Magazine*, 27/7 (2002), pp. 300–5.

4   Cokayne, *Complete Peerage*, quoting Sir Henry Craik's description of Henry Jermyn in his *Life of Clarendon*.

5   G. E. Cokayne, *The Complete Baronetage* (Exeter 1900–9): 1665–1770, under Davers of Rougham.

6   Ibid.

7   Bartle Davers Rushbrooke is commemorated by a memorial in Rushbrooke Church, where many members of the Jermyn, Davers and Rushbrooke families are buried.

8   *Bury Free Press*, 1 November 1919.

9   Knight, Frank & Rutley, *Sale Catalogue 10/11 December 1919* (SRO(B) 728.8).

10   *Bury Free Press*, 13 December 1919.

11   The National Trust, *Ickworth* (London 1998).

12   *Bury Free Press*, 6 December 1919.

13   *Country Life*, 24 June 1922, p.870: letter from A. P. Powys.

14   *Country Life*, 22 July 1922, p. 99: letter on Lord Islington's purchase and Estate Market article.

15   L. G. Pine, *New Extinct Peerage* (London 1972): under Islington.

16   Plans for the house by Stanley Hall & Robertson, dated March 1938, bear the initials CP (for Claude Phillimore): Royal Institute of British Architects, British Architectural Library, Drawings & Archives Collections (PA763/1).

17   W. C. Bellenger, *Rushbrooke 1938–1998* (privately printed 1999). This work gives an account of the history of the house and estate in the first sixty years of Rothschild family ownership.

18   *Bury Free Press*, 15 July 1949.

19   The Report of the Committee on Houses of Outstanding Historic or Architectural Interest chaired by Sir Ernest Gower (1950). The Committee recommended the creation of the Historic Buildings Councils for England, Wales and Scotland.

20   *East Anglian Daily Times* and *Eastern Daily Press*, 21 March 1961.

21   N. Pevsner, *The Buildings of England: Suffolk* (2nd edn) (London 1974).

STOKE PARK, pages 144–147

1   Farebrother, Ellis & Co. (in conjunction with Robert Bond & Sons, Ipswich), *Sale Particulars 4 July 1918*, Notes p. 2 (SRO(I) SC242/86).

2   The inheritance by William Acton of Bramford of his cousin's interest in Stoke Park is recorded in a bound notebook of Sir William Fowle Fowle Middleton dating from the years 1813 to 1824 (SRO(I) SA/1/2/21).

3   J. Kirby, *The Suffolk Traveller* (Woodbridge 1829).

4   Hodskinson's Map of the County of Suffolk 1787 and Smith's Map of Suffolk 1801 (SRO(I)).

5   Burrell's account books for various periods between 1807 and 1846 survive (SRO(I) SI/16/1.1 and 1.2). His Contingency Expence book for the years 1834 to 1846 records the sale of £15,228 of investments in May 1840 and the payment of £16,300 to the Ipswich Bank with the annotation 'to purchase Stoke'. Burrell's account books disclose substantial investment transactions during the years prior to his purchase of Stoke Park.

6   Farebrother, Ellis & Co., *Sale Particulars 4 July 1918*, Notes p. 2.

7   Tithe Map 1840 (SRO(I) P461/152).

8   Richard Makilwaine Phipson: for biographical details, see Bramford Hall, note 9. Evidence of Phipson's involvement in the rebuilding of Stoke Park rests on the survival of a drawing of a design for the ceiling to the staircase (Christchurch Mansion Museum, Ipswich: Phipson Drawings Collection). In the obituary of Phipson in *The Ipswich Journal*, 3 January 1885 Stoke Hall (which as noted in the text was a different property) is mentioned as one of his designs, and it is also listed as such in C. Brown, B Haward and R. Kindred, *Dictionary of Architects of Suffolk Buildings 1800–1914* (Ipswich 1991). The omission of Stoke Park in these sources gives rise to uncertainty in relation to Phipson's involvement in the rebuilding of Stoke Park.

9   Farebrother Ellis & Co., *Sale Particulars 4 July 1918.* These sale particulars provide a detailed description of the house, outbuildings and gardens.

10 Conveyance by Lady Henniker Heaton to Cox Long & Co. Limited, London, covering the whole estate except one lot adjacent to existing development on the edge of the estate near to the outskirts of Ipswich (SRO(I) HD432/5).

11 Farebrother Ellis & Co. (in conjunction with Robert Bond & Son), *Sale Particulars 6 September 1921* (SRO(I) fsc 242/33).

12 The conveyance of Home Farm for £10,000 included the release of Barker from covenants regarding rights of way and fencing that he had given when he bought other parts of the estate as he had by then bought 'the rest of the estate' (SRO(I) HD 432/7).

13 Minutes of Ipswich Borough Council, 22 June 1927. In addition to the gift of the land Alderman Paul undertook to build a keeper's house and fence the land. It is clear from the offer letter that the gift was motivated by a desire to provide a public amenity in an area that was becoming residential (SRO(I) DA8/151/18).

14 Robert Bond & Son, *Sale Particulars 20 June 1928* (SRO(I) SC242/104).

15 Charles Francis Annesley Voysey (1857–1941) was one of the leading architects of domestic buildings in the late nineteenth and early twentieth centuries. A contemporary of Sir Edwin Lutyens, he espoused the principles of the Arts and Crafts movement, and his buildings were notable for their use of buttresses, bay windows, long sloping roofs and tall chimneys. His work incorporated chimneypieces and architectural metalwork specifically designed for individual buildings. His style was adopted by many architects in the period before World War II.

16 Information provided by the Hon. Jill Ganzoni (the first Lord Belstead's daughter).

SUDBOURNE HALL, pages 148–153

1   W. A. Copinger, *The History of the Manors of Suffolk*, 5 (Manchester 1909), p. 177. Copinger states that Jane, daughter of Sir Michael Stanhope, married Sir Edmund Withypool. However, *Burke's Peerage* (105th edn) states that it was a daughter of Sir William Withipole (not of Sir Edmund) who married Leicester, sixth Viscount Hereford.

2   Address given by J. F. Burns to the Parent–Teachers' Association of Wallace High School, Lisburn, 20 April 1980. Sir Richard Wallace served as MP for Lisburn from 1873 to 1884 and made a number of charitable endowments to the town (www.lisburn.com/books/historical_society/volume3_2).

3   A copy of the indenture of 22 February 1873 setting out the terms of the settlement confirmed the Irish estate to Sir Richard Wallace and the £400,000 compensating payment to Sir George Hamilton Seymour and Arthur Henry Seymour (SRO(I) HB 83: 1379/2).

4   In 1872 Sir Richard Wallace transferred his lands at Chillesford in trust for his son but reacquired them in 1879 for £28,000 (SRO(I) HB 83: 1379/2).

5   J. Allen, *The Wallace Connection* (Orford 2008) and *Country Life*, 23 February 1901, p. 240.

6   James Wyatt (1746–1813): for biographical details, see Fornham Hall, note 5.

7   T. Cromwell, *Excursions through the county of Suffolk*, 2 (London 1819), p. 87.

8   J. Kenworthy-Browne et al., *Burke's & Savills Guide to Country Houses, III – East Anglia* (London 1981), p. 264.

9   K. Bradley-Hole, *Lost Gardens of England* (London 2004) contains a description of the gardens in 1901.

10 One of these 'cottages ornees' is sited on the B1084 road near its junction with the B1078 between Sudbourne and Chillesford.

11 Fryers & Penman were a firm of Scottish architects who practised at Largs but also in Manchester. Initially engaged on building suburban houses, in 1905 they secured the patronage of the Coats family of Paisley, and this connection with the cotton industry, no doubt, explains why they were engaged by Clark to make alterations at Sudbourne in 1907.

12 Knight, Frank & Rutley, *Sale Particulars 31 May and 1 June 1918* (National Monuments Record SC1018).

13 Ibid.

14 Ibid.

15 Ibid.

16 Ibid.

17 *East Anglian Daily Times*, 5 March 1948.

18 Provisional List of Buildings of Architectural or Historic Interest 1949: Deben Rural District Council.

19 *East Anglian Daily Times*, 22 August 1951.

20 *East Anglian Daily Times*, 2 December 1959.

TENDRING HALL, pages 154–157

1 J. Seymour, *The Companion Guide to East Anglia* (London 1970), p. 352.

2 *Stoke by Nayland & Leavenheath Community News*, June 1998. This article also states that an overmantel from the Tudor house was reused in the eighteenth-century replacement house and was later installed at Scotland Place in Stoke-by-Nayland.

3 W. Goult, *A Survey of Suffolk Parish History*, I (Ipswich 1990): under Stoke-by-Nayland.

4 The settlement is referred to in the 1748 Act of Parliament vesting the paternal estates of Richard Williams in assignees for his creditors (Rowley Family Archive SRO(I) HA108 Acc 10515 Box 4 No. 19).

5 Bargain and Sale dated 19 March 1750 (SRO(I) HA108 Acc 10515 Box 9 No. 135). For the lineage of the Rowley family, see *Burke's Peerage* (1970 edn): under Rowley of Tendring.

6 1915 inventory of heirlooms with notes (SRO(I) HA108 Acc 10515 Box 12 No. 192).

7 Sir John Soane RA (1753–1837) trained under George Dance. He was responsible for the design of a large number of public buildings and houses (both town and country). His work included the Bank of England (rebuilt in the twentieth century), Dulwich Picture Gallery and many houses in East Anglia (including Shotesham Park, Burnham Westgate Hall, Honing Hall, Earsham Hall, Letton Hall and Saxlingham Rectory). He built two houses for himself, Pitzhanger (Middlesex) and 13 Lincoln's Inn Fields, London (now Sir John Soane's Museum), which he left to the nation and which now houses his eclectic collection of artefacts.

8 Soane's plans and drawings, his Precedents in Architecture (a record of work undertaken) and his account books (Journals 1 and 2, Ledger C) are held at Sir John Soane's Museum.

9 P. Dean, *John Soane and the Country Estate* (London 1999) notes that many of Soane's houses had similar bows, citing Saxlingham, Sydney Lodge, Tyringham and Pell Wall as examples.

10 The arbitrators were George Dance (junior), John Johnson and Richard Norris (Soane's Ledger C). The detailed cost figures were:

	£
Dwelling House	6,798
Kitchen Court and Offices	1,148
Stable Buildings	1,665
Kitchen Garden and Hothouse etc.	659
Lodges	250
Park Paling	1,130
Farm buildings	400
	12,050
Work not executed	1,530
	10,520
Additional costs	1,282
	£11,802
Amounts paid to Soane (£9,976 + £992)	£10,968

11 E. Hyams, *Capability Brown and Humphrey Repton* (London 1971), p. 149.

12 Repton's Red Book for Tendring is held in a private collection (English Heritage, *Register of Parks and Gardens of Special Historic Interest: Part 39 – Suffolk*).

13 Sir Robert Taylor (1714–88), a sculptor and architect whose work included Heveningham Hall (Suffolk), where he was responsible for the exterior, only the interior being entrusted to James Wyatt, Barlaston Hall (Staffordshire), Sharpham House (Devon) and the Bank of England.

14 E. Martin, 'Garden Canals in Suffolk', in *East Anglia's History: Studies in Honour of Norman Scarfe* (ed. C. Harper-Bill, C. Rawcliffe and R. G. Wilson) (Woodbridge 2002) attributes the canal to Sir John Williams.

15 The lease, dated 6 February 1931, required Davies to maintain the gardens and driveways and employ four gamekeepers (SRO(I) HA108 Acc 10515 Box 14 No. 199).

16 1915 inventory and notes (SRO(I) HA108 Acc 10515 Box 12 No. 192).

17 Vesting Assent 1932 (on succession of Sir Charles Samuel Rowley) endorsed with notes of sales of land including the Western Area of the estate (823 acres) by auction on 24 June 1939 (SRO(I) HA108 Acc 10515 Box 14 No. 204).

18 Raymond Charles Erith (1904–73), who practised in Dedham, just over the Essex border from Stoke-by-Nayland, has been described as 'one of the few genuine classical designers in Britain, his work not a pastiche of a past style but a serious attempt to make classicism work in the second half of the 20th century'. Erith's plans for Tendring Hall, his correspondence with Captain Joshua Rowley (later seventh Baronet) and the contract (undated) with the demolition contractor are in the British Architectural Library (ERR/25/3 & 4).

19 Dean, *John Soane*.

THORINGTON HALL, pages 158–160

1 W. Goult, *A Survey of Suffolk Parish History*, 2 (Ipswich 1990).

2 J. Kirby, *The Suffolk Traveller* (Ipswich 1735), p. 124.

3 Will of Alexander Bence, proved 8 October 1759 (Records of the Rous Family, SRO(I) HB26/412/1034) and Marriage Settlement of 16 January 1762 (SRO(I) HB26/412/1035).

4 K. Anderson, 'East Riddlesden Hall and the Kentwell Connection', *Long Melford Historical & Archaeological Society Newsletter*, February 2004.

5 T. Cromwell, *Excursions through the county of Suffolk*, 2 (London 1819), p.109. C. Brown, B. Haward and R. Kindred, in *Dictionary of Architects of Suffolk Buildings 1800–1914*, state that the new house was on the site of the old hall. However, Hodskinson's Map of the County of Suffolk 1783 shows the (old) hall on a different site, and a 1954 report on rights of way over the estate refers to an Order of 1820 when the site of a road to old Thorington Hall was closed as 'useless and unnecessary': this is unlikely to have been the case if Bence's new hall was on the site of the old (Suffolk County Council, Rights of Way Sub-committee minutes, 26 May 2004). Archaeological evidence reported in Suffolk County Council Sites and Monuments Record TNG015 (SF12765) also supports the view that the old hall was on a different site from the new.

6 Brown, Haward and Kindred, *Dictionary of Architects* state that the new house was 'probably by T. Hopper'. Thomas Hopper (1776–1856) is best known for his Gothic Revival architecture but, as he himself stated, 'It is an architect's business to understand all styles and be prejudiced in favor of none,' a rule that he himself followed, designing buildings that varied from Tudor and Jacobean to Palladian and Greek revival. The author has not been able to verify the attribution of Thorington to Hopper, but its entrance portico is markedly similar to that at Leigh Court, Abbott's Leigh, Somerset designed by Hopper.

7   White, *Directory of Suffolk 1844*.

8   Hampton & Sons, *Sale Particulars 12 September 1945* (SRO(I) SC410/1).

9   Ibid.

THORNHAM HALL, pages 161–165

1   W. A. Copinger, *The History of the Manors of Suffolk*, 3 (Manchester 1909), p. 312.

2   The Great Hall appears not to have been open to the roof but ceilinged in a similar manner to that at Sir Nicholas Bacon's Redgrave Hall.

3   John Peter Deering, formerly Gandy, RA (1787–1850) was a pupil of James Wyatt and had a considerable reputation both as an authority on Greek architecture and as a practising architect. His work included the south front of Shrubland Hall for Sir William Fowle Middleton. In 1828 he inherited a Buckinghamshire estate, changing his name in consequence, and gradually gave up his practice to manage his property and engage in public affairs.

4   Deering's designs for the north and south fronts survive (Henniker Archive, SRO(I) HA116 Acc 8254/5–8).

5   The Henniker/Kerrison Marriage Settlement provided (in addition to Sir Edward Kerrison's £20,000 payment as a marriage portion) for a jointure of £3,000 p.a. in Anna Kerrison's widowhood (this compared to a jointure of £2,000 for the third Baron's widow), annual 'pin money' of £500 and jointures for younger children of the marriage (SRO(I) HA116 Acc 4530: 10).

6   Sydney Smirke: for biographical details, see Oakley Park, note 6.

7   H. R. Barker, *East Suffolk Illustrated* (Bury St Edmunds 1908/9), p. 473.

8   Correspondence between Smirke and Lord Henniker and other papers regarding the works (SRO(I) HA116 Acc 4861: 2 and 3). Smirke's plans and drawings (SRO(I) HA116 Acc 8254/1, 2, 9, 10–12, 14–17, 18–30 and HA116 Acc 4530/14(2), (4) and others).

9   Grimes's account (SRO(I) HA116 Acc 4861/3).

10 Grimes's 'sundry alterations' account (SRO(I) HA116 Acc 4861/2).

11 The account (undated) of C. F. Bielefeld (a leading producer of plaster and papier-mâché mouldings) for the plasterwork shows the cost to have been £730 (SRO(I) HA116 Acc 4861/3). The pinnacles were supplied by Mr Stamper of the Zinc Works, 15 New Road, Fitzroy Square, London and had to be returned as defective in April 1840.

12 James Kellaway Colling (1815–1905), an able draughtsman interested in art foliage and the writer of books on this subject and on Gothic architectural detail. His proposals for Thornham were formulated in March 1872 and May 1873 (SRO(I) HA116 Acc 4530/14/1 and 2).

13 The Hughes tenancy ended with some disagreement between the landlord, who wanted an inventory of furniture taken, and the tenant, who said that his family must be trusted, having been tenants for over thirty years during which the Henniker-Major family had changed the furniture and imported additional items on the death of two of its members.

14 Correspondence regarding the future of the house and possible lettings (SRO(I) HA116 Acc 4861/29).

15 Report and correspondence regarding demolitions and alterations (SRO(I) HA116 Acc 4861/5).

16 John D. Wood & Co., *Sale Catalogue 24 May 1937*: 1,600 lots were offered for sale (950 furniture and effects, 200 pictures and 450 books) (SRO(I) HA116 Acc 4861/20 and Acc 4861/30).

17 Perry & Phillips Limited, *Sale Catalogue 30 June 1937*: included in the sale were the 'carved oak Jacobean mantlepiece with raised mouldings forming panels, figure pilasters and carved pediment and frieze decorated with centre panels of fruit' from Lord Chancellor Hatton's Hammersmith house, which fetched £50, and the drawing room panelling 'purchased in Paris' (SRO(I) HA116 Acc 4861/21 and Acc 4861/30).

18 The contractor was F. Sparrow, Riverside Works, Needham Market, who had also been engaged to modernise Bramford Hall, where the Hon. John Henniker was agent for Sir Percy Loraine (SRO(I) Acc 4861/5).

19 *East Anglian Daily Times*, 23 November 1954. The reporter, clearly unaware of the reduction of the house in 1938, wrote that the house had thirty-nine bedrooms.

UFFORD PLACE, pages 166–169

1 The history of the house in the seventeenth century is not clear. It is possible that the original house in the park at Ufford was on a different site and that this was the house sold in 1627 by Joan, widow of Thomas Ballett to Margaret Father, who is said to have left it to Edward Hammond. William Hamant and Miss Sarah Hamant are recorded as having houses with six and seven hearths respectively in 1674. It may be that William had a new house and that Sarah lived in the original one.

2 J. Kirby, *The Suffolk Traveller* (Woodbridge 1735), p. 163.

3 *Burke's Landed Gentry* (17th edn) (London 1952): under Brooke of Ufford Place. Reginald Brooke was the second son of Sir Thomas Brooke, who traced his descent through nine generations from Francis Brooke of Woodbridge.

4 Maps and Plans of Ufford (SRO(I) HD80/1/1 no. 12, formerly part of the Brooke Archive).

5 SRO(I) HD80/1/1 no. 13.

6 SRO(I) HD80/1/1 no. 14.

7 Hampton & Sons, *Sale Catalogue 15–19 September 1930* (SRO(I) SC429/1).

8 The Brooke and Blois-Brooke Archive contains deeds of land, cottages and other properties acquired in the eighteenth and nineteenth centuries as the estate was built up (SRO(I) HA401/1).

9 Garrod Turner & Son, *Sale Particulars 27 September 1921*: the sale included land in Ufford, Bawdsey, Hollesley, Martlesham and Melton (SRO(I) SC429/5).

10 Hampton & Sons, *Sale Catalogue 15–19 September 1930*.

11 Garrod Turner & Son, with W. C. Mitchell & Sons, *Sale Catalogue 28/29 September 1956* (SRO(I) SC429/2).

12 *East Anglian Daily Times*, 30 June 1956.

13 The date of demolition of Ufford Place is quoted in various sources as 1953, but as it was furnished until June 1956 when the contents were sold its demolition in that year appears correct.

14 Designs for the conversion of the orangery by John Penn (Royal Institute of British Architects PA1016/14(1–5). John Penn (1921–2007) was a Suffolk-based architect responsible for the design of buildings in the modern idiom.

BIBLIOGRAPHY

This bibliography lists the works cited in this book together with some other works on the subject of lost houses. Books on the lost houses of a number of English counties have also been published, and a list of these can be found in Giles Worsley's *England's Lost Houses*. In this bibliography works of reference of which there have been a number of editions are listed once, noting the date of the earliest edition cited or that most frequently cited.

Adolph A., ' "and in My Lady's Chamber" Jermyns and Stuarts: Illicit Liaisons', *Genealogists Magazine*, 27/7 (2002), pp. 300–5

Airs M., 'The Designing of Five East Anglian Houses', *Architectural History*, 21 (1978), pp. 58–67

—— *The Tudor and Jacobean Country House: A Building History* (Stroud 1995)

Allen J., *The Wallace Connection* (Orford 2008)

Allibone J., *Anthony Salvin: Pioneer of Gothic Revival Architecture 1799–1881* (Columbia 1987)

Angus W., *Seats of the nobility and gentry, in Great Britain and Wales* (Islington 1787)

Anon., *The Book of Bramford: A Suffolk Parish and its People* (Bramford 2003)

Barker H. R., *West Suffolk Illustrated* (Bury St Edmunds 1907)

—— *East Suffolk Illustrated* (Bury St Edmunds 1908/9)

Benton, the Reverend G., 'Wall-paintings Discovered at the Manor House Mildenhall', *Proceedings of the Suffolk Institute of Archaeology and Natural History*, 22, part 1 (1934), p. 108

Binney M. and Milne E. (eds), *Vanishing Houses of England* (London 1982)

Bradley-Hole K., *Lost Gardens of England* (London 2004)

Brown C., Haward B. and Kindred R., *Dictionary of Architects of Suffolk Buildings 1800–1914* (Ipswich 1991)

Builder (The), 21 December 1850, 16 March 1867, 10 January 1885, 17 June 1899, 18 May 1901, 1 June 1901 and 16 February 1912

Bunbury Sir C. J. (ed.), *Memoir and Literary Remains of Sir Henry Edmund Bunbury (bart)* (London 1868)

Burke's Genealogical and Heraldic History of the Landed Gentry (17th edn) (London 1952) and other editions

Burke's Peerage and Baronetage (105th edn) (London 1975) and other editions

Burrows K., *Mildenhall in Edwardian Times* (Mildenhall 1978)

Cannadine D., *The Decline and Fall of the British Aristocracy* (New Haven and London 1990)

Cokayne G. E. (ed. The Hon. V. Gibbs), *Complete Peerage*, 1 (London 1910)

—— *The Complete Baronetage* (Exeter 1900–9)

—— (ed. H.A. Doubleday and Lord Howard de Walden), *The Complete Peerage*, 7 (London 1929)

Colvin, H., *Biographical Dictionary of British Architects, 1680–1840* (3rd edn) (New Haven and London 1995)

Copinger W. A., *The History of the Manors of Suffolk*, 1 (London 1905); 2–7 (Manchester 1908–11)

Cornforth J., *Country Houses in Britain: Can they Survive?* (London 1974)

Cromwell T., *Excursions in the county of Suffolk*, 1 (London 1818); 2 (London 1819)

Davy H., *Views of the Seats of the Noblemen and Gentlemen of Suffolk* (Southwold 1827)

Dean P., *John Soane and the Country Estate* (London, 1999)

Dring C. M., *Mildenhall in Old Postcards* (Zaltbommel 1993)

Dymond D. and Northeast P., *A History of Suffolk* (Chichester 1985)

English Heritage, *Brodsworth Hall and Gardens* (London 2000)

Evans N., 'The Tasburghs of South Elmham: The Rise and Fall of a Suffolk Gentry Family', *Suffolk Institute of Archaeology and History*, 34, part 4 (1980), pp. 269–80

Farrer, the Reverend E., *Hardwick Manor House* (c. 1928)

Fitch, the Reverend J. A., *The Church in the Forest – St Mary the Virgin, Santon Downham* (1996 edn)

Gibson R., *Annals of Ashdon* (Chelmsford 1988)

Goldstein E., *18th Century Weapons of the Royal Welch Fuziliers from Flixton Hall* (Gettysburg 2002)

Goult W., *A Survey of Suffolk Parish History*, 2 vols (Ipswich 1990)

Harris J., *No Voice in the Hall* (London 1998)

—— *Moving Rooms – The Trade in Architectural Salvages* (New Haven 2007)

Harrison W. and Willis G., *The Great Jennens Case* (Sheffield 1879)

Hyams E., *Capability Brown and Humphrey Repton* (London 1971)

Johnson D. E., *Some Notes on the History of the Church and Parish of Acton, Suffolk* (5th edn) (Acton 2003)

Kelly, *Directory of Suffolk* (London 1883) and other editions

Kenworthy-Browne J. et al., *Burke's & Savills Guide to Country Houses, III – East Anglia* (London 1981)

Kirby J., *The Travellers Guide and Topographical Description of the County of Suffolk (The Suffolk Traveller)* (Ipswich 1735, London 1764, Woodbridge 1819, Woodbridge 1829)

Lymn I., *What's In a Name? (A History of Ousden)* (Ousden 2001)

MacCulloch, D. (ed.), *Letters from Redgrave Hall: The Bacon Family 1340–1744* (Woodbridge 2007)

Mackley A., 'The Construction of Henham Hall', *The Georgian Group Journal*, VI (1996), pp. 85–96

McCann J., *Dovecotes of Suffolk* (Ipswich 1998)

Mandler P., *The Fall and Rise of the Stately Home* (New Haven and London 1997)

Martin E., 'Garden Canals in Suffolk', in *East Anglia's History: Studies in Honour of Norman Scarfe* (ed. C. Harper-Bill, C. Rawcliffe and R. G. Wilson) (Woodbridge 2002)

Meyrick R., *The Ousden Clock* (Bury St Edmunds 1981)

Mordaunt Crook J., 'Sydney Smirke: the architecture of compromise', in *Seven Victorian Architects* (ed. J. Fawcett) (London 1976)

Muthesius H., *Das Englische Haus* (Berlin 1904/5; English translation, London 1979)

National Trust (The), *Ickworth* (London 1998)

Paine C. R., *The Culford Estate 1780–1935* (Ingham 1993)

Pevsner N., *The Buildings of England: Suffolk* (2nd edn) (London 1974)

Pine L., *New Extinct Peerage* (London 1972)

Post Office, *Directory of Suffolk 1865*

Redstone V. B., *The Suffolk Garretts* (published privately 1916)

Sampson A. (comp.), *A History of Mildenhall* (Mildenhall 1893)

Sandeen E. R., 'The Building of Redgrave Hall 1545–1554', *Proceedings of the Suffolk Institute of Archaeology*, 29, part 1 (1961), pp. 1–33

Sandon E., *Suffolk Houses* (Woodbridge 1977)

Schoberl F., *A Topographical and Historical Description of the County of Suffolk* (London 1818)

Seymour J., *The Companion Guide to East Anglia* (London 1970

Sheehan J., *Redgrave Reflections* (Redgrave 1993)

Smith D., *Assington through the Ages* (1974)

Strong R., Binney M. and Harris J., *The Destruction of the Country House* (London 1974)

Stroud D., *Henry Holland – His Life and Architecture* (London 1966)

—— *Capability Brown* (London 1975)

Suckling, the Reverend A., *The History and Antiquities of the County of Suffolk*, 2 (London 1848)

Suffolk County Handbook (Ipswich 1939)

Thompson F. M. L., *The Landed Estate in the Nineteenth Century* (London 1963)

Tricker R., *St Margaret of Antioch, Cowlinge: Brief History and Guide* (1993)

Walford E., *County Families of the United Kingdom* (London 1886)

Waterson E. and Meadows P., *Lost Houses of York and the North Riding* (York 1990)

White, *Directory of Suffolk* (London 1844) and later editions

Whitehead R.A., *Garretts of Leiston* (London 1974)

Williamson T., *Suffolk's Gardens & Parks* (Macclesfield 2000)

Wilson R. and Mackley A., *Creating Paradise – The Building of the English Country House 1660–1880* (London 2000)

Worsley G. A., *England's Lost Houses* (London 2002)

Wright S., *Drinkstone Revisited – More Stories from a Suffolk Village* (2007)

INDEX OF NAMES

Printed and bound by CPI Group (UK) Ltd, Croydon, CR0 4YY

09/06/2025

14685720-0001